A Civilian in

Lawton's 1899 Philippine Campaign

The American Military Experience Series
John C. McManus, Series Editor

The books in this series portray and analyze the experience of Americans in military service during war and peacetime from the onset of the twentieth century to the present. The series emphasizes the profound impact wars have had on nearly every aspect of recent American history and considers the significant effects of modern conflict on combatants and noncombatants alike. Titles in the series include accounts of battles, campaigns, and wars; unit histories; biographical and autobiographical narratives; investigations of technology and warfare; studies of the social and economic consequences of war; and in general, the best recent scholarship on Americans in the modern armed forces. The books in the series are written and designed for a diverse audience that encompasses nonspecialists as well as expert readers.

A Civilian in Lawton's 1899 Philippine Campaign

The Letters of Robert D. Carter

Edited by Michael E. Shay

University of Missouri Press
Columbia and London

University of Missouri Press, Columbia, Missouri 65201
Printed and bound in the United States of America

5 4 3 2 1 17 16 15 14 13

Cataloging-in-Publication data available from the Library of Congress
ISBN 978-0-8262-2008-0

∞™ This paper meets the requirements of the
American National Standard for Permanence of Paper
for Printed Library Materials, Z39.48, 1984.

Design and composition: Jennifer Cropp
Printing and binding: IBT/Hamilton
Typefaces: Minion and Thonburi

Drawings from Carter's letters are reproduced courtesy of the Robert Dexter Carter Collection, Rutherford B. Hayes Presidential Center, Fremont, Ohio. Photographs of the Philippine-American War are used courtesy of the Library of Congress and the Military History Institute. Photograph of Maj. R. D. Carter reprinted from *Bingham Military School for Boys Catalog for 1920* courtesy of the North Carolina Collection, Pack Memorial Public Library, Asheville, North Carolina. Photographs of the Second Reserve Hospital, Manila, reprinted from Mary C. Gillett, *The Army Medical Department, 1865-1917* courtesy of the National Library of Medicine.

For Edward J. Shay and Mary P. Shay

from their “Affectionate Son”

Contents

Illustrations

Preface

During the research phase of my biography of Major General Clarence Ransom Edwards, I eventually found my way to the papers of Robert Dexter Carter. In 1898, at the start of the Spanish-American War, Edwards, a career Army officer, accepted a commission as a major of Volunteers, and he was eventually assigned to the staff of Major General Henry Ware Lawton as his Assistant Adjutant General, 1st Division, 8th Army Corps. The division was posted to the Philippines, and in January 1899, Lawton, his family, and staff—including Edwards—sailed from New York aboard the United States Army Transport (USAT) *Grant*. Also aboard was twenty-two-year-old Robert Dexter Carter, who, as the son of a former colleague of General Lawton's, was appointed as a temporary civilian quartermaster clerk in his headquarters.

I began my background research for the Philippine-American War with the classic *Schoolbooks and Krags* by John Morgan Gates. In his footnotes, the author referred to the Carter papers at the Rutherford Hayes Presidential Center in Fremont, Ohio. Hoping to find some references to Lawton, and possibly to Edwards, I made the fortunate acquaintance of the curator, Nan Card, and, in turn, the Robert Dexter Carter Papers. Nan graciously answered my questions and copied Carter's nearly forty letters, along with the diary of his voyage to the Philippines, as well as articles and fragments of articles that he wrote hoping for their publication—in sum, literally hundreds of pages mostly in the young man's crabbed handwriting, virtually devoid of punctuation. Thank you, Nan.

Carter's father, Robert Goldthwaite Carter, who retired due to a service disability, was a war hero and a longtime friend of Lawton, both having served in Texas under Col. Ranald S. Mackenzie in the 4th Cavalry in the 1870s. Young Carter obtained his position through the influence of Lawton, and his respect for and awe of Lawton is clear throughout his writings. Carter was a frequent visitor to the Lawton's home, where he was introduced to notables like Brig. Gen. Frederick D. Grant. Understandably, his letters home, particularly to his father, are full of news and gossip related to his father's friend. We also get to see the kindness and generosity of an Army spouse, Mary Lawton, who took the time to look out for Carter while he was in the hospital, and at other times, by lending him books she thought he would like.

Robert was also a keen observer. Through him, we get a glimpse of life in Manila—the sights, the smells, and the native peoples. He was not completely deskbound, and he served in the field from time to time. In addition to his letters, Carter's diary and several related articles present a firsthand account of the historic voyage of the USAT *Grant*, which carried Lawton, his family, and his command through the Suez Canal to Manila in early 1899. Carter's papers are important, because they help form a picture of the war from the standpoint of a noncombatant, although some of his experiences in and outside of Manila could be described as harrowing. All too often, the role of support troops in war are either minimized or ignored. His article written one Sunday while traveling along the Manila-Dagupan Railway to Calumpit colorfully illustrates the massive logistical tail supporting Generals Lawton and MacArthur during their first campaign into Central Luzon. All in all, Carter opens a window onto the everyday experiences of an ordinary young man during an extraordinary time.

My thanks also go to Luther D. Hanson, Curator of the U.S. Army Quartermaster Museum at Fort Lee, Virginia. Luther generously searched out materials, including information about the USAT *Grant*, prior to my visit, and he was there to answer my questions. Also, thanks go to Richard Baker and Rod Foytik of the Military History Institute at the Army Heritage & Education Center in Carlisle, Pennsylvania. Both of them were most helpful in accessing the vast collection of materials and photographs pertaining to the Philippine War; their help made the visit productive. Thanks once again to Suzanne Christoff, associate director for Special Collections and Archives at West Point, who helped me access the great on-line digital collection there. Ginny Roth, curator of Prints and Photographs at the National Library of Medicine in Bethesda, Maryland, found several old photographs of the 2nd Reserve Hospital in Manila circa 1899, and she patiently scanned and re-scanned them for me. Likewise, Zoe Rhine, librarian at the Pack Memorial Public Library in Asheville, North Carolina, located and scanned the only photograph of Robert Dexter Carter that I was able to find. Thank you both.

Finally, the book would not have come about without the help of my best friend and traveling companion, Marilyn. It was through her curiosity, after many years of passing and re-passing the sign on the Ohio Turnpike, that we first went to Spiegel Grove, the home of President Rutherford B. Hayes in Fremont, Ohio, and, more important, the location of his Presidential Center. Marilyn, "Spike," and I travel about the country doing research. Her patience and insights (not to mention her camera work!) are invaluable. Here's to her!

Editor's Note

In the process of reading and transcribing the letters of Robert Dexter Carter, I found that, although his spelling was generally good, his punctuation was almost nonexistent. Moreover, his sentence structure was poor, as he used run-on sentences. Capitalization was "hit and miss," and in his haste to get his letters posted, he often left many articles and prepositions out altogether. In addition, some pages were missing or torn, while in other places some words and phrases were indecipherable. In order to make the text more readable, I have inserted a word or two, some obvious, where it fit the context, while some were my best guess. In any case, I kept such insertions to a minimum. Hopefully, I have remedied these deficiencies without altering the text or disturbing the flow of the young man's thoughts.

His principal correspondents were his mother and father, as well as his older sister, Mell. Sadly, none of their letters survive. He tended to write in batches, as he received his mail in batches, so some of his letters to all three are repetitive regarding certain topics. Accordingly, I have compressed some of the correspondence by eliminating much of this duplication where it would not harm the thread of the story. For instance, the reader does not need to know over and over again that Carter was paid $83.33 per month (a fact that galled him, knowing that the other clerks were paid $100). I have chosen not to use ellipses, since I believe that they are a distraction and would disrupt the flow.

Finally, it is quite apparent that white Americans, even middle-class northerners like Carter, viewed African-Americans and the native peoples of the Philippines in a much different light than we do today. Epithets ranging from the obviously racist ("coon," when referring to a black cook; "nigger," with reference to the native Filipinos; "dago"; "gu-gu") to the paternalistic ("little brown brothers," used by governor (later president) William Howard Taft) appear throughout.[1] As offensive as this speech is to me, as well as the modern reader, to "sanitize" this work would, I believe, deprive the reader of an authentic nineteenth-century voice. For that reason, I have chosen to leave the terms in the text.

MES

A Civilian in Lawton's 1899 Philippine Campaign

"No body ever heard of a quarter Master in history as such or in relating any brilliant action."

—Quartermaster General Nathanael Greene
(Letter to Gen. Washington, April 24, 1779)

Introduction

The Quartermaster Department

If, in accepting General Washington's orders to assume his new duties as quartermaster general of the Continental Army, Nathanael Greene viewed the assignment as the supreme vote of confidence in his abilities by the commander-in-chief, which it most certainly was, it would be difficult to glean that fact from his initial response. "Whoever heard of the exploits of a quartermaster," an obviously disappointed Greene groused to a friend. A Rhode Island Quaker turned soldier, he was ambitious and had thirsted for a significant combat command. Although somewhat sensitive to slights, he was also devoted to Washington, and if only for that reason, with great reservations, and with the understanding that he could keep his line commission, he accepted the job.[1] Admittedly, the supply situation was a mess, and some viewed the position of quartermaster as a means to profit first and a chance to advance Washington's "Glorious Cause"[2] a distant second. Although the ethics have changed (then making a profit was acceptable), Washington needed a man whom he could trust; one who would suppress his own ambition; and one who would strive to provide for the common soldier, who was always in his thoughts and prayers. After all, it was the soldier who bore the heavy burden. "Sunshine patriots"[3] need not apply!

Greene hewed to that task for more than a year, and when he resigned (following the stunning failure of General Horatio Gates, the hero of Saratoga, in the Carolinas) and was returned to the command of soldiers, there were those in the Continental Congress who sought to sanction him. Washington's defense of his subordinate was swift.[4] Greene went on to re-form the army in the South and to lead a dogged drive against a skilled General Cornwallis, inexorably wearing him down and forcing him north to meet his fate at Yorktown.

The function of the quartermaster, while often unglamorous, as Greene lamented, was, nevertheless, no less vital to the ultimate success of the Continental Army, or for that matter, any army in any age. In another era, General George C. Marshall observed: "The army with the higher breaking point wins the decision."[5] If the combat arm wins the battle, the support arm provides the critical staying power. The job of quartermaster encompassed the transportation of baggage and supplies, procurement of horses and mules, as well as forage for their maintenance. In addition to powder and ball, the quartermaster transported food and necessities to the army, whether stationary or on the move. Today we would call it logistics. By the time of the War with Spain, and the Philippine War that followed on its heels, the Quartermaster was one of several departments that made up the United States Army, each department head a virtual law unto himself, reporting, in effect, only to Congress.[6] It was an inefficient system, as was clearly evident with what happened with the support of General Shafter's forces in Cuba, and it would change, but not until after President Theodore Roosevelt declared the war over in the Philippines in 1902, and then only grudgingly.[7]

In the course of our foreign wars, beginning with Mexico in 1846, and later the War with Spain, the distances that the Quartermaster had to transport troops and supplies were relatively short, being wholly within our own hemisphere. The Philippine War was something very different, and, in a very real sense, the precursor to the massive missions the Army would undertake throughout the twentieth century, in the two world wars, Korea, Vietnam, and the Gulf. With each succeeding conflict, the military built a more powerful and efficient Quartermaster arm, capable of "delivering the goods" literally to every inch of the globe. Given the scope of the First Gulf War, the relative speed with which the combined military acted was superb; the scale of the effort in landlocked Afghanistan is truly astounding. Again, the expanded mission really began on a global scale in the Philippines, and in so doing, the role of the Army Quartermaster Department had certainly come a long way since the days of Nathanael Greene.

It was to this department that young Robert Dexter Carter was assigned as a "temporary" civilian clerk at a division headquarters. He had, therefore, an excellent vantage point from which to observe, firsthand, the operations of a quartermaster, the Army's unsung hero, both from an administrative standpoint, as well as service in the field. In addition, he witnessed firsthand army politics, as well as the opportunities for graft by a few venal characters. Carter was also, to his extreme frustration, the victim of the inertia inherent in any bureaucracy, especially one so well entrenched in old attitudes and methods. He was an acute, articulate observer, if somewhat biased toward his father's friend, Major General Henry Ware Lawton. His letters offer valuable insights from the standpoint of the lower ranks, particularly by those serving in less-heralded branches, which are more often than not the best sources—history from the bottom up.

Taken by themselves, Carter's writings are important, since they help fill out the picture of service in the Philippines during the war with the nationalists. However, it is also within the larger context that they achieve importance, since they were written during this very important moment in time, which marked the transition of the United States from an inward-looking republic to, as some would characterize it, an outward-looking empire. For it was at this time that the United States solidified its interest in the Pacific and began the process of expanding its power both militarily and economically around the globe.[8] Could an Isthmian canal be very far behind?[9]

The Carters

Robert Dexter Carter was born August 10, 1876, the son of Robert Goldthwaite Carter and Mary Maria Dexter. His father, a Civil War veteran whose gallantry as an enlisted man earned him an appointment to West Point, had hopes of a long military career. However, a disability contracted while in service in the southwest ended those plans, and he turned to other endeavors, including writing. Carter taught school and was the Washington bureau chief of the Public Service Publishing Company of New York.[10] Twice brevetted for gallantry, he was belatedly awarded the Medal of Honor in 1900 for his actions while serving with the 4th Cavalry at the Brazos River in Texas in October 1871. Despite retirement, Captain Carter maintained close contact with influential former colleagues, including Maj. Gen. Henry Ware Lawton, with whom he had served in the 4th Cavalry.[11] Undoubtedly, it was through Lawton's influence that his son, Robert Dexter Carter, received an appointment to the Quartermaster Department as a civilian clerk, specifically in Lawton's headquarters in Manila. Robert viewed this as a "stepping stone" toward reaching his ambition to be an Army officer like his father.

Young Robert was the third of four children of Robert and Mary, and their only son. Carter graduated from the Business High School in Washington, D.C., in 1894,[12] and he went to work at a stock brokerage up until the time that he went to Manila. On January 16, 1899, the day before his departure, he married Helen F. Wright,[13] the daughter of Charles and Mary Wright. Her father was a patent attorney in Washington, D.C.[14] Carter was particularly close to his oldest sister, Mellie ("Mell"), and she, along with his father and mother, were his most frequent correspondents during his tour of duty in the Philippines. Although he signed a few letters to Mell with his family nickname, "Tod," perhaps with an eye toward posterity, the majority are signed with a strained formality, "Robert Dexter Carter."

The young man could at times be somewhat stuffy, and he definitely had a chip on his shoulder regarding officers his own age, obviously delighted when they were brought up short. Clearly, he wanted to be respected for the obvious skills and pride that he brought to his job, but he often failed to fully

Casa del Ayuntamiento (City Hall), U.S. Army Headquarters, Manila, P. I.

appreciate the fact that his colleagues might well have looked at him as Lawton's pet. His standoffishness (he did not drink with them) and frequent visits to the Lawton's home only served to solidify this impression.

Carter's letters are liberally sprinkled with references and anecdotes about his patron, Major General Lawton and his wife, Mary ("Mamie") Craig, as well as other important military figures. The glimpse into the Lawton's family life, in particular, the sympathetic portrait he paints of this loyal army wife is both a reflection upon her fine character and a demonstration of her genuine concern for the men under her husband's command.

Henry Ware Lawton

Physical courage was never in short supply with Henry Ware Lawton. A large, mustachioed man, he built a reputation as a profane, hard-driving, hard-drinking man of action. Much of his reputation was undoubtedly reinforced by the man himself, simply by living up to it. And if his troops complained at all about the hard marching, he was always there to set an example. He led from the front—where else would the commander be? He had no use for desk-bound generals, like his immediate superior, Major General Elwell

Otis. Lawton was also a family man, the father of three girls and a boy, Manley, who was clearly the apple of his eye. From a young age, the boy accompanied his father, often dressed in a miniature army uniform. Lawton's wife, "Mamie," came from a prominent Kentucky family. She willingly followed her soldier-husband once again to his latest assignment in the Philippines, despite her own ailments.[15]

Maj. Gen. Lawton with Mary Craig Lawton and son Manley

Lawton was born in Manhattan, Ohio, now a part of Toledo, on March 17, 1843. At an early age, he moved to Fort Wayne, Indiana, where he spent his formative years. A large boy, at the outbreak of the Civil War, he enlisted in the 9th Indiana Infantry and became one of three sergeants. He later joined the 30th Indiana Volunteer Infantry where he became 1st lieutenant. Lawton eventually saw service in what is now West Virginia, and later at, among other battles, Shiloh, Stone's River, and Chickamauga. He emerged from that war a lieutenant colonel, and was later awarded the Medal of Honor for his actions at Atlanta near its close. His luck was incredible, never having suffered a wound, despite all the derring-do. He briefly tried the law as a career, but he quickly returned to the Army, where he remained for the balance of his life.

As with most postwar soldiers, Lawton's service took him to the southwest. He, along with Carter's father, served in the 4th Cavalry under the legendary Col. Ranald Mackenzie. Carter became disabled, and Mackenzie suffered a mental breakdown, but Lawton's star rose higher in the firmament. In 1886, he had the good fortune to lead the force that captured the Apache leader Geronimo.[16] When war with Spain erupted, Lawton played a prominent role in the fighting in Cuba, capturing El Caney and protecting the flank of Roosevelt and his Rough Riders.[17] He was a logical choice to play a major role in the Philippines.[18]

William McKinley, Cautious Imperialist

William McKinley was a cautious, savvy politician, much more adept at gauging the public mood, as we are now coming to find out. When faced with an important decision, his philosophy was to, in his words, "make haste slowly."[19] Much of his political support came from the business community, which was understandably nervous about a war with Spain, as the nation was just coming out of a deep, prolonged depression. With McKinley, though, it wasn't just about politics. He himself was reluctant to rush to war, having lived through arduous service during the Civil War. As a quartermaster sergeant at Antietam, he braved withering fire to rush much-needed food and ammunition to the front line. For this he was commended and promoted, ultimately to the rank of major, a title he bore proudly the balance of his life. "I have been through one war. I have seen the dead piled up, and I do not want to see another," he would often say.[20]

Although he did not rush to war with Spain following the sinking of the battleship *Maine* in Havana Harbor in February 1898, he was canny enough to rush through Congress a $50,000,000 appropriations bill to fund one, just in case.[21] In addition, he placed a call for volunteers. The response was

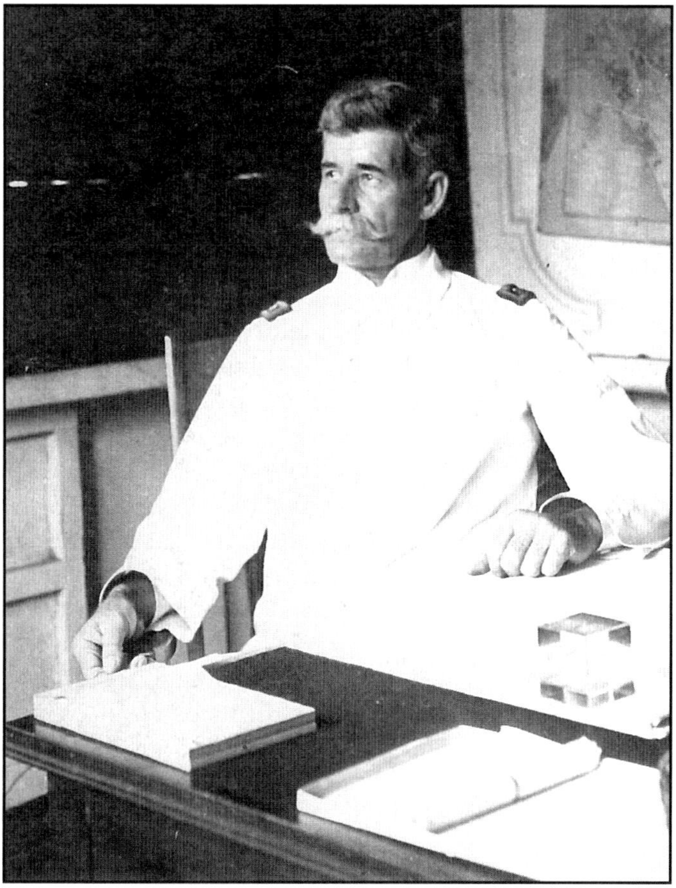

Maj. Gen. Henry Ware Lawton, U.S. Volunteers

overwhelming. Young men, and even some older ones like Theodore Roosevelt, raised on the Civil War exploits of their fathers and grandfathers, flocked to the colors. During the debate on the defense appropriations bill, the warp and the weft of the American political fabric was on full display, and the Teller Amendment was added, specifying that the United States would have no colony in Cuba.[22] War with Spain did come, and it was over in the blink of an eye. However, although we eschewed a colonial interest in Cuba, the Platt Amendment was added to another appropriations bill in 1901 that authorized the United States to intervene in Cuban affairs in the event of political instability, among other reasons.[23] Moreover, as it was important to our hemispheric ambitions, Puerto Rico was seized and retained without too much fuss or fanfare. The real dilemma came with Dewey's equally swift victory at Manila Bay.

The year 1898 turned out to be one of the most pivotal ones in United States history. Victory in Cuba was followed by an even swifter one in Puerto Rico. Like falling dominoes, Hawaii was annexed, Guam was seized,[24] and finally, the fate of the Philippines moved right to the forefront of the national debate. An already deep divide continued to widen between those who wished to expand America's role in the world by projecting its strength, primarily by means of a modern navy, and those who did not. A vociferous debate took place in the halls of Congress and on the front page of the nation's newspapers. The first group, the so-called expansionists, or "imperialists," like Alfred Thayer Mahan, Henry Cabot Lodge, and Theodore Roosevelt, pushed for the seizure of the entire archipelago. In opposition were the "anti-imperialists," just as vocal, just as committed, like Mark Twain, Samuel Gompers, and William James, who argued that an empire was antithetical to the notion of a democratic republic.[25] Allied to the former were many in the country who hewed to the hubristic notion that it was the mission of the United States to Christianize the native Filipinos, most of whom were, at least nominally, Catholic.[26]

True to character, while the treaty with Spain was being negotiated in Paris, McKinley stumped the country testing the mood of the electorate. To the shock of some, particularly the Spanish, the president, who had earlier told a colleague that he doubted that he could even find them on a map,[27] decided to keep the entire Philippines. He was, he rationalized, compelled by "duty and destiny."[28] By the time the treaty was signed, thousands of troops had been sent there, enough perhaps to hold Manila, but more, many more, would be needed to pacify the populace.

At the time of the War with Spain, the American Army was extremely small. Approximately 28,000 officers and enlisted men were scattered all over the country, mainly in the west, many in small, two-company posts. Each state had its own militia, poorly equipped and indifferently trained.[29] Although the militia was potentially a ready-made pool of troops, for the most part, the officers were more than likely men who were popular in their local communities or had political connections. The problem for the president and the Regular Army was that by law, these troops could not serve outside of the United States. As a result, resort to a stratagem was taken. Each member of a militia unit would resign with one breath and, en masse, join as a volunteer with another. Thus was born the U.S. Volunteers. Not only did it more than solve the immediate manpower problem, it also provided an opportunity for some ambitious Regular officers who would be assigned to Volunteer units to advance in rank in what was normally a glacially slow promotion process. Hundreds of officers and their political godfathers bombarded the adjutant general's office seeking one of the limited number of appointments.[30] Volunteer units were among the first to see service in both Cuba and the Philippines. Technically, however, their tours of duty were supposed to end within sixty days from the end of hostilities with Spain, and soon after Carter arrived in Manila, there were calls to bring the boys home. The McKinley Administration played for time, ultimately interpreting this period of service to end upon the ratification and signing of the treaty in June 1899.[31] Meanwhile, the Regular Army scrambled to fill its ranks, sometimes with less than ideal recruits, as Carter was quick to point out.[32]

United States Army Transport *Grant*

During the evening of January 17, 1899, as the big ship began to ease away from the dock at Pacific Street, Brooklyn, a steel mooring cable became fouled in the starboard propeller, very nearly ending the historic voyage of the vessel then known as the USAT *Grant*.[33] Earlier in the day, Major General Lawton, his staff, and many of their families, along with nearly two thousand men, composed of the 4th Infantry Regiment and a battalion of the 17th Infantry,[34] had boarded the troopship in anticipation of sailing to the Philippines the following morning. The route would take the ship across the Atlantic Ocean, through the Mediterranean Sea and the Suez Canal, across the Indian Ocean, and finally to Manila. She would be the first American troopship to do so. Given the length of the trip, prudence dictated that the ship be inspected. Accordingly, she was towed to Liberty Island, where, the following morning, two divers pronounced the ship sound.

Visiting dignitaries, including the adjutant general of the Army, Maj. Gen. Henry C. Corbin, and Secretary of War Russell Alger, who had been taken from the Adam's Express Company pier in Jersey City to the *Grant* aboard a quartermaster craft, took part in an inspection and the ceremonial send-off. The vessel then steamed up the Hudson River to Grant's Tomb, witnessed more fanfare, and returned downriver to moor, once again, at Liberty Island. The ceremonies done, the voyage would finally get under way the next morning.[35]

What better way to introduce the young man than through the brief diary of his historic voyage halfway around the globe?

USAT *Grant* salutes Grant's Tomb, January 18, 1899

Chapter One

The Diary

"My little pocket diary which I had with me on ship was lost for quite a little time. Yesterday I found it. A few extracts from my daily life might be of interest."

—Robert Dexter Carter

January

Mon. 16 Appointed. Married. Left for NY.

Tue. 17 A beautiful day, magnificent sunrise, Hudson full of floating ice, the sun behind the great skyscrapers in NY. 23rd St. Ferry. Went to Hotel St. Denis, 11th & Broadway, fine breakfast. Found Percy, went down Broadway, crossed Brooklyn Bridge, went aboard *Grant*. Spent afternoon on deck and quay with H.[1] Pulled out to the Liberty [Island] in evening.

Wed. 18 A fine day. Gen. Corbin[2] and officials were on board, band played, salutes fired. About 4 P.M. got under way and went up Hudson to Grant's Tomb, cheering crowds on ferry boats, bitter cold. Saluted. Anchored off Cortland St.[3] Many men left, cooks, etc. Wrote many letters. Years may pass before I again set foot in my native land. Dropped down off Liberty [Island] during night. Lawton overhauled Baker.[4]

Thur. 19 Snow during night. Got under way about 10 A.M. Went down in hold and worked getting up stores. Rec'd postal from Father. The last word from home. Am glad H. is home at last safe. Passed Sandy Hook. Disappearing batteries fired salutes. Swarms of gulls follow ship. Adjust compass. Had to change quarters. Have not been sick.

Fri. 20	Have passed no ship since leaving [Sandy] Hook. Rather heavy swell. In the hold in morning. We are crossing the Gulf Stream and the temperature is gradually getting warmer. We made up to noon 280 mi. So far have not been sick, headaches. Have heard quite some tales of Manila, smallpox, etc. Every night I look toward west at sunset. Behind I have left the whole world to me behind.
Sat. 21	One poor fellow died last night. Made 240 miles. Engine stopped 2 ½ hrs.
Sun. 22	218 miles today. Feel fine, worked hard in store. Heavy sea. Talked with Mrs. L.[5] Passed the British tramp *Laura*. Slight squall in morning. Issuing fruit all morning. We are not making very fast time. It seems like Sunday. This evening I sit alone and think of one week ago with H. Now on the sea, how brief the time, how great the distance.
Mon. 23	301 miles. Rough night. Am feeling well. Rained in morning, heavy blow in evening. Making fast time. Talked with Gen. L. He seems to think I want to stay in Manila the rest of my days. That is out of the question. Moonlight on the water. Will write some tonight. The sea, the sea, the sea.
Tue. 24	292 mi. Heavy swell, dishes flying. In the hold hunting L's box. Wrote on my article. Slept badly.
Wed. 25	294 mi. About half way. Hard work in the store this P.M. Heavy roll. Vessel getting lighter from taking out coal. Wrote H. I have made up my mind to go off the ship at Manila and stick to Lawton.
Thur. 26	282 miles. Over half way. May sight the Azores tomorrow. Not a hard day. Showers every few hours. My head aches, no appetite, stomach alright. Wrote some on my article. Shall write to H tonight. This is my night with her at home.
Fri. 27	Longest run yet, 308 mi. Hard work in store, sold 600 cans fruit. Musical in Saloon Last eve. A beautiful morning, heavy sea, and wind in P.M. Tomorrow possibly *land, land*. Talked with Gen. L. last evening on deck.
Sat. 28	A fine day, 280 miles. Passed Santa Maria, southern island Azores. Great mass of rocks, mountains, etc., bronze color. Played cards in evening. Not feeling well.
Sun. 29	Much work. One would never know it was Sunday. Worked a long time in store. Did some writing.
Mon. 30	245 mi. Rainy. Worked in office. Game evening.

Tue. 31 — 285 [mi], fair. Not much doing. Only the ocean. Passed some vessels distant. 3300 mi. so far. Tomorrow will probably land us on the "Rock." About 8 P.M. engines stopped. Land in sight. Will enter Straits of Gib[6] in morning. A beautiful day, heavy thunderstorm during night.

February

Feb. 1 — [Wed.] A cold rainy morning. Passed through Straits. Long lines of jagged cliffs and mountains. Passed "Ape's Head," one solid gray rock 2800 ft. The "Rock" is a beautiful sight. Came to anchor, health officer aboard, heavy sea, quarantined, salutes from sea and 1st Line of Defense. Japanese torpedo boat in harbor, also *Princeton*.[7] Great swarms of gulls. Tugs having a hard time. One of the after launches slipped from davits throwing sailors into water. Musical in evening.

Feb. 2 — A succession of heavy squalls increasing in P.M. Too rough to coal.[8] Moored anchorage at 10 A.M. between *Devastation*[9] and American steam yacht. Very rough. Even L & staff and Gen. H.[10] went ashore. Torpedo destroyer circled around us at high speed. HMS *Griffon*. Two Englishmen aboard. One gave me considerable information.

Fri. 3 — A good day. Checked coal until 4 P.M. Went ashore. Bought some things. Came on ship. Went back 8 P.M. with Engineers. Saw the town. Was with two English soldiers, R.A.[11] Hotel Cecil Café Universal, Spanish dancers. Got on board 12:30. Came on launch with officers who went to masked ball, all drunk.

Fri. 4 — Checked coal. Was presented with box yesterday from Father. One today from H. Cleared the port about 2:30. Now in Med.[12] To Port Siena Nevada. Starboard Mts. of Atlas. Ceauta.[13] Colonial Penal Settlement in sight.

Sun. 5 — Sunday, when that day comes I can not but think of my H. All day in sight of the undulating hills of Africa. Weather fine. Very little motion.

Mon. 6 — Rainy in forenoon, cleared in P.M. Passed points at entrance to Algiers Bay. Drew, wrote.

Tues. 7 — Islands, high rocky ones. South of Sardinia. Worked in hold and store. Am in doubt but think the Island of Malta is in sight. Cool and clear. Sighted many vessels.

Wed. 8 Beautiful day, the finest so far. Very busy below. No land in sight, passed Malta during the night. Water calm, a summer day.

Thur. 9 Showery, big run, 301 mi., will be in Said tomorrow night. No land today, [we] are now south of Greece and north of Egypt. Quite cool in evening. Vaccinating men this week.

Fri. 10 Clear. Big run, 305 mi. Water changes from the River Nile's delta. Was paid $55 gold on a/c.[14]

Sat. 11 Entered Said[15] in Suez Canal about 11 A.M. Went ashore in afternoon, a great old town. Left about 12 P.M. The *Princeton* and *Raleigh*[16] are here. Rec'd news of great battles in Manila. Sent letter & mans [manuscript] home. Sent H $45. Post Office, Bank, Photos [taken] Day before [:] Egyptian Christmas, police, American sailors, boats coaling ship, E. India boat coming in, ornaments, circus, ships draped.

Sun. 12 Passing through Canal all day. Saw Ismaila,[17] a beautiful spot near Bitter Lakes. Mid-Arabians, totally nude ran for miles beside ship, [crying] "Bacheech." Got into Suez about 9 P.M. Associated Press correspondent, Mr. Collins, came on board. Waited all night to get soldiers and firemen who were left in Said. Soldiers singing at night. (desert, camels, dredges, stations)

Mon. 13 Foggy. Sailed early in morning, passed to stern of Italian mail steamer, passed French transport, men all in white. Gulf of Suez, red sandstone cliffs. About 5 P.M. passed mountains on both sides. Mt. Sanaii,[18] very ragged. Beautiful sunset.

Tues. 14 300 miles. A fine sunset. Distant glimpses of land. Now in Red Sea at evening, the distant peaks of mts. 60 miles away were discerned. Quite a celebration last night. Valentines delivered, a supper afterwards. Have very little time.

Wed. 15 Weather fine. Nothing of interest. Sea calm. Hot.

Thur. 16 Fair. Hot. Calm.

Fri. 17 Heavy sea, rain in A.M. About 4 P.M. entered harbor [of] Perim Island, English, black rock covered in sand.[19] Coaled. Black divers. Barren black soil. Somalais[20] from Africa, wild fellows. 30 white men on island, English club. First American ship. Snakes extremely venomous, houses built up in air. Capt. B full.

Sat. 18 Weather fair. Nothing of note. Distant land.

Sun. 19 Saw the last of Africa. Eng. ship was near us signaled "Good Luck."

Mon. 20	Fair. The sea.	
Tue. 21	Fair. The sea.	Superb
Wed. 22	Fair. The sea.	Salutes.Moonlit
Thur. 23	Fair. The sea.	Nights
Fri. 24	Fair. The sea.	
Sat. 25	Beautiful day. Saw in the dim distance mts. at the end of India. Floating coral, flying fish, whale, porpoises. Passed close to several ships. Got into Colombo about 12 P.M., anchored in rear of Russian transport.	
Sun. 26	*Very warm*, fair. Went ashore, P.O.,[21] got photos, rode in ricksha, heard of more fighting in M.[22] The boats are green. Church music. Very beautiful flowers, sweet perfumes. Breakwater. Coal dust streaks. Cleared about 12, passed signals with "Good Luck." Alan Robertson. Launches selling jewelry.	
Mon. 27	Showers during night. Fair. Boxed up my overcoats and winter stuff.	
Tue. 28	Nothing of note. Clear.	

March

Wed. Mar. 1	Clear.
Thur. 2	Clear.
Fri. 3	Sighted land. Lay too [to] for hrs. to get soundings in Straits of Malacca.
Sat. 4	Cloudy. Many islands. Got into Singapore about 7 P.M. Went ashore. Ricksha, Chinese coolies, stores, Royal Oak Hotel, Japanese Quarter, Tanjong Pagan,[23] Up all night.
Sun. 5	Cloudy. Heavy sea.
Mon. 6	Heavy sea. Superb sunset.
Tues. 7	Clear. Nothing except water, quite a heavy sea. Remola. Learned finger exercise on typewriter.[24]
Thur. 9	Clear.
Fri. 10	Clear. Got into M about 9 A.M., salute, etc. Met *Monterey*[25] on way in. British ship *Narcissus* manned the yards and went home, fine sight. Unloaded the 17th Infantry in cascoes.[26]
Sat. 11	Dewey[27] came aboard. Met Capt. Lamberton.[28] The 4th Infantry went ashore. I went ashore in P.M. and mailed package to Father and letter. Got 2 letters from H. Wrote Percy.
Sun. 12	All day in the hold getting out baggage. Fire on shore, fight among firemen, engineers, etc. Got 2 letters from H, answered them.

Mon. 13	Heavy firing all day and last night. The *Baltimore*[29]came in.
Tues. 14	In the hold. Big fire at night.
Wed. 15	In hold.
Thur. 16	In hold.
Fri. 17	Clear. Unloading ammunition. Gen. L received his assignment.
Sat. 18	Clear. Went ashore, got a Spanish dinner, went through burnt district. *Oregon*[30] arrived in evening.
Sun. 19	In hold.
Mon. 20	In hold.
Tues. 21	In hold.
Wed. 22	In hold.
Thur. 23	In hold.
Fri. 24	Went to Spanish hotel. Was paid off $114 + left ship, damned glad of it. Old westerner who had been to India in same room.
Sat. 25	Ate breakfast at American restaurant at Bilibad [sp].[31] Went to Gen. L's Hdqtrs.[32] Major Edwards[33] and I went to Palace.[34] Was sent out on *Grant* for transfer papers. Was assigned to Capt. Walcutt Chief, Q.M[35] 1st Div., 8 A.C.[36] Ate lunch on *Grant*. Got off for last time. She sailed in P.M.
Sun. 26	No entry.
Mon. 27	Wrote H of my assignment. Sent her MO $60.[37]
Tues. 28	No entry.
Wed. 29	No entry.
Thur. 30	No entry.
Fri. 31	No entry.

April

Sat. Apr. 1	Sent H $20. Was paid for balance of month from 24th.
Sun. 2	No entry.
Mon. 3	No entry.
Tues. 4	No entry.
Wed. 5	No entry.
Thur. 6	No entry.
Fri. 7	No entry.
Sat. 8	Clear. Started in P.M. with money box and in soldiers traps [sp] to Gen. Lawton's house. There embarked in launch *Maria*;[38] went up Pasig.[39] Bad night's work, launches are all aground at San Pedro Macati. Look on troops. Dined on gin-

	ger snaps and a bottle of Apollonaris.[40] 3 A.M. all in lake, got started up lake.[41] No sleep. Walked on all night.
Sun. 9	Beautiful sunrise. At noon consultation. Afternoon moved on Santa Cruz,[42] shelled woods, landed troops. Went around in front of city, enemy not in sight. Walcutt arrived at night. Came off in early morning covered with mud.
Mon. 10th	Gen. [Lawton] was up before daybreak. Opened on city, cleaned niggers out in short time. In evening went ashore, carried much money. Wounded on wharf. Slept in Palace.
Apr. 11–30	No entries.

May

May 1–5	No entries.
May 6	Went to Palace in P.M. Horse ran away into mounted orderly, threw us on ground.[43] Got paid, sent H $55.

End of Diary

Chapter Two

January—February 1899

Getting There

At this time, the Army Transport Service, part of the Quartermaster Department, was responsible for the transport of its own troops and supplies.[1] During the run up to the Cuban expedition, the Navy had stolen a march on the Army when it quickly supplemented its own fleet with the charter or purchase of private vessels, including some pleasure craft.[2] As a consequence, there was a serious shortage of suitable transport at Tampa available to carry General Shafter's force to Cuba, let alone supply it.[3] Not wanting to be left out of the "great adventure," anxious troops and their commanders engaged in a wild scramble to secure a place in those few ships. Notwithstanding the aggressive creativeness of Colonels Wood and Roosevelt, a very disappointed contingent of the Rough Riders had to be left behind.[4] This situation, along with an inefficient supply system, would increasingly call into question the competence of Secretary of War Russell Alger. Eventually, Alger would become a scapegoat and his name synonymous with incompetence (i.e., "Algerism").

With the defeat of the Spanish fleet at Manila Bay on May 1, 1898, Admiral Dewey asked for a sufficient number of troops in order to garrison Manila. Once again, the Army would be challenged to transport troops, this time halfway around the world. As a result, the Quartermaster Department purchased a number of passenger steamers which they renamed in honor of prominent Civil War generals, like *Grant*, *Sherman*, *Sheridan*, *Thomas*, *Hancock*, and *Hooker*. While some of these ships were utilized throughout the Caribbean, the majority were sent to the Pacific, where they made twice-monthly runs between San Francisco and Manila.[5]

USAT *Thomas*

In addition to his diary, young Carter maintained a regular correspondence with his family while aboard the USAT *Grant*. His letters at this time are necessarily short, as he undoubtedly wanted them to be sent home on the next available westbound boat.

USAT *Grant*
January 18, 1899

Dear Mother,

My time is short. I send this by one of the party who came on board this a. m. with Sec. Alger.[6] Have just been talking with Mrs. Lawton. She thanks you for your kind note. Says she is sorry she has not time to answer it. I got on board in plenty of time yesterday. Poor Helen, I felt so bad to leave her. Percy was very kind and took her to the train. For my sake treat her nicely and do all you can for her. I want to find out about whether I get any allowance for traveling expenses. As it is now, I am paying at the same rate. Enclosed find $5.00. Give this to Helen and tell her I am sorry I could not send her more, but my money was in sad shape, small bills and Gold, that I did not dare to send it by letter. They say sea voyages in the Mediterranean were very beautiful. We are now anchored off of the Statue of Liberty. Time is short. Must say good-bye in haste.

Your affectionate son,
Robert D. Carter

January 28, 1899

Dear Sister,

I take this opportunity while waiting for my lunch to write you. I have hardly a minute to spare or would have written you from day to day. It is a beautiful, clear day. Very much as we have in the early part of April and May. Nearly all day we have been in sight of land, the first we have seen for many days. In fact, since our departure, we are now passing the extreme southern island of the Azores, Santa Maria. It looks in outline somewhat like this and from this distance, seems a massive mass of bronze colored rocks. The trip so far has been smooth and pleasant. I have not been sick at my stomach since departure. The only effects felt was a severe headache and dizziness when I went down in the fore part of the vessel due to the extreme pitching there. A great deal of the routine of the ship, and various like incidents, you will probably find in a letter which I will mail Helen at Gibraltar. That is if you get her to read it or show you it. Today is the first day that I have not had to hustle [torn and indecipherable] blessing on a trip like this. My duty so far has been to really be a commissary clerk and sell fruits and stuff and various articles to the soldiers. Nothing clerical whatever.

When you write me, let me know if you got my letter written from New York to you, [and] also, if Helen got money I sent her. Off Sandy Hook, I received a post [from] father. Have been writing up a dry and salty article which possibly may do [to] start the *Star* on. I understand him to say Harries had fixed it O.K. Commencing at "Gib" there will be something to write. Since leaving New York, there has been nothing of interest to write about. The sea—miles upon miles of waves flecked with foam, that's all. Someone left a camera here, as they never returned for it, I consider myself in [luck]. The question is now, for films and how to preserve them until I can get them developed. If you get a chance, read a book called *Yesterdays in the Philippines* by Stevens.[7] It is good and if things are as he says, then it will be O.K. An officer said you can live out there and have a servant for $9.00 per month. Let us trust it is so.

Mrs. Lawton, and especially the children, were dreadfully seasick. The General said he felt it more than he ever had before. In fact, I think he was pretty sick. He is in citizen's clothes and does not seem to mingle much with the other officers. Speaks to me every day; wants to know how I am, etc.

On ship board one has a very light appetite. The grub is grand—steamed oysters, salads, etc. for lunch, roast wild duck, goose, turkey and all meats with preserves for dinner; likewise ice-cream and varied desserts. Sometimes we have large fat partridges for breakfast. No "embalmed" meat here.[8] This is no horror ship. There's money and grub to burn. One man died about the second day out of meningitis; sealed him up and put him in the hold. Will land him at Gibraltar. Evenings, the talented people get together in the Dining Room, and sing individually and collectively. One fellow plays a violin grandly. Over in the corners, the old pikers, not so talented, run a game.

Captain Baker[9] is a man very similar to Fowler—good-natured, but yet a hustler. Mail me newspapers whenever you can, so I may keep in touch with Washington. Also illustrated papers, or magazines. Send by way of Frisco. Captain Baker told me today that I would not be charged a cent, so my living expense is nothing. Hurrah! General Lawton showed a good eye going as [a] passenger. He draws 7 cents per mile, $245.00 just to "Gib."

The manuscript has been written when I had a minute to spare, is crude, and needs overhauling. I wanted to type write it, but could not get a chance. If it will cost [but] a trifle, will you have it put in shape. I could greatly improve it by going over it. Let [Pa] overhaul it before having it put in shape.

An Irishman is leading the ship. [So he says:] "You stiffs lower these trunks into the basement." Another said, "I have seen the wind dig up graves in Dakota, but it can't touch this (meaning [the] ocean breeze). While passing Santa Maria, one guy said, "It would take a man who could see a coyote four miles off to see that (island)."

Tell Helen to get some of those little pictures taken. She knows; on F Street. You have some, too.

Love to all,
Tod

Gibraltar and Beyond

Shortly after his arrival in Gibraltar, Carter wrote the first of three travelogues with an eye toward publication in a magazine or newspaper. He would later tell his sister that he had thought that one day the collection might well be made into a book. His description of the famous "Pillars of Hercules" depicts not a sterile rock, but a place teeming with life. With the second article, he continued his story, fleshing out the diary entries with a description of a stop at Port Said, a transit of the Suez Canal, and the voyage across the Indian Ocean to Ceylon (now Sri Lanka).

On Board U. S. A. Transport *Grant*
Mediterranean Sea
February 10, 1899

At last, after many days, the engines are stopped, and we are at rest, gently rising and falling on the undulating swells of the Atlantic. The Tarifa Light marking the entrance to the Strait of Gibraltar, or the "Gut" so called by the mariners, is in sight. All night, crashes of thunder, incessant flashes of lightning and heavy rain are proof that we were now in the semi-tropics. To starboard, as we enter, are the jagged cliffs and rocky mountains of Barbary or Morocco. On the port, long lines of saw-toothed rocks of considerable size and height mark the Tarifa or Spanish coast, extremely rugged and wilder than New England's, here the mountains meet the sea. Waves have worn coves and grottoes among their rocky sides, and the surf whitens their base. Here we are in sight of two continents. On the African side the mountains of Atlas lift their snowy summits skyward. A singular thing about them is that for their great height, there are comparatively no foot hills or ascending grades, each standing separate, a sharp cone of matted rock standing out boldly. It is Mons Abyla, called by the Moors "Apex Hill" and has an altitude of three thousand feet. An old Moorish legend declares that from this point came into Europe the wild monkeys, a few of whose descendants still inhabit the Rock of Gibraltar. They have the distinction of being the only wild ones in the whole of Europe.

Gibraltar, anciently called Calpe and Abyla, were the legendary "Pillars of Hercules," and to the ancients marked the boundary of the Western world. Turning north, before us majestically towers the Rock—"In the dimmest north east dawned Gibraltar grand and gray." —How well England commands the entrance to the Far East is easily determined, a grim sentinel indeed.

As we approached the southern end, Point Europa, we see, ascending in tiers, parapets surmounted by the finest rifled guns, from every port and vantage point bristle heavy cannon. The middle slope is occupied by long lines of barracks and villas shaded among groves of stunted orange trees. Yet further up, on an inclined plane, is a bright green parade ground which lends color to the perpendicular block cliffs beyond and the yellow ledges in the immediate foreground.

As we approached the town, one is uniformly impressed with the architectural effect, the houses being square and severely plain, built in rows and in tiers, one above another, all of a straw or drab hue, occasionally a bright blue one to break the monotony. Nothing but stone or wood is allowed in their construction, a prevention against fire in case of siege. Opposite the old mole, or "Devil's Tongue," a land battery projecting into the harbor at the northern end of the rock, we cast anchor. To the western end lies the Bay, over eight miles in length and upwards of five in breadth. On the western curve facing Gibraltar is the old Spanish town of Algeciras. The harbor is studded with numerous craft. A great fleet of coal hulks painted somber black, a Japanese torpedo destroyer, and an Italian cruiser are anchored near. Every flag can be seen in this port. As one looks across the vast expanse of azure water, the names of Britain's naval heroes, Howe, Nelson, and Collingwood, whose great ships so often rested upon these waters, come to mind.

On the northern side, basking under sunny skies is the village of *Las Roque*. Beside it the hill of the "Queen's Seat." The story runs that during one of the great sieges, the Spanish queen swore she would not leave her seat on the summit of the hill until England's banner was hauled down. The English courteously lowered the flag long enough for Her Majesty to leave, then re-hoisting it, commenced a vigorous bombardment of the hill. The background of this grand picture are the green mountains of Ronda, whose slopes so often were whitened by the camps of the besiegers.

From our ship a twenty-one gun salute was fired in honor of the Governor, and from the water battery and high up among the misty clouds came answering booms. The climate, as a whole, is genial, winter losing all of its severity, and summer heats are tempered by refreshing sea breezes. In December and January there are violent thunder storms with gales almost tropical in their fury. It was our misfortune for the first two days in port to encounter the coldest and roughest of the season, hail falling quite thickly. During the height of the storm, the U. S. Gunboat *Princeton* passed out on her way to join Admiral Dewey's fleet. From the shore swarms of long, slender, chunky bum boats and many tugs and launches raced through clouds of spray to our ship. It is surprising how these watermen manage to row such small boats through these heavy seas. Yesterday P.M. an accident happened in lowering one of the launches. The tackle slipped, throwing a couple of sailors into the water. One hung to the boat, the other, heavily dressed in oilskins, swam like a duck (he looked like a big yellow turtle) around to the stern. A line was thrown and he was quickly drawn on board. One of the engineers was inside and went down with the boat to the water's edge where he hung by the stern. He seemed to be entirely disconcerted, and stepping out, was hauled on board still smoking a cigarette.

The health officer, vice-consul, and friend came aboard. All others were ordered away. Notwithstanding this, however, the bum boats lingered, deluged by heavy seas for hours until discouraged, they pulled back to shore. Many of the Spaniards thought it was because of their nationality that they were allowed on board to sell their wares. One eloquent spokesman with imploring look and gesture said: "Me no Spanisha man, American me English." Upon being greeted with shouts of laughter, he then said he was an "Italio man, no do harm!" Being refused and ordered away, he swore fiercely in Spanish and gesticulated wildly. Thousands of sea fowl keep up a great din, struggling, squawking heaps in the water indicating where the ship's refuse had been thrown.

To our sorrow, due to some ancient cases of measles, we are strictly quarantined. The yellow flag was hoisted and no one was allowed off or on, but sorrow was turned to joy in the morning when the orders were revoked, and we hoisted anchor and moved into the inner harbor.

We anchored between the second class battleship *Devastation* and a large American steam yacht, a worthy craft from which to fly the Stars and Stripes. The battleship has a low free board resembling somewhat one large double-turreted monitors is painted black with yellow funnels and forcibly reminds one of Britain's Empire of the seas.

In the afternoon, Gen. Lawton and staff, with Gen. Hall went ashore to be informally received by the Military Governor and also to call on the American Consul. Hundreds of grimy Spaniards are coaling the ship. It is astounding to see the small, slim-waisted and narrow-hipped youths carrying heavy coal baskets from sunrise to sunset, laughing, smiling, smoking and singing, apparently not exhausted with such heavy labor. Many of them are soldiers returning from Cuba and Puerto Rico, a villainous looking lot. The British torpedo destroyer *Griffin* circled the ship at high speed, hearty cheers being exchanged by the tars and U. S. soldiers.

The Rock of Gibraltar, England's pride, her "Crouching Lion," forms a promontory, rising seaward to a height of 1,400 feet, connected with the mainland by a low, sandy isthmus. The Rock is divided into two unequal parts by a ridge running north and south, the principal points being "Rock Mortar," 1,350 feet, "Signal," 1,276 feet (a large signal station is here covering a wide range of vision), and "Sugar Loaf" at the south, 1,439 feet. The western section is a gradual slope broken by precipices, but the eastern, which faces the blue Mediterranean and the north facing Spain, are steep and inaccessible. The ridge is honeycombed with galleries, is about two miles long, about one-half mile in breadth at its base, the entire circumference being between seven and nine miles. At the base of the northwest slope lies the town of Gibraltar, about 20,000 inhabitants. Along the sea wall are mounted heavy batteries in casemates suitable for 1,500 men. Fragments of old Moorish walls can be seen ascending the slopes. From the summit is a beautiful view. At one's feet are many batteries intermingled with villas and gardens. To the westward the Spanish hills and rocky coast of Tarifa. To the east a vast expanse of deep blue water, the Mediterranean. To the north roll the hills of Ronda, the little town of San Rocque nestling on the summits and yet beyond, mute, lost in long banks of clouds the snowy caps of the Sierra Bermejo, well-named "Snow Saw."

Facing north commanding the sandy isthmus with Spain, is the "Rock." It is here the large eight and ten inch guns project their black muzzles from galleries hewn in solid rock. The "Windsor" galleries and "Hall of St. George" were made during the great siege. In the latter, Nelson was entertained prior to the battle of Trafalgar. The grand range of batteries whose parapets, etc. contain over one thousand guns. England's activity is ceaseless. Each year sees old batteries displaced by the latest ordnance. At the present time, a big cut is being made in the center of the ridge to mount guns firing east or west. The present garrison numbers over eight thousand picked men.

Upon landing, I crossed a drawbridge over a wide, wet ditch filled with water, passed under a stone archway with a former governor's name and date of term inscribed upon it, and found myself upon a narrow, ascending roadway. Passing through casemates and pyramids of ancient cannonballs on either side were beautiful gardens, luxuriant with subtropical flora, clinging vines, large rose bushes and graceful palms. Surrounding these, parallel with the sea wall, are parapets on which ceaselessly pace sentinels in red coats and white helmets. Upon entering the streets one soon sees that architecture has been sacrificed to solidity. There are a few Spanish houses with *mirandas* or towers, from which the inmates, without leaving their houses, can view the ample prospect of the Bay and purple hills of the neighboring coasts.

The two or three principal long streets run parallel to the sea. Branching off in every direction are narrow alleys and lanes with flights of broad stone steps called "ramps." In the main street are to be seen every type of civilization. Riding in light wood, double-seated pony carts are English officers, travelers and English women on their way to market or shopping. On the sidewalks, barely permitting two people to walk abreast, crowding and gesticulating, undersized Spaniards incessantly smoking, pass to and fro. Barelegged Moors, fine looking fellows, abound, and striding along in hobnailed shoes, his little hat one inch from his right eye, passes "Tommy Atkins" the beau ideal, crack English soldier. I was much impressed with these strong types of the British army. They are indeed splendid specimens of manhood, robust and hardy. The different regiments are graded in size, the larger men belonging to organizations wearing white jackets, the smaller ones wearing the red coats of the artillery and engineers.

In appearance, the Spanish women fell far short of my expectations, being coarse featured, with heavy eyebrows and painted cheeks. Their redeeming features were their dark, lustrous eyes and graceful carriage. Every type of a Spaniard can be seen, from the coal-begrimed stevedores, and uncouth, loud-voiced mule drivers, to "sporty" ones with curved "love lock" on his forehead, and brilliant sash on his waist—the genuine "Don."

On entering the bazaars one is greeted with profound salaams and much rubbing of hands. Asking the prices you are amazed at the high figures asked. Americans especially seem to be the "good thing" of all Europe. Starting at their first outrageous sum, after much haggling and many drops in the price, you start for the door and immediately off comes a shilling, until at last exhausted with bargaining you secure your purchase and make your escape to the street. Following one on the street are swarms of gamins on each and every corner you turn; horrible looking beggars thrust forth their hands, all asking for coppers. Entering a café, I asked for some candy. Staring at me for some time, the Spanish salesman at last said: "Do you mean taffy?" I stood corrected; however, there is no good candy to be had in "Gib." The only kind being French preserved fruits and cakes of chocolate filled with cream.

Near the seawall at the terminus of the main street is the Moorish market. Live poultry seemed to be their principal stock in trade. The Moors are very picturesque in fezzes and turbans, with long, flowing garments, the younger ones barelegged, the older ones wearing heavy ribbed hose and red or yellow slippers. Fruit is very bountiful and fine. The oranges are small, but exceedingly juicy. The tamarinds are most delicious. Seedless lemons, thin skinned and larger than American oranges, are to be had on all sides. The figs seem dried and packed in small boxes, are very nice. For convenience, all fruit is delivered to you in woven grass baskets.

Liquor in price runs from very low for cognac and wines to quite high for good American whiskey. In the evening, with two bright young soldiers of the Royal Artillery, I saw the various places of amusement frequented by the soldiers and the streets by lamp light. In the Café Universale sat hundreds of soldiers at tables sipping wine, smoking and chatting, quite similar to our beer gardens. On a small stage were some Spanish dancers. Their dance seemed to comprise several glides, a movement from the hips and a pirouette, the whole accompanied by guitars and clattering castanets. For my part, I think them quite inferior to our music hall dancers.

All night, through the many winding streets slowly tramps the patrol, six stalwart troopers led by a corporal. Befuddled Jack Tars tack about on the "Ramps" at a loss for their warship. Skulking Spaniards and Portuguese disappear into the gloom of blind alleyways. In some quarters it is exceedingly dangerous for English or Americans to venture out at night. Sitting in a latticed café the soldiers drank ale and spin yarns, many of them have been nearly all over the world. The recent events in Cuba and Puerto Rico have made things quite lively around "Gib," for some time. Consequently, it was chiefly the Spanish-American War that they talked.

As the war progressed, the Spanish accounts in their "*El Calpense*" grew, from day to day, more and more exaggerated at the successes attending their arms. They could scarcely restrain their rage, however, when the London papers arrived contradicting all their reports. At one time they started to erect fortifications over by San Roque, and on the Moorish coast, but stern warnings from the English governor caused them to speedily desist. During their construction there occurred a mishap which nearly occasioned serious trouble. One of the hundred ton guns in the Rock was being exercised at targets on the rocky headland across the Bay; the shot ricocheting struck one of the small Spanish earthworks and knocked it into a "cocked hat." Luckily no one was injured. Before the war, the soldiers, when on leave or pass, would take the little steamer and cross the bay to Algeciras or "Spanish Town." Their return pass would be signed by the Governor reading: "Governor of Algeciras, Alameda and Gibraltar, temporarily in the hands of England."

This farce has continued since 1704. One or two venturesome Americans who crossed the isthmus into Spain during the late war were nearly killed, one being stabbed quite severely. This caused a suspension of fox hunting on the hills of Ronda by our British cousins until more congenial times.

Between the Spanish boundary marked by towers and the north face of the "Rock" is the neutral ground, the only land approach from the mainland. From this neck, Gibraltar is impregnable. The lower batteries, termed by the Spanish "the Mouth of Fire," can blow away the narrow causeway at a single discharge. Several tiers of guns extending to the seawall and "Willie's Batteries" halfway up the crag peep out through the fissures and are called "The Old Lady's Teeth." In addition, the "Devil's Tongue" projecting into the harbor sweeps this narrow neck of land.

After four days stop at this mightiest and historic peninsula, the Rock of Gibraltar, we got under way and started for our next coaling place, Port Said, on our voyage to the Far East. As we steamed out of the Rock, to leeward with fast fleeting shadows playing over it, it never appeared more majestic and beautiful. To starboard, we passed the little white U. S. Gunboat *Castine*, which had cast anchor. Boats filled with British soldiers waved their hats and cheered lustily a final adieu. It was with much regret that we saw the last of Gibraltar. Rounding Europa, over by Mount Abyla, on the Moorish Coast, Ceuta could be clearly seen. It was on this rocky point that Spain kept all prisoners brought from Cuba and her other colonies. Here on this desolate spot many political prisoners have met an unknown fate, either by lingering merciless death or rapid execution.

To the south the low purple, undulating hills of Africa outlined against an azure sky. To the north, enveloped in great banks of fleecy clouds, the lofty summits of the Sierra Nevadas can be faintly seen through blue haze. In our wake the perpendicular cliffs of Gibraltar broken by great banks of yellow sand gradually fade from our gaze, the fiery African sun slowly sinks in a gray cloudbank. The darkening shadows grow as night closes in. We are once more alone upon the sea.
Robert D. Carter

February 10, 1899

My Dear Father,

Your letter received at "Gib." I was very glad to hear from home, also that Helen's welfare will be attended to. As to the requisition, I shall forward one from Manila. It will do no harm, even if it is not allowed. The manuscript and drawing will need to be corrected somewhat, [as] my time was short and conveniences few. I should judge it ought to run about three columns. The little history can be inserted wherever you think best or left out entirely. The chart gives a better idea than photo, although I enclose photo which gives the precise view of the Rock as seen from the ship. The roads and walls appear more distinctly than in the larger. The large one may do to make a true print from. For myself, I think the plan does very well, although they might not like the printing.

We had a fine voyage across the Atlantic. In my letters to Helen and in the papers I have covered "Gib" pretty well. On the "Med" it is smooth and the air Spring like. I think we shall [have] a cool trip. It is just right so far. I still wear heavy flannels [and] have not needed [an] overcoat more than one day out from New York. From Said we go to Aden, then a long trip, 3,600 miles, or 14 or 15 days, to Colombo, Ceylon, where we coal. The engineers say, "Hell will be cool [compared] to the Indian Sea."

See very little of General Lawton. He seems to keep to himself most of the time in his stateroom. Mrs. Lawton does not think she will do any writing. At present, she is hard up with a vaccinated arm. I think I will get my arm vaccinated at Manila or further along on the trip when we are not so busy. Shall have to get me a mackintosh at Manila for when it rains there it rains. Tomorrow, we will be in Said. The stop will be short.

Am well and have been free from sea sickness. On the "Med" we were in sight of [the] African shore [for] about two days. As my time is short, [I] will close with love to hound and all, I am

Your affectionate son

Robert D. Carter

P. S. Got letter from Helen at "Gib." Tell her.

On Board U.S.A. Transport *Grant*
Nearing Colombo, Island of Ceylon
February 25, 1899

For some days after leaving Gibraltar we were within sight of the low, undulating hills of Africa; the sky was cloudless, the air balmy and a very slight swell rippled on the deep blue waters of the Mediterranean. Occasionally a ragged island comes to view and many vessels passed us at too great a distance to speak. Malta, we passed during the night; after which, we saw no more land until about one o'clock on Feb. eleventh, when the distant outlines of Port Said assumed shape and emerged in splendor, apparently from the sea. On either side no land could be discerned. The distant shipping, domes, minarets and tall chimneys seemed to rest upon the bosom of the sea, a strange, yet beautiful mirage.

The waters of the Mediterranean are here, at intervals, streaked with the yellow, muddy waters from the deltas of the Nile causing a curious contrast with the deep blue. A trim little "Pilote" boat soon came out to meet us, passing a great stone breakwater which extends far out into the sea; by the Dutch warship

Piet Hein, whose crew crowded the deck and gave us a rousing reception. At last we were moored by great cables to buoys in the inner basin. Coming directly into the heart of the city from the sea, made it seem not unlike Venice. The waterfront is a great beach of yellow sand, on which break incessantly long green ridges of surf with a resounding boom. Near the beach is quite a large area, bare of habitations, the level stretches of sand reflecting the rays of the sun. Ships coming in from the sea enter directly into the canal, or a series of great basins at its entrance. Our ship is directly opposite the Suez Canal Company's building. It is by far the most impressive edifice in Said constructed of olive colored tiles; with three great domes, a signal station on the center one, it can be seen from all sides. Standing apart, on a fine stone pier, its modern lines contrast strongly with the plain buildings of the neighboring section of the city. Along the waterfront are hundreds of neat little boats, manned by a motley throng of native boatmen. Among them are all types of the Holy Land, Turks, Egyptians, Arabs, Syrians and ebony Nubians. A fine force of uniformed harbor police wearing the square Egyptian fez compel order.

Directly before us lies the USS *Raleigh* returning from Manila; on either side of her are a Dutch warship painted white, and a small, black English torpedo gunboat. To our port, their bows to the channel are moored the U.S. gunboat *Princeton*, a Dutch cruiser and several merchant craft. Dotting the harbor are trim little launches, boats from the many warships propelled with the long regular man-of-war's stroke, coal barges, and numerous wherries with picturesque natives at the sweeps. Floating over the water is heard the prolonged chanting of the coalers, who in an endless stream from a distance, appearing like ants, pass in and out of the ships. These stevedores are dirty, wretched working human beings clothed in but a single ragged garment. They coal a ship very rapidly, working much faster than the ones so far encountered. As night approaches, the primitive beacons, crude iron baskets filled with chunks of coal, cast a weird light on little groups, eating their simple fare, a coarse loaf and a little fruit.

For three pence I was rowed ashore, there to be almost literally carried away by a swarm of couriers wearing brass insignias, donkey drivers and herds of foul urchins howling "baksheesh."[10] The streets near the waterfront are wide, partially paved and fronted by substantial stores and buildings. Crossing a little bridge, passing between twin rows of olive, orange and fig trees, I came to the market. Here, sprawling, by filthy booths, were all shades of men and women; swarms of flies fill the air, and the odor from decayed fish and vegetation, not to mention the natives was indescribable. Being besieged "tooth and nail" by donkey drivers, I was at last obliged to halt; determining that my only escape lay in mounting one, I got on my first Egyptian donkey, and trust it will be my last. Once upon the beast, I was informed that the pay was in advance. After jabbering, haggling and cussing, two shillings was advanced, and I thought my troubles ended. Alas! 'Twas but the beginning. Beaten with a stout club from behind, the little beast dashed off around corners at a great pace to the immediate peril of my neck. The stirrups, instead of being a support, are a deception, sliding from side to side with every pressure of the foot; with the bridle but a mere halter and loaded with belts, it is difficult, once started, to come to a stop. The louder I yelled and tugged, the faster the club descended, and the greater the pace, until at last, I know not how, we came to a halt, and I, sore and bruised, alighted. Here I was again asked for money. The first payment, I was told, was for the master; this was for the driver. I concluded the next payment would be for the mule, so I refused, and presto! My conveyance disappeared. The boy in the bazaar which I entered told me that the owner got nothing, so I surmise the drivers are the winners at this game. One has to arise early in the morning to beat these sons of Egypt. An English penny to the natives is big money, when compared with their coin subdivided into infinitesimal fractions. The bazaars are filled with knickknacks of every sort; silverware depicting the Sphinx and pyramids or covered with prayers in Egyptian or Arabic from the Koran predominate. Here, relics from the Holy Land can be had by the cartloads; stones from Jacob's well, ornaments of olive wood from Gethsemane, and pieces of the True Cross are seen on all sides.

Port Said well sustains its name of the "wickedest place in the world." On sale are the vilest photographs imaginable, while the city fairly teems with the scum of Europe, Asia, and Africa, the latter being pretty bad. The day of our arrival was an Egyptian holiday, it being the day before Christmas, so the warships and transports were gaily dressed in honor, and in town, a little more laziness was visible than usual. The further from the waterfront the more scattered the habitations, the greater evidences of African filth, until, on a broad stretch of level land near a grave yard called "Little Arabia," I came upon a crowd celebrating the Egyptian festival. Beating drums, flutes and bells furnished music, to which were danced the seven or more varied dances, foremost of which was the famous "*Dance du Ventre*." Horrible looking old fakirs were pulling trained monkeys and snakes through their antics. There were several Bedouin tents which I could not summons courage to enter due to the horrible odor from the crowd inside. To one who has never been near an Egyptian of the lower class, the odor is appalling. No description can do it justice. Water to them is evidently unknown for bathing purposes, and their garments finally drop from them by reason of decay and age. Surrounding the fair were numerous groups, quite similar to those at our pleasure parks, in which gyrated and gesticulated wild looking men, each trying to outdo his neighbor in violence and exertion of swinging. Upon leaving, I entered upon one of the main streets leading to the waterfront. On the sidewalks every nationality was represented, Egyptians, French and Italians seemed to predominate. Sailors from the warships on don-

keys and afoot were celebrating the holiday in a style of their own. Little bob-tail train cars drawn by a doubtful assortment of beasts rolled along, filled with fat Frenchmen, Egyptian women of higher class, lace veils covering their faces to the eyes, Arabians in turbans, Syrians, Turks and Egyptians in the red fez. Rows of gnarled trees, thick in foliage, line the main streets. Little parks and statues surrounded by neat iron fences lend attractiveness. The police in neat blue uniforms, red fezzes and smartly polished shoes are much in evidence. On the whole, for an Eastern city, it is quite clean and [well] constructed. It is probably the most cosmopolitan city in the world.
Robert D. Carter

Chapter Three

March 1899

On the Cusp of Empire

With the defeat of the Spanish fleet at Manila Bay on May 1, 1898, Commodore (soon to be Admiral) George Dewey asked for a sufficient number of troops to garrison Manila, then occupied by the Spanish forces. Shortly thereafter, on June 30, 1898, nearly nine months before Lawton's arrival, the first wave of American soldiers, a contingent of approximately 2,500, arrived under the command of Brig. Gen. Thomas M. Anderson. The troops consisted of the 14th U.S. Infantry, the 2nd Oregon Volunteer Infantry, and the 1st California Volunteer Infantry. They would be followed by Brig. Gen. Francis V. Greene with approximately 3,600 more troops. Overall command would initially rest with Maj. Gen. Wesley Merritt, who arrived with Brig. General Arthur MacArthur and an additional 4,800 troops on July 25.[1] Although his tenure would be brief, Merritt would eventually command a mixed force of approximately 20,000 Regulars and Volunteers, which would form the 8th Army Corps.[2] By mid-1900, this number would increase to approximately 60,000.[3]

The insurgent forces under the command of Emilio Aguinaldo had surrounded Manila and laid siege to it. Upon arrival, Anderson's force camped south of the city. As more and more American troops arrived, General Merritt convinced his Filipino "allies" to allow American troops to occupy a portion of the line adjacent to Manila Bay on the left. Aguinaldo was only too happy to accommodate him. After all, Dewey had ordered the Navy to transport him and other insurgent leaders back home following their exile. Moreover, with no clear directive from Washington, Dewey may have sent mixed signals to Aguinaldo.[4] Of more significance, earlier in the year, E. Spencer Pratt, the American Consul General at Singapore, had assured

Aguinaldo that America had no colonial designs on the Philippines whatsoever and would assist him in reclaiming them from Spanish rule.[5] The insurgent leader was so confident with these assurances that he declared Philippine independence on June 12, 1898.[6]

American politics, however, complicated matters. As peace negotiations with the Spanish in Paris dragged on, McKinley tested the will of the electorate through a series of speeches. Simultaneously, Dewey and Merritt were conducting negotiations with the Spanish garrison commander, this time, however, with clear directions from Washington, to the effect that the insurgents were to be deliberately left out of the process, that no assistance was to be provided to them, and that under no circumstances were they to be allowed to occupy Manila, not even jointly with American soldiers.[7] Eventually, an agreement was reached whereby Spanish honor would be preserved with a token exchange of fire, and the garrison surrendered to the Americans, who, in turn, were expected to keep the insurgents out. The surrender occurred on August 13, 1898, with minimal loss of life,[8] and the 2nd Oregon Volunteers were quickly hustled into the Old City for provost duty.[9] Aguinaldo and his forces were understandably upset. In their eyes, they had been betrayed by the Americans.[10] Matters only got worse from that point on.

Merritt was recalled to assist in the negotiations in Paris. His place was taken by Maj. Gen. Elwell Otis, a cautious, desk-bound man, unpopular with his subordinates, and known as "Granny" or "Grandma" to his troops.[11] In addition, he was a notorious micromanager, something that would contribute to that animosity.[12] Some of the criticism of Otis is unfair. He was a wounded Civil War veteran, a scholar, and a lawyer, and, given the success of his later offensives against the insurgents, he could also be considered a good strategist who was prepared to carry out McKinley's policy of "benevolent assimilation."[13]

The American forces formed a thin fourteen-mile ring around Manila, starting in the north next to Manila Bay and the adjacent marshes, and then looping around to the south, again touching the Bay.[14] The Pasig River, which flows through Manila, divided the American force into a North and a South Line, each section the responsibility of a division, at this time, the 2nd and 1st Divisions respectively. The Americans themselves were surrounded by the Filipino forces, many occupying abandoned Spanish blockhouses and earthen works. One soldier likened it to a "state of siege."[15] The situation deteriorated daily with the sporadic firing upon and taunting of the Americans. According to one officer: "House servants became provocative in their attitude toward their employers. Along the outposts the situation daily became more trying. Filipinos taunted Americans with profanity and obscenity recently learned

Maj. Gen. Elwell Otis, U.S. Volunteers

from the latter."[16] All this gave the impression of American weakness. Everyone was on edge. Largely inexperienced Volunteers returned fire at the drop of a hat, especially at night. Things finally came to a head during the night of February 4, 1899, with an exchange of fire between members of the 1st Nebraska Volunteers and a small party of insurgents. From that point, the fight was on, with the Americans now trying to break the stalemate and to push out the lines, first to the north, and eventually to the south. For their part, the insurgents fought back, giving way grudgingly, only to occupy new defensive positions. They also infiltrated the American lines in order to cause trouble in Manila as they did on the night of February 22/23, when they set fires. As a direct result, a 7:00 P.M. curfew was imposed.[17]

This was the situation on the ground at the time Carter arrived as part of Lawton's force on March 10.

"A Floating Row"—Life Aboard the *Grant*

In a long letter to his father, Carter goes to considerable lengths to describe his voyage to the Orient aboard the *Grant*, at one point describing it as a "floating row," which is in sharp contrast to his travelogues in which he maintains a more upbeat tone. Aside from the petty rivalries among the crew members, there were numerous opportunities for graft, whether with the purchase of coal from the Spanish in Gibraltar or the illegal sale of liquor on board ship. To the latter, he indicates that he turned a blind eye and said nothing. He even hints that Captain Baker, lawyer turned Volunteer quartermaster, whose recordkeeping skills were nonexistent, took advantage of his many opportunities to line his pockets. Baker even ousted the commissary and assumed his functions, thus compounding the problem. Throughout his correspondence, Carter draws a clear distinction between the efficiency and integrity of Regular officers serving as quartermasters compared with Volunteers performing the same duties.

The contrast between a Regular quartermaster and one in the Volunteers is striking. He allows as how a depot quartermaster, who is responsible for the award of contracts to those provisioning vessels in his area, is in line to accept bribes, and at Gibraltar, more than likely did so. Later, rumors would circulate about kickbacks involving General Otis which went nowhere, unlike a major scandal involving the commissary in Manila in 1901 that did.[18]

As a case in point, Carter describes the coaling of the ship at Gibraltar which was, at best, a very dirty and laborious job.[19] While there, he and another man were each assigned to a hatch to keep a tally of the baskets of coal as they were loaded on the ship. The American tally called for 21 baskets to the ton, while the Spanish held that 20 baskets constituted that weight. The young man faithfully recorded the correct tally at his hatch. Later on during the voyage, the chief engineer accused Carter of accepting a bribe to short weight the ship on coal while at Gibraltar. Carter was incensed and nearly came to blows with his accuser.

Moreover, as far as Carter was concerned, the two-month voyage was a lost opportunity to learn his job as a quartermaster clerk. He told his father that although Captain Baker was kind to him, which could well have been Baker's recognition that Carter was under the protection of General Lawton, at the same time, he received no training. Yet Baker could also have had an ulterior motive. As further evidence of this point, Baker took pains to keep Carter in the dark about the goings on aboard the *Grant*, especially with the accounts. Again, this was more than likely precautionary, afraid that Carter would pass something on to Lawton.

In addition, there was some resentment of Carter by other crew members, who thought that they should have been Baker's clerk. However, as standoffish as he might have been, Carter did mingle with some of the Regular infantry officers like Lt. John C. Gregg, later killed in action. Later on, in Manila, he would be clearly pleased when more senior officers made the connection with his father.

A New Assignment

With perhaps a brief excursion or two ashore, after arriving in Manila, Carter remained on board the *Grant*, as he described it, "in the hold," awaiting his assignment on shore. The suspense was undoubtedly stressful, and it was literally at the last minute when he received his orders. No surprise, he was assigned to Lawton's headquarters located in a large house on 38 Nozaleda Street in Paco. In fact, the general's office was next to his. Once ashore, much of what he found in Manila and its environs concerned him. No detail is too small, as he describes everything from the noisy hotel where he spent his first night ashore, to the weather, to the rate of exchange and the cost of living. Prices for many items were high and food was bad. "Nearly everything," he reported, "has a suspicious smell." Doing laundry, let alone having an adequate supply of proper clothing, was problematic. Overall, there was the constant threat of attack by insurgents infiltrating Manila. As a precaution, sufficient small arms and ammunition were kept at his office. On the positive side, Carter, who was for the most part a loner, enjoyed evening walks on the *Luneta* ("little moon"), a popular oval promenade with bandstands at either end adjacent to the Old Walled City (known as the *Intramuros*), where he got his exercise, or simply sat and watched spectacular sunsets over Manila Bay and the distant mountains.[20]

Throughout his correspondence, Carter shows his disdain for the native Filipinos, referring to them at times as "nigger," "dago," "gu gu," and "umbria," among others.[21] A good early example is his lack of concern for the fate of the Filipino driver who broke curfew so that Robert could retrieve his laundry. He is almost amused at the thought that that person might be "calaboosed." General Otis banned the use of such derogatory terms, to no avail.[22]

Carter was entitled to a commutation reimbursement for his travel to the Orient, but collecting it involved paperwork. In the end, he let the matter drop, reasoning that he had had free room and board on the ship, courtesy of Captain Baker, and he anticipated significant bureaucratic red tape. However, it was his pay status that would cause him problems throughout the coming year. Appointed as a temporary civilian clerk by a Volunteer officer (Law-

A gate to the old walled city or Intramuros, Manila, P.I.

ton), he would rise or fall with the quartermaster to whom he was attached at any given time. While on the voyage to Manila, he was treated as a civilian transport clerk and paid $1,000 per year, whereas permanent civilian quartermaster clerks were paid $1,200 per year after six-months' service. The initial difference was justified by the fact that as a civilian quartermaster clerk, room and board would be his responsibility.

Once ashore, without the shipboard perks, after Carter had assumed the duties of a quartermaster clerk, doing the same work as his companions, he expected to be paid the same as they were. For him, though, it was a case of simple fairness. He observed that Regular quartermasters had full-time clerks who were assigned to them and who were paid the full salary of $100 per month. Moreover, such clerks had better job security.

The powers that be in Washington appeared deaf to his attempts to collect what he thought was his just due, and the failure of the Army to rectify the situation was a constant and increasingly frustrating experience. So much so, it became an obsession, and he mentions it in virtually all of his succeeding correspondence. As he sorted through the problem, it became clear that his situation more than likely stemmed from his temporary appointment. He told his father that perhaps he had misunderstood the nature of his appointment. In truth, the appointment came through Lawton's influence, and, in any event, he considered it a stepping stone toward his ultimate goal of becoming an army officer, or at the very least, a Civil Service employee in Washington, D.C.

Early on, Carter remained hopeful that his bride, Helen, would be able to join him in Manila, and he expressed the hope that he would be able to take on some side work while there. Using his colleague William ("Willie") Leathe, who brought his intended bride over to get married, as an example, Carter felt certain that he and Helen could make a go of it. Moreover, he pointed out that there were numerous women presently in the Philippines, who were not wives, but who took advantage of the free travel to go on a junket. Both he and she blew hot and cold about the prospect, which plan was ultimately abandoned when the Army changed its policy. In the meantime, like most soldiers, Carter joined a mess group composed of fellow clerks. In addition to drawing the standard ration, they were able to pool resources in order to purchase better food locally and from the commissary.[23]

Carter would learn his job with the help of Leathe, a permanent clerk assigned to the division quartermaster. Some of his correspondence during this period, although thankfully very little, is fragmentary. He sprinkles many of his letters with whimsical sketches. In one early letter, he used his free time on the *Grant* to roughly detail his view of Manila Bay from the deck, as well as the warships floating at anchor, which he refers to in a letter to his father.

[Fragment of letter dated on or about March 17, 1899]

[My dear father,]

Let me know if any of my articles have been published. Received two letters from Helen awaiting me. They were sent to Brooklyn after we had sailed, were dated the 18th. The one I got at "Gib" was a later one. There may be mail ashore for us. The *Oregon* is said to be about due. She will be a welcome addition. Mrs. Lawton and the General have been very nice to me. I am worried now about my orders. I am afraid the General will get busy on the line and forget to detach me from the ship. Prices are enormous—25 cents to wash a shirt! Twenty-five cents per pound of ice. And my kind of a shack commands big prices. Shall get shirts, clothes from quartermaster of infantry, private's stuff, all to work in.

Will write you in full regarding my commutation allowance order, as soon as I know more fully. Am now making out vouchers. Complicated affairs. General Lawton says: "If you are entitled to it, you will get it right here." When I get all [paperwork] made out in duplicate, will get him to sign. He saw your letter regarding it. If it is not allowed here, shall forward to Washington to you.

Am feeling fine. I have a good stock of quinine. I am afraid it is a hard old town to exist in at reasonable rates, but there should be good chances for me to make money on the side. Shall investigate the gold report first. Shall keep writing to the home papers, and if they pay anything at all, it should be a good item to me.

Love to all, I close

Your affectionate son,

Robert D. Carter

P. S. General Hall[24] has just been talking to me. He said he was at San Antonio when you came out. Also remembers Mother. (Spoke of Olmstead, inquired concerning your health, and ended by saying, "that was a good many years ago, so perhaps you may see, I have known of your father longer than you have." Very nice. General Hall is a man of few words, and very much of a gentleman. He is the first officer that knows you or has spoken to me of you.

Carter refers to his Sketch of Manila Bay when he writes:

[Fragment of letter dated on or about March 19, 1899]

This is the view in front of me as I write. The ships constantly swing in circles, so are constantly changing. On our other side are the *Oregon*,[25] HMS *Pauncefote* and the fleet of merchant ships and the transports. Went ashore yesterday. Great place. I have not received any shore assignment yet. The *Grant* sails for home on the 25th if not before. Tomorrow if I get a chance am going to make a good drawing of the city from the Bay. Some of the little photos I forwarded give a pretty good idea of the places we stopped.

[Your loving son,

Robert D. Carter]

March 19, 1899

My Dear Sister,

You cannot imagine how glad I was to receive your letter, along with one from Mamma. The news was very welcome. I am so glad that it turned out well, and hope Helen will not worry, and will be patient until I get things fixed for her. She mentions bringing the hound. That is not to be thought of. He must stay with you because it would be a tremendous job to bring him here, and he could not be with me. When she comes, send some picture papers, *Harpers*, etc., also fudge. Likewise a few Washington papers with articles of interest to me. Of course, I told you about our trip to New York, how nice Percy was, etc., and my letters and descriptions home covered the different stopping places. Our whole trip was remarkably free from bad weather. When Helen comes, I hope she can get a transport from New York. It would be a saving in car fare, and the trip is much finer. If not, she must work it from Frisco. I did not receive your special to New York. It seems peculiar [it's] two months later to a day. I should be answering your letter. I sit on the afterdeck facing the battleship *Oregon*.

Send me duplicate clippings of my articles. The "Old Man" has been assigned to the 1st Division, formerly General Anderson, yesterday. I expect mine will be something soon in the night.

I think Pa would enjoy the trip down here, not only for the beautiful sights, but for the benefits from the long trip on water. I gained flesh, appetite, etc. [and] am feeling as well as I ever did. Of course it would be hard on his sleep. The engines, etc., also rolling in case of heavy weather. I sleep next to the engine room with an electric fan buzzing in the room at night and sleep like a top. It is very hard to work one's brain here. I feel drowsy all the time. Have had hard work since I got into this post, but today am enjoying a snap, having finished my [work].

Your affectionate brother,
Tod

March 20, 1899

Dear Father,

Received your letter at Gibraltar, also two here. I got four letters in all from Helen, nearly all forwarded, two from Mamma enclosing [a] stack [of] clippings, which I greatly appreciate; also, one from Mell. I have stepped foot on shore but twice, then but for a few hours. All my time has been devoted to the hold, getting out cargo. I manage to work the "Dagoes" for all they are worth. General Lawton has said nothing about my assignment ashore. Mrs. Lawton and the children are still on the ship. I am gaining by staying on the ship while she's here, for it would cost me more to live ashore. When I go ashore permanently, I shall have to hustle for an abode.

You say General Lawton contemplated a civil position for me; in just what line? I understood in Washington that I would be assigned to the Quartermaster Department, and would be in the Army for awhile until I saw a favorable opening. To be in this place, not in a government position, is rather a risky business. So in as much as I am under government employ, I feel secure, in as much as I will get my money, and also receive transportation to the U. S. sometime. In a civil position, I have no idea what day will find me adrift in a foreign land, destitute. And sailors say this is the worst spot on the globe for a man to get stranded. I will feel OK when I know just what will come next. I think this place has been overdrawn. The climate, so far as it goes, is not severe. I do [not] find it so uncomfortable as in Washington during the hot spell. My health [is] excellent. I have gained flesh and am all right. As soon as I am detached from the ship, I will forward my voucher to Washington for $150.00. I hardly expect to get [it]. The other clerks traveling out here [are] in the Adjutant General's Office and had their orders [read]: "You will proceed, etc."They got their money from one of the quartermasters here.

As it now is, I am very glad that Helen did not come. With this uncertainty, it is well that she were safe in Washington. As soon as I know what I am to do, I will fix it up for her. There should be no difference for her to come on some of the U. S. transports, as there are lots of women [who] have no business out here. Friends, relatives, etc. of officers that have come out and returned, a kind of junket, so I think there should be no trouble about her coming and orders, and I trust she can sail from New York because Percy can look after her, and the expense will be small. By way of Frisco the fare will be quite an item, not to mention the trouble she might have locating the transport at the docks, her length of stay in Frisco, etc.

Each day, the Filipinos get a little worse licking. They do not [attack] in masses, but keep up a harassing guerilla warfare.

March 23, 1899

While the weather yet remains good, there will be great activity on our part to end the war. Lawton is having the rapid fire guns taken off the transports and placed on small river-going boats.[26] From what I hear, a general move to clear them out is contemplated by the end of the week. The *Sherman* came in yesterday. She is the sister ship of the *Grant*. They can hardly be told apart. She had several deaths and encountered tougher weather than we did.

Went to Lawton's Headquarters yesterday. He was not there. The ship sails in two days, and I have not yet received my assignment. I understand a clerk in the Quartermaster Department receives a raise from $1,000.00 to $1,200.00 after the first [six] months. I am anxious to be transferred from this Department because there is a greater chance of permanency in the position and besides, it will be but a [few] months before I get a raise.

[Manila] is a hard old town. The eating is [bad]; nearly everything has a suspicious smell. It takes a great quantity of clothes to be presentable. Since leaving New York, I have had no chance to have my washing done. My [changes] I have washed myself, and at ["Gib"] I got considerable stuff which [will see me] through. Got a letter yesterday from Mamma enclosing a great number of stories, etc. Today the long lost special delivery of Mell's of the 18th of January arrived [and] a letter from Helen. Tell Mr. Thompson, I thank him very much for his kindness in sending me the *Army-Navy Journal*, and just as soon as I get ashore will send him personal news of the officers, etc. I suppose he does not want the "Volunteer's," only the Regular Officer's letters.

March 26, 1899

I have but a minute. I have been holding this to know just where I am [assigned]. Yesterday, I got my assignment a firm [one]. Am well. Helen can come out. I wrote her more fully today. I write at each opportunity covering everything [about the] trip, Manila, etc. We got a severe repulse yesterday [on] the left of the line.[27] Your letters received, the last dated January 30, I think. I want to thank you for your kindness to Helen and your many efforts in Washington on my behalf. I can never forget it.

Love to all, Natalie, hound, Thomas Keedle, Little Annie, etc., Mrs. T, in fact [to] all. I am well fixed. The climate is all right. I only regret Helen will get here during [the] rainy season.

Your affectionate son,
Robert D. Carter

P.S. Love to Grandpa & Aunt Nellie and thank them for their nice letter and present to Helen. I am well fixed, best section of city, big house for office.

March 31, 1899

Dear Father,

Yesterday I received a letter from you, one each from Helen, Mell and Mrs. Choate, the latter enclosing a copy of the "Star Spangled Banner" and much patriotism. There were also two illustrated papers and a bundle of newspapers. From the time of my arrival in the Bay, until I left the ship, I was constantly in the hold, and so did not get ashore. On the very last day, I got transfer papers from Baker and was assigned a clerk to Captain Charles C. Walcutt, Jr., Chief Quartermaster, 1st Division, 8th Army Corps.[28] So you see, I was assigned directly at Lawton's Headquarters. The other clerk, Mr. Leathe, is one man in a hundred, a very fine fellow and splendid clerk. He has taught me more in the week here than I would have learned in ten years under the outfit on the boat. The clerk there has been with Baker a year, and neither he nor Baker know one paper from another, so consequently, I learned nothing on my entire trip in the clerical line. Baker personally is a very nice man, agreeable, good-natured, and considerable of a hustler. Yet his position is due to political influence. He was a lawyer and prominent politician, a regular ward heeler, and it is his strong line.

If he does quit this transport business rich, it's not his fault or the clerk's, who is a champion cheap thief.

The Depot Quartermasters in large cities, charged with loading transports, are getting rich, and the Quartermaster of a big transport is a gold mine. For instance, dealers from whom goods are bought will give, on the quiet, a big bonus to get the ship's order. For instance, at "Gib" one firm thrown nice work!! — got all the contracts to the detriment of larger and more substantial houses. Why? Who knows. Here at this office, there are books for everything. Every part that comes in or goes out is put in a book, copied and numbered, and all the channels through which it came numbered. Walcutt has been a Regular quartermaster for ten years, and things are kept OK here. I have regular books to keep and I keep them; and the other clerk has other duties and he does them.

Baker's correspondence went to hell for all he cared; accumulated papers of six months were scattered about; and he lost my original order. Had I not had a copy sworn to on the boat in advance for such a contingency, there would have been complications. When I went for my transportation papers, the outfit clerk, Jesse M., and the Commissary didn't know what to do, although there is a transfer form. Through some wire pulling, there being jealousy between the Commissary and Quartermaster Department on board transports, Baker had Major Wilkins,[29] the "was to be" Commissary on the *Grant* ousted, and Baker was both Quartermaster and Commissary on the trip, and a nice tangle stores and papers are in. An old clerk out here said it would be lucky if in a year he cleaned things up.

There was a gang who were working to have the clerkship which I got, and they were dead sore on me for being in a place I had a right to be. I took everything and did not give anyone one word, except the Chief Engineer. He had been an engineer on big tramp steamers all his life, an ignorant, coarse man. At "Gib" Baker put me to work tallying the coal at one hatch, an employee of the Engineer Department was at the other, for two days, without being relieved, missing breakfasts and lunches. I was at that and I afterwards found out it was not by rights my work at all. The Spaniards count 20 baskets to a ton; we count 21, however, as it is brought in, we count with them 20 baskets, and at the end, divide the total sum of baskets by 21, deducting it into our count. My account at my hatch tallied basket for basket with the Spanish, and after being divided at the end coincided with his account. The Chief Engineer was having a drink with the Spanish coal man, received a box of cigars from him, gave him a letter of recommendation to the next transport, etc. When my sum was rendered, he had evidently finished the transaction with the man, and had Baker pay him.

One week later, the Chief Engineer saw me and said: "You made a deal on that coal at "Gib," the bunkers are not filled to what they ought to be; there was dirty work." In fact, he charged me with stealing on the counting of the coal, cussed me, threatened me, etc. I said: "Will you come upstairs and put that in writing before Captain Baker. Will you come up there to the office and back your claim." No, he would not, but if I ever was put on work calling for dealing with him, he would "buck my face." I got mad then; told him I had been used to handling money, dared him to make a charge, and told him I was not an enlisted man, bound under no Articles. He had no more authority over me than the steam galley cook, and that furthermore, my status on the ship was just that on land, a citizen; that if he hit me, that he would get it back, and that he could go to Hell, and be damned, report the whole transaction if he desired. He said he did not desire, and I had further official dealings with him, and things were quiet. I minded my business and he kept his "yap" shut. The charge of "peculation" against me did not go higher, as I wished, and I wonder who does the dirty work.

One can say what they please on board ship; it is a floating row. This was mostly among the ship's crew, fighting in the steward's department, wordy rows and official smells among the higher ones. In fact, if one did not keep his end up when compelled to, he got to me a small gun.[30] When the ship was delayed in New York, and they had only one half-frozen diver at work on the cable, "Old Man" Lawton took a leading role, giving Jesse some points which he will not soon forget. In fact, he was so scared of the "Old Man" that he would not go down by Lawton's quarters for nearly half the trip.

I had a hard role to play. They (Baker and the clerks) wanted to keep me out of the way when anything was going on in accounts, for they seemed to think that I would tale bear to Lawton, or Hall, what was going on. It was none of my business to report, but in spite of what they tried, I was not so thick that I could not see when profits were being made, when liquor was being sold in express violation of the Transport Regulations, etc., etc., and if I desired, I could write a report on the inside of Army dealings under Volunteer Quartermasters that would rival the beef scandal. Whatever I saw, I shut my mouth about. I looked at it that in my position, "silence was golden," and although I got the tough end for being in a position by an authority they cared not dispute, I was endured and that was about all. So they put me as far away as possible from the scenes of active operations. More upon this anon. I could fill pages with stuff about the ship voyage, etc., at present will defer it until I have more leisure.

With the exception of a few days while in port here, I have not one day's work in the government employ from 6 A.M. to 11 P.M. that would commence to be what I did in Fowler's between 9:30 to 3:30, although I am now getting four times the amount, I do about 1/6th the work. Thus one progresses.

After coming ashore and getting my assignment, I got a room at the Spanish Hotel at 25 cents American per night. A Spanish hotel is a great place. There is but little privacy, a lattice work top and big cracks through the partition through which issue much cussing and lengthy discussion on "Grandma Otis," Bill Shafter, and Dewey. The bed is a four-posted concern with lofty canopy, from which hangs a mosquito net [which is] indispensable here. No mattress, only wicker work over which is spread a fine matting to keep the mosquitoes from the underside. A Jersey mosquito is a hollow-chested wreck compared to one of these.

After seven o'clock the streets are deserted, not a "Pino"[31] or a Chinaman to be seen. If he is, he is "calaboosed."[32] One night I went from the Headquarters over to the city, about two miles, to get my laundry, and I had time to get a rig. At last, I got into a horse one, a Victoria covered. At first, the native, when I told him the district, demurred. Said he would be "calaboosed," but I gave him a grand bluff, got into the carriage, and drove ahead. It being dark, and my wearing a white helmet, and being well under the covered top, also being a two-horse rig, the guard thought I must be some "main guy," so when I crossed the big bridge at a smart pace, I was not challenged. On the contrary, they came to present arms. I was well back in the carriage. So instead of having a two-mile walk with a big bundle of clothes, I rode in style. I expect when the "umbria"[33] returned with the empty rig, he was jugged.

I cannot help but notice at Headquarters what a difference it makes when the "Old Man" is around.

American money is just double the miscellaneous silver coin here. Strictly speaking, the Spanish and Mexican dollars are worth 47 2/10ths, but in ordinary transactions, they count as 50 cents.

The nights are very damp. One has to sleep under a blanket! It is bad here when there is not a big breeze blowing. Altogether it is much cooler here now than we have it in Washington in the summer, although much moister. After I came over from the hotel, I bought me a cot, or rather a small native bed, but not having bedding for the first two nights, I had a hard time—no pillow, nothing to cover the holes in the wicker and the mosquitoes did not do a thing to me.

When Helen comes, here are a few things which I would like to have her bring. One is for her to get a small camera and a few films. I can get materials, etc. to develop it, etc. after it comes, but it would be well for her to bring some with her. It will be invaluable to me here for newspaper work, and I never before required so much, not having before requesting so much not having one with me on my trip. Had I one, I would have gotten a fine picture of Dewey, Otis, Lamberton,[34] and so many things of interest. Also: these Spaniards live like hogs: never any sheets or pillow cases. [Bring] a thin blanket, some sheets and some pillow cases. Also, have a big clothes bag of washable material made. To buy one at the present prices would be going into insolvency. Thin cotton drawers cannot be bought, and those made do not fit and cost. So a few good American ones would go a long way. These people wear only white clothes next to their hide (undershirts and socks, the best can be had here, in abundance).

I have been vaccinated again. This time I think it will take, as my arm is beginning to swell. There is a fine shower bath attached to the house, so I take one every morning. Tub baths are unknown here.

My companion clerk's prospective bride is to be here in a few days, [and] he will be married. As she did not get transportation in a government boat her fare over will be quite an item. He has an entire floor, four big rooms and several small ones, which he furnished himself, for which he pays $20.00 American per month. Two servants, daily expenses, etc. do not amount to $15.00 American more. So you see, I can get some rooms, barely furnish them, have two servants, a cook, and a *muchacho* (kid) for a very small sum, $25.00 or $30.00 per month, which also includes daily supplies,[and a] better class of groceries I can buy at the Commissary. At present I am living at a mess of the clerks, [which] costs me $12.00 American per month; my room, nothing. I am in with three orderlies. For breakfast, I get oatmeal, eggs in any form, bread, sometimes batter cakes, coffee, and about every other morning canned fruits, always canned butter and jam. This is a breakfast impossible to get at any dining room in Manila. At noon we have potatoes in various forms, chicken, duck, or beef for a main dish, canned vegetables, tea, rice, tapioca, etc., [and] a light meal similar at night. I drink water sparingly; have not touched native fruits, although I tasted mangoes on the boat and do not like them—too much like petroleum.

April 1, 1899

Today, I shall send Helen a money order for $20.00. Tell her so she may know about when it's due. I sent her a money order for $60.00 on the 27th. I think she has enough to go here, if not, I will send her more if she will cable "money."

Lt. Gregg,[35] a very fine officer of the 4th Infantry [and] an ideal soldier, met a soldier's fate the other day—shot through the heart. He was over six feet, very handsome, fine-proportioned, [and] a distinguished marksman. I saw much of him coming over. He was one of the finest looking men I ever saw, similar to Captain Capron.[36] Just a day or so before, he saved General Hall's life, as they were standing out by the lines. Gregg saw a native in the bushes about to fire on Hall. He pulled his pistol and with a rapid shot killed him. They brought back the "bloody shirt" etc. of the native. He would have probably been in line for a medal. It was very sad that he, of the officers who came over on the *Grant*, should be the first to fall. The outlook is now favorable for a complete clearing up of the surrounding territory to Manila of insurgents before the rainy season.

This month and the next, May, are the most unhealthy ones of the year. Nearly all the young men at Headquarters who have been here seven or eight months look the picture of health. Those sick have chronic dysentery. Monkeys are everywhere, tied up by a long rope in the yards, as common as house cats at home. In a few days, I will send something in the newspaper line illustrated with sketches.

The "Dagoes"[37] have simply been slaughtered. The ground is six and eight thick with them all knocked to pieces along some of the lines. Whenever the Springfield hits them it kills. There are arms here for the civil employees, so in case the natives should rise, that there will be a small garrison at Headquarters awaiting them. A Krag[38] and a Colt apiece ought to do some execution.

If Helen can make the *Grant* from Frisco, returning [on] it would be well, that is in case she cannot possibly go from New York. This is the last money order I shall send her until she cables she has started or is not coming. The latter in case she cannot get Army transportation. My address is now Headquarters, 1st Division, 8th Army Corps. As I wish to mail this and get to town, I will close with much love to all.

Your affectionate son,
Robert Dexter Carter

P.S. If Helen can go on U. S. transport and will have enough money, have her buy me a lightweight mackintosh. I think she can get a light, cheap one at "The Hub" [on the] corner [of] 14th and Pennsylvania Avenue for about $4.00. The same here are about $15.00 or $20.00. I see by my order, I am designated "temporary clerk" and by a recent order from the War Department, I see all clerks designated temporary, their service ceases with the muster out from the Volunteer Service of the Quartermaster. Now the one I am with holds a Volunteer rank, although he was a Regular Quartermaster and belongs to the 8th Cavalry, and was a regular Quartermaster for five years previous to the war. Now that temporary has stuck, and I am put on the rolls that way, although I am appointed under just the same circumstances as all these clerks who have not had that "temporary" put on a handle by which to throw them out. Now, Mr. Leathe is designated clerk and started at $100.00 per month under Captain Pope[39] and was transferred by him to Walcutt, identically the same. I think that under the rulings of the War Department, a clerk in the Quartermaster has to serve six months before he gets an increase. Most of them started at $100.00. I am the lowest, $1,000.00, at Headquarters. Now on July 16, I will have completed my six months service. See if you can get Shreiner[40] to send an order taking effect from that date, or sooner, if that regulation is not in force, putting me on a $1,200.00 basis. I did the same work as Baker's clerk. He was on $1,200.00 and am doing the same work as Leathe at $1,200.00. Neither Baker's clerk or Leathe were experienced at starting and were not permanent clerks, although borne on the rolls as such. That "temporary" in my orders has gone in the roll, so I am liable to be among the first bunch dropped in case of a mustering out of the officer to whom I am assigned, while the other clerks can be reassigned, and thus keep their position. Could it be possible for an order similar to the one they sent Walcutt giving him authority to pay his clerk $100.00 in gold be sent, also including the $1,200.00 basis. Give him a talk about the "war rates on everything," that I am married, that Leathe is not, that living in the Philippines is high, etc. He could do the trick in a minute. I don't see but what I am entitled after my six months apprenticeship to the regular clerk's salary, which inexperienced men have been drawing from the outset, not appointed from the War Department either as I was, but got their money through an order from the War Department authorizing the officer to pay them that sum. In the order, my being designated "temporary" on the rolls could be rescinded, thus giving me an equal chance with these other fellows to be assigned by the Chief of the Department of the Pacific, in case the officer (a Volunteer) should be returned to the Regular service or mustered out. I do not fear that Walcutt will be mustered out for a long time, for he is a Division Quartermaster, a good one, and as long as they keep a corps here, and Lawton is here, he will not be mustered out, being an experienced man. Tell Schreiner that the extra $17.00 per month cuts big ice here in living, a little smooth work and an order authorizing Walcutt, [the] Chief Quartermaster of 8th Army Corps, to pay Robert D. Carter, clerk ("designated" clerk not "temporary" clerk), also telling [the] Chief Quartermaster to have me designated and borne on the rolls as a "clerk" to be paid at the rate of $100.00 per month gold, that order to Walcutt or [the] Chief Quartermaster would fix me on a firmer basis. If the "temporary" part cannot be worked (I do not see why not, as Leathe and Baker's clerks are not termed "temporary") then have him work the $100.00 part, at least after six months to take effect from July 16, 1899. Of course, that is in case the War Department regulation is in effect. If it is not, why just as soon as possible, if all these fellows were put on a $100.00 basis at start, I do not see but what I should be getting that way out in the Philippines, doing war work, when clerks in the War Department, inexperienced, were started at that figure. Do not place it in the [nature] of a claim, but as a favor.

I should not put in for $150.00; do not think it will be allowed. Baker did not charge me a cent, which was nice. So I may put in just my actual expenses in New York, etc. en route to ship, a small amount, to which I will swear to, and which under regulations I am entitled to.

I want to thank you very, very much for your kindnesses to Helen, your fine present to her and myself, and for your efforts in my behalf. I shall always remember them. Love to all.
Robert D. Carter

Chapter Four

April—May 1899

Driving the Insurgents—The Northern Line

It is clear that the American public craved stories about their soldiers serving in the distant Philippines, and the would-be journalist still held out some hope that he would see one of his articles published in a popular magazine like *Harper's*, *Leslie's*, or *Scribner's*. As a quartermaster clerk, in addition to his clerical duties, Carter was sometimes called upon to accompany the division quartermaster in direct support of the troops in the field, which could involve anything from transporting ammunition to packing stubborn mules. This field duty would also provide him with new material for his writing. In general, the early fighting took place in the trenches surrounding Manila, and it eventually encompassed a substantial portion of the island of Luzon. Although there were other Filipino leaders, Emilio Aguinaldo was clearly the most influential leader of the independence movement and, arguably, the most effective. Ruthless in his consolidation of power, he was implicated in the elimination of Andrés Bonifacio, a rival and founder of the Katipunan Society. In fact, in the eyes of the American Army, he came to symbolize the independence movement, and his capture and the destruction of his army became a major objective.

The Philippine archipelago stretches approximately one thousand miles north to south and is comprised of nearly seven thousand islands. The largest is Luzon in the north, which is primarily Catholic, followed by Mindanao in the extreme south, where the indigenous population primarily adheres to Islam. At least a dozen dialects can be heard throughout the country, the dominant being Tagalog, particularly in Luzon.[1] Aguinaldo was a native of Cavite Province in southern Luzon and spoke the Tagalog dialect. So, given the symbolic importance of Manila, and the origins of the independence movement against the Spanish, it is not surprising that most of the early fighting took place in Luzon. More important, it is where Aguinaldo chose to plant the flag and to make his stand.

For the American Army, it was important to consolidate its hold on Manila and to nip the independence movement in the bud. The insurgents had surrounded Manila with entrenchments from which they regularly sniped at the Americans and infiltrated the city. Otis was determined to push out from Manila toward Malolos, a small town chosen by Aguinaldo as the capital of the Philippine Republic in a ceremony on January 23, 1899. That task was assigned to Maj. Gen. Arthur MacArthur, who had been awarded the Medal of Honor and a commission for his exploits during the Civil War as a young enlisted man. After that war, he remained in the Army and had a very distinguished career. However, a diminutive Volunteer from Kansas, Frederick Funston, would garner the glory in the fighting north of Manila in March. It was during a daring crossing of the Bag-Bag River near Calumpit, by a small force on a raft, that Funston earned the sobriquet "Fighting Fred."[2]

Brig. Gen. Fred Funston, U.S. Volunteers

Through a series of sharp fights, the men of MacArthur's Second Division were relentless and enjoyed repeated success in their efforts, and they managed to drive the insurgents from a succession of entrenchments from Malabon to Calumpit, eventually forcing Aguinaldo and his diminishing forces to abandon the "capital" at Malolos in order to seek sanctuary in Central Luzon near San Isidro. However, despite these early efforts, Aguinaldo and his forces always managed to elude capture.

Santa Cruz Campaign (April 1899)

In early April, Otis thought the timing was right for a thrust at the *insurrecto* supply bases to the south of Manila, principally at and around Santa Cruz. Carter accompanied Maj. Gen. Lawton on what would be the first major offensive thrust into the region south of Laguna de Bay, a large lake connected to Manila Bay by the Pasig River. The operation encompassed the period April 8 through April 17, 1899.[3] Utilizing some captured Spanish steam launches and refitting them with guns and some armor, the American forces had, up to this point, achieved some small-scale successes in and around Laguna de Bay.[4] The villages surrounding the lake produced food for friend and foe alike, and insurgents utilized the area to bypass Manila on the way to northern Luzon. A coordinated plan of attack evolved using the gunboats *Laguna de Bay*, *Napindan*, and *Oeste* for transport and to support Lawton's forces during the fighting.[5] The soldiers were told to draw two hundred rounds of ammunition and ten days' rations.[6] At the same time, a proclamation was prepared for distribution among the populace of the captured towns reassuring them of the good intentions of the United States.[7]

Late in the afternoon of April 8 the troops scrambled aboard eight launches, seventeen *cascos,* and two *bancas*[8] at San Pedro Macati on the Pasig River. Carter, carrying the cash box, accompanied Lawton on the captured steam launch *Maria*, which served as his floating headquarters. The press corps followed on the steamer *Oriente.*[9] While awaiting the start of the operation, the young man had a dinner aboard the launch consisting of bottled water and some ginger snaps.[10] That night, the loaded *cascos* and *bancas* were then towed upriver by the steam launches toward Laguna de Bay. Progress, however, was agonizingly slow as the boats became hung up on the numerous sand bars and mud flats, due to the inability of the pilots to find the main channel. Once out on the lake, choppy waters impeded progress even more. It was well into the daylight hours of April 9 by the time the expedition approached its destination, and the anticipated element of surprise was thereby lost. The attack scheduled for dawn had to be postponed for one day.[11]

Steam launch on the Pasig River as viewed from an artillery battery

Cascos on the Pasig River

The infantry waded ashore late that day, moved into a line perpendicular to the lake shore opposite the town of Santa Cruz, and prepared to settle in for the night. The ground over which they struggled to get into position was a mix of "marshy rice fields . . . underbrush, sugar cane fields, and jungle."[12]

Early on the morning of April 10, with a protective fire coming from the *Napindan*, the cavalry landed on the north side of the town, attacked the fortified positions there, and drove the defenders into the town. At the same time, the infantry formed up for the attack. As was his custom, Lawton was a conspicuous figure in the front line. Bisecting the road south of the town was a small river with a lone stone bridge, which was the only means for the troops to cross over dry shod. The insurgents were entrenched behind the river. The Americans charged in one continuous line carrying all before them. Although the bridge was forced, most of the men simply jumped into the stream and waded across. Once within the town, those rebels that were not killed outright slipped out of the jaws of the pincer, fleeing through the adjacent thickets and rice paddies to the northeast. Dozens more were killed in that effort. American casualties were very light. The nearly deserted city was secured, and the proclamation was posted at various places throughout.[13]

The expedition then moved north and east along the shores of the lake. Throughout the operation, the *insurrectos* were never very far away as was evidenced by their ability to set up ambushes. The jungle and the looming mountains surrounding the lake were as familiar to them as they were forbidding to Lawton's men. Nevertheless, they seized several vessels in the Pagsangan River, overcame sand bars and obstructions to navigation there, and captured Lumban, all the while brushing aside the rebel blocking forces. By now the American fleet, including the captured vessels, was quite large. It continued to move northeasterly along the shoreline of Laguna de Bay in concert with the land force, all the while seeking an advantageous spot to re-embark the American troops now that the operation was winding down. A small unit was sent forward to reconnoiter the town of Paete, when it met with resistance along the way. A sharp firefight followed with some loss of life. More troops, including the artillery, were brought up, and the force was aided by fire from the *Laguna de Bay*. After an hour the enemy was disbursed, and the Americans entered Paete on April 13.[14]

Over the course of the following four days the expeditionary forces, along with their captured vessels, were assembled at Paete, Santa Cruz, and the mouth of the Santa Cruz/Pagsanjan River in preparation for their return to Manila. The tired men undoubtedly reflected upon the events of the week past. As the soldiers looked back toward the receding shoreline, it must have been dispiriting to see the insurgents re-occupying the towns that they had just seized by force and then abandoned. The troops arrived back in Manila on April 17.[15]

Sadly for historians, what follows here is a mere fragment of Carter's firsthand account of that campaign, couched in his colorful prose, detailing the return of the soldiers to Manila following the successful completion of their mission. Other than his brief diary entries, lost is a firsthand description of his role in the fighting, particularly from the standpoint of a quartermaster.

Santa Cruz Campaign

. . . launches over the bar. At last they were all pulled out, not over the bar, but through a small channel discovered close to the shore among the bamboo obstructions which masked the river's mouth. During the entire stay of the expedition, continual signal smokes were noted on the mountain sides and along the shores of the lake, evidently marking the location of insurgent bands mobilizing. Words fail utterly to picture the beautiful scenery of the San Juan River; such a wealth of luxuriant vegetation, bright flowers, graceful palms, festooned vines, and amid the foliage of giant trees fluttered birds of rare plumage such as seldom falls to the lot of civilized man to see. Daily the gunboats scoured the shores of the head of the lake and wherever entrenchments or *insurrectos* were discovered a bombardment speedily followed. Night was turned into day by the flames of burning villages still remaining in the enemy's hands. They expected a raid on their towns any day and preferred to destroy them by fire rather than to see them fall into our hands; thus the towns we did not take, we were saved the effort of taking by the thoughtful energy of our foes. A trip along the shores of the lake brought more closely to our view the wonderful natural wealth of this practically unexplored Eden. The great mountains are clothed in giant forests, primeval, seldom penetrated by the footsteps of man, where the hum of insects, songs of wild birds and the howls of wild beasts alone disturb the solitude. The tiny emerald isles are the homes of the giant empire bats which roam abroad at night, a terror to the poultry and small stock of the Filipino farmer. Partially hidden among the leafy bowers, diminutive huts of bamboo raised on stilts, stand amid the waving green of rice fields, while on every side are glossy green leaves of the banana and palm trees waving in the gentle breeze like the billows of the ocean. The purple mountains, on whose precipitous sides flit the ever-changing cloud shadows, are the rim of this great basin wherein sparkles the lake, a gem of purest ray.

Loathe we were to leave this 'Garden of the Gods' and to return to the sultry days awaiting us in Manila. Towing the captured launches in the advance, the column forms; cascos loaded to the water's edge with the hardy, sun-burned soldiers of Uncle Sam, plunge onward through the foam-capped waves, and

the white towers of Santa Cruz are lost in the mist of approaching night. Overhead the tinge of azure, as twilight advances, begins to assume purple and violet hues; the sun slowly sinks behind the mountains and the sky is colored with the exquisite tints of a pearl shell or a fine opal. There are few fairer spots on this great earth and fitter frame for the picturesque lake than these mountains, and a finer setting for the glorious sunsets of the Philippines will not be found."
Robert D. Carter

"Kick the cat for me"

All soldiers yearn to stay connected to their homes and families. Letters were the link,[16] and it is quite apparent from Carter's letters home that he was interested in even the most mundane bits of information and family gossip, including news of the dog ("Teddy") and the cat ("Thomas Keedle"). The U.S. Army transports that carried the mail trans-Pacific took approximately thirty days each way. So, the reality was that letters to and from Manila often crossed in the mail, news from home was always at least a month in arrears, and answers to specific questions could take as much as two months or more for a reply. In addition to his own articles, Carter often referred his family to national newspapers and magazines that contained stories of the fighting or the personalities involved, in particular, his father's friend, General Lawton. Undoubtedly, had he been able to continue his military career, the elder Carter would have been in the thick of it. Naturally, he looked forward to any stories that pertained to his former colleagues like General Lawton.

In addition, for some time, Carter had hoped that his new bride, Helen, would join him in Manila as had so many other wives. He found that the cost of some essentials was high, though overall, he felt that they could live fairly comfortably. Better still, if she could travel by Army transport from New York or San Francisco, the cost would be negligible. However, the couple dithered too long, and when Carter found that the Army had changed its policy regarding the transportation of servicemen's families, his disappointment was palpable. In addition, he showed the first signs of dissatisfaction with his status as a clerk, while every "Tom, Dick, and Harry" was being commissioned.

April 23, 1899

My dear Mother,

You will think that I have forgotten you, but I have kept in mind your many nice letters and interesting enclosures. Between work, writing to Helen, writing my newspaper stuff, and a little correspondence home, I have pretty well covered the ground and consumed my time. But I take this time now that the office is well deserted, all being away on a raid into the enemy's country to answer your letter of March 9.[17]

I did not expect any mail at Said because we moved so rapidly that I knew there would be no time for the mail to catch us. My wheel[18] I am sorry to hear is sold. It was worth more than $10 to me here and could have been crated at a bicycle store and shipped to me here. Wheels are much ridden in the cool of the evening.

My greatest disappointment is to hear of the order keeping the ladies from coming out on the transports. I am probably bound out here for two years or more. I wanted Helen to come. She could have come by transport so cheaply, now it will nearly break me. So many, many women are here. We live so nicely and for so little here, and I know Helen does not want to remain a minute in Washington. It is pretty hard luck to have that order come now, for it knocks her out of returning on the *Grant*. I am much put out over it.

Got the *Journals* with account of Lawton O.K. The old warhorse is doing great deeds here now. He will, if he is not snowed under by Otis, acquire a big name. I see "Tom, Dick, and Harry" got commissions in the Regular establishment. A word from Lawton and I believe I could be secured a place. Too late now, everything gone wrong. So many fine opportunities lost by a hair.

April 28, 1899

I am at present arrayed in clothing of all nations. My shoes were bought in Singapore, my socks were seized in the Palace at Santa Cruz (silk, finely striped), my underclothing comes from Manila, my shirt from Gibraltar, my pants from the hold of the *Grant*, my coat from Washington, D.C., and my "bonnet" from Colombo, Ceylon. Am going over to Mrs. Lawton's today to see her house and draw a sketch of her bath-room for her.

Was very busy first part of this month, then was in the field ten days, and owing to the forgetfulness of a clerk, my mail, which I told him to stamp and send, was not sent until I returned, then I started to catch up with my work, newspaper article on Santa Cruz and my correspondence. I sent a Spanish mantilla to Helen in the bundle of papers. Will write Mell next.

Much love, your affectionate son,

Robert D. Carter

P. S. Kick the cat for me.

[Undated Fragment of Letter to his Sister Mell prior to San Isidro Campaign]

[Dear Mell]

. . . present indications point to Lawton's establishing his field headquarters

at Malolos. I may have to go out there, perhaps to remain in the field beyond, for months, in which case, you may not hear so much from me. Mr. Leathe was first ordered to Malolos today, so it looks as if I would run the city office, in which case, I will have a great snap, almost no work and the whole office. If Helen were here, we could have a fine time. I have had so many opportunities to get nice establishments from officers or clerks who are obliged to stay in the field. Well, with much love to all, I remain, your affectionate brother,
Tod

P. S. In case Lawton's Headquarters should be in the field or at Malolos, first address my letters: Q.M. Clerk, at General Lawton's Office, 38 Calle Nozaleda, Manila, P.I.[19] Then if I am at the front, they will be forwarded.

The San Isidro or Northern Expedition

Just days after Lawton's men returned from the Santa Cruz Campaign, Major General Otis decided to build upon his success in pushing the insurgents away from Manila and to strike at Aguinaldo's retreating forces, in hopes of capturing him and ending the rebellion once and for all. The plan called for a two-pronged attack into Central Luzon, during which MacArthur's Second Division would push north along the narrow-gage Manila-Dagupan Railway. At the same time to the east, Lawton and his First Division would push along narrow wagon roads and tracks through the mountainous jungle, taking with them only rations and ammunition, as well as fodder for the animals. The objective was to catch Aguinaldo in a pincer near San Miguel. The plan looked good on paper, but when all was said and done, MacArthur's troops reached their physical limits at San Fernando and were unable to join Lawton's men, who had won a series of battles and skirmishes and had also reached their limits at San Isidro, where they had outrun the ability of the Army to supply them. In addition to the *insurrectos'* bullets, the ranks of both divisions were daily decimated by sunstroke and disease, in particular dysentery and malaria.[20] The expedition lasted from April 22 through May 30. Despite a determined effort on the part of the American forces, as the pincers never closed, Aguinaldo managed to elude his pursuers, at least for the time being.

From its assembly point at La Loma Church on the outskirts of Manila, Lawton's division made its way north into central Luzon. The plan was to eventually utilize the Manila-Dagupan Railway line, which MacArthur's division was simultaneously clearing, to supply both wings. Initially, Lawton's supplies followed along behind. Later, as his division pushed farther out from Manila, he established a forward supply base, first at Bacaue, and then at Malolos. His chief quartermaster, Captain Walcutt, who also served as temporary chief commissary of subsistence, took charge of the supply train.[21] Walcutt's clerk, William Leathe, had been sent ahead to Malolos.

Manila-Dagupan Railway

However, Walcutt's task was made particularly difficult as the heat and the strain resulted in the death of the carabao bulls pulling the supply carts. These large, slow, indigenous beasts of burden proved totally unsuited for the job. So slow, in fact, that after only one day, the supply column, guarded by a troop of Cavalry, was four miles behind the main force. Those carabao that did not die had to be periodically unhitched and cooled off in one of the many streams or waterholes. But die they did, and given the shortage of Army mules, the task devolved onto Lawton's exhausted troops themselves to pull the loads, thus slowing movement to a crawl.[22] Wherever found, Walcutt was forced to seize carabao from the natives in order to replace those that had died along the way.[23]

Further compounding Captain Walcutt's problems were numerous hills, valleys, and streams that needed fording, as well as the fact that just north of Novaliches, the road had suddenly became a "mere footpath."[24] Not only did Walcutt have to contend with the climate and terrain, but also with a multitude of other problems, from uncooperative mules and inexperienced packers[25] to the Chinese bearers, who had a tendency to wander off from their assigned units to commit various depredations among the native population.[26]

As both columns moved north, it became apparent that the ever-lengthening supply line could not keep up with Lawton's forward progress.[27] Accordingly, it was decided to take advantage of the Manila-Dagupan Railway to, in effect, shorten the 1st Division's supply line. Thus, when Lawton reached the vicinity of the towns of Norzagaray and Angat between April 25 and 26, a telegraph line was run west to the town of Bocaue situated on the railway. Rations and ammunition were routed overland to Lawton at Angat from that point, and the sick and wounded were returned to Manila via wagons to Bocaue.[28] Walcutt was hands-on, moving back and forth along the road, thus assuring a steady flow. At one point, the officers' subsistence was not delivered to Bocaue, nor did all the rations arrive. Lawton ordered forward all that could be delivered, and told Manila that his officers would make do with the field rations. His column moved along, and a new supply route would have to be established.

Shortly thereafter, on May 2, when Lawton's force had reached the vicinity of Bustos and Baliuag, he detached a company of the 22nd Infantry to nearby Quingua in order to secure the telegraph and supply lines to and from there to Malolos. The operation was taking a toll on the men's clothing as well, and Lawton ordered a fresh supply of shirts, pants, underwear, and shoes.[29] Otis held Lawton in place there for several days, and it was at this time that Carter took his ride on the rail line. Once again, Captain Walcutt was back and forth between Malolos and Quingua conducting the supply train bearing ammunition and rations to Lawton, as well as ambulances returning from the battlefield with sick and wounded. He had to contend with high water and a difficult ford at the Quingua River, where the wounded had to be unloaded and carried across one by one. Adding to the quartermaster's troubles, Lawton's supplies were not waiting at Malolos as anticipated.[30] The supplies did arrive the next day, and Walcutt loaded them on forty wagons, along with block and tackle in the event that the water at the ford had risen, and he set off for Quingua.[31]

When Lawton resumed his drive, the division moved north through Maasin, San Ildefonso, San Miguel, and Tarbon Bridge, culminating with the taking of San Isidro. MacArthur was originally ordered to join Lawton at San Miguel. Instead, he sent a mixed force of infantry and artillery, joined by gunboats, along with supplies for Lawton's men, northeast along the Rio Grande de Pampanga to Candaba. Shortly thereafter, Lawton's division, its task done, made its way back to the rail line at Calumpit, and eventually to Manila. The last unit to arrive back in Manila was the division supply train on May 30.

At the end of the campaign, Lawton was unstinting in his praise for Walcutt in his dual role as chief quartermaster and acting commissary. "Few quartermasters," he began, "ever had greater difficulties to overcome, and none could have rendered more cheerful and untiring service." During the campaign, from the first day to the last, "he spared himself neither night nor day in his indefatigable efforts to render the expedition a success."[32] Carter heartily concurred.

An earlier letter to his mother and the above undated fragment of a letter to his sister indicate that Carter remained behind at headquarters, at least for a while, as Lawton moved north. However, in a later letter to his father dated May 13, 1899, during the middle of the joint expedition, Carter states quite clearly that he had been under fire at Calumpit. Although this could be an exaggeration, it implies that he did, in fact, follow Lawton's division north at some point, perhaps as far as Malolos, there to join his colleague Leathe, or perhaps simply to satisfy his curiosity.

On May 4, Carter took advantage of a Sunday lull to take a ride along the Manila-Dagupan Railway, at least as far as the temporary "end of track" at Calumpit, in order to catch a glimpse of the scenes of the recent battles. What follows is a vivid description of the Army's logistical tail along the way out and back. Carter is dismissive of some of the efforts to win the "hearts and minds" of the Filipino people, such as the program to buy back "serviceable" weapons for $30.00 silver apiece. Not only were the weapons likely to be old and useless, but also some enterprising American soldiers had attempted to collect the reward for themselves for weapons captured during the fighting. This attempt was quickly rejected by headquarters in Manila.[33] He is also skeptical of the bona fides of the Filipinos, the so-called "*amigos*," many of whom fought the Americans, then quickly hid their weapons and passed among the general populace. He describes one such fellow as having no weapon, but the dirty sweat ring of a cartridge belt around the waist of his shirt. Carter also seems to lump all Filipinos together, as he describes several Macabebes, who, in fact, were not only enemies of the Tagalogs, but also loyal fighters for the Americans.

A Sunday Ride on the Manila and Dagupan
("Kansas and Utah Short Line") Railroad
Manila, P. I., May 4, 1899

Nearing nine o'clock each morning the diminutive train on the narrow-gage road running from Manila to the North starts from the quays at the River Pasig, well-loaded with supplies for the soldiers encamped along its line. The train consists of several cars armored with railroad iron, a few box and quite a number of compartment cars. These last, although on a much smaller scale, are similar to the European railroad carriages. The trip out is very tedious, a stop being made, seemingly at every ant hill. Wherever a small detachment is camped, there, several quarters of beef, canned goods and large galvanized tins of pure drinking water are unloaded. As the outskirts of Manila are left behind, a beautiful country is unfolded to our vision. Toward the Bay, the rolling green is studded with clumps of dark, glossy foliage. A large white tower stands silhouetted against the clear blue mountains across the Bay. It is the prominent landmark which indicates the town of Malabon. Here was fought one of the most desperate engagements of the present rebellion. On the gently undulating ground to the north of the town and nearing Caloocan the gallant General Egbert[34] fell and the distinguished Lieutenant Gregg[35] met a soldier's fate. At Caloocan many deserted trenches furrow the ground, and an engine house riddled with holes stands a mute reminder of the fierce fighting here with the insurgent forces.

The country beyond Caloocan is a vision of great agricultural wealth, and the greater part is green with growing crops. Broad expanses of fertile meadowland rolls away to meet the harder soil of the rising ground, broken here and there by little streams whose banks are hidden in copses of feathery bamboo. Deserted blockhouses and partially destroyed entrenchments dot the land-

Section of captured Insurgent trenches near Manila

scape, while upon the ground are numerous evidences which mark the bivouacs and battles of an army. Fragments of clothing, insurgent hats, empty cartridge shells, meat cans, and scattered about, a few lonely yellow mounds mark the final resting places of the unknown dead. Fresh detachments of regulars, which are arriving from the States on every transport, are marched out to the important points along the inner line, there to do the hum-drum guard duty, thus allowing the hardened troops to go to the front and engage in the active campaign. These regulars, fresh in their clean khaki and new equipment, are in marked contrast to the volunteers and regular troops who have been in the field off and on for nearly a year. The friends at home would hardly be able to recognize their soldier boy in his field clothes, unshaved and often unwashed. Every conceivable headgear is worn while in the field, from tattered campaign hat to the broad dish-shaped hat of the Chinese coolie. The uniform consists of a variegated assortment of shirts and greasy pair of "cast-iron" pants deeply dyed in the rich mud of the Philippines. All are bronzed, the hair uncut, the beard untrimmed; fine, healthy, robust men, in their wild appearance not unlike the portraitures of Robinson Crusoe.

An enterprising individual on the train conceived the idea of running an amateur bakery. And his "lead pipe" pies, "galvanized" cakes, and "corrugated" buns disappear as mist before the morning sun under a spirited onslaught of our soldier boys. As soon as the "Kansas and Utah Short Line," as the train is termed by the soldiers, is brought to a standstill, it is at the pie car that the howling mob are shouting "give me 'er peach, 'er cherry etc.," and they eat with great gusto every particle of these flabby pies, a mouthful of which would give an able-bodied ostrich gastritis. Paper boys from Manila do a thriving business, and their rivalry is keen; the smaller the boy, the better his patronage. One small boy, arrayed in a soldier's khaki uniform, equipped with a large pistol, seems to do the best of all. Honesty is virtue among the soldiers, and the trader trusts the busted soldier boy for a pie, newspaper or any of his little wants, seldom loses by his confidence, for at the end of the month, the warrior bold "antes up." The famous camps of Bohemian gypsies could not approach in picturesqueness the temporary camps of our soldiers along this railroad. Wherever a very strong entrenchment has been vacated by the enemy, a detachment of our boys have occupied it and remain there as a guard to the railroad. Surrounding the little settlement will be a stone, bamboo, or mud embankment, nipa huts, bamboo shacks, dug-outs, lean-tos, shelter tent flys, in fact, any old thing that will protect from the scorching heat by day and the frequent showers of the night, are utilized, and it would astonish the wizard Edison to behold the ingenuity displayed in their construction. Far away from the city's roar, the boys in brown, in dishabille, recline in the shade of their own little domicile. A pair of dirty feet, a tousled head projecting from one of these crude huts is all that represents the dominion of Uncle Sam in this locality.

Water is scarce out here; liquor even scarcer, and by the time the train arrives, the boys look forward eagerly for their water supply for the next twenty-four hours, having accumulated a pretty strong thirst. Imagine then the horror with which they saw the pole on which the water can was slung break and the precious fluid for which their parched palates thirsted absorbed by the ground. Long and loud were the cuss words, and the "Chinos"[36] who were the unfortunate carriers may thank their lucky stars that actual violence did not occur. Oh, "there was no joy in Mudville that night."[37]

After much puffing, creaking and groaning, the wheezy iron steed was stopped at Malolos. That mighty capitol of a great and free republic, that might have been, is in reality a dirty, torrid little station. The capitol buildings and city proper is not visible from the car line. Malolos comprises one long street flanked with verdant banana trees, among whose shadows are thickly clustered the long line of native houses. There are in the entire town no more than six substantial structures; of course the church and palace are most prominent. Although the rifle pits and strong entrenchments are much in evidence, as the train nears Malolos, the stern determination and the presence of the brave band of defenders is painfully apparent by their scarcity. At the present writing, it looks very much as if the boastfulness and sand were rapidly disappearing from the anatomy of that Spartan band of Filipinos who, but a brief time ago, promised us that they would be in Manila in twenty days. The twenty-day part of the boast may still be good, but it will be under guard that they will enter.[38]

American troops enter Malolos

Everywhere great trenches, almost impregnable in our hands, mar the landscape, and their positions from a strategic standpoint could not have been better chosen. Beyond Malolos the train moves very slowly and the line of track is carefully guarded. The view is superb; the land is as level as a billiard table, the never-ending rice fields, marked into squares by tiny dikes, are works of art. At present, they are dry and hard; in a few months this same territory will be a sea of mud and water. In the broad meadows, where scarcely a hillock or stone could be found, there is ample room to encamp a whole army, not a tree to break the great expanse of level ground. Again we pass large fields of waving corn; groves of huge umbrella shaped trees shade the little homesteads which peep from beneath their foliage, and far away on the horizon, basking in the sunlight, are the great mountains partially hidden in the folds of the purple cloud banks. This country carries one's mind back to the dear old States; the familiar corn fields undulating in the cool sea breezes, reminds me very much of the beautiful valleys of New England. At intervals, roads cross the tracks, and through these little vistas of green we see the long wagon trains, troops of cavalry and herds of mules being loaded by the skillful western packers. The rough country, the scene of General Lawton's operations, is found to be impassable for wagon trains, so the old army pack mule was again called into service. This aggressive warfare, carried into their chosen strongholds, is a great surprise to the insurgents. Our men have surmounted every difficulty; advancing into the mountains, such wagons as are taken had to be hauled up sheer precipices and through rocky *cañons* and mountain torrents by main strength, one hundred men sometimes pulling on a single ammunition wagon. The larger force of the enemy awaited the attack in the valleys, but our men who comprised the flying columns scaled the mountain trails in single file in the same manner as when campaigning against the Apaches. Marching rapidly along the crests of the lower line of mountains, they came upon insurgent bands entrenched in the gorges; a brief fusillade and the insurgents were sent scurrying in a disordered mass to their next line of defense. Sometimes their lines would be pierced in the center and the two wings separated and left to the rear of the advancing column. Their alternative then was to make a fight or disintegrate, and they generally chose the latter course. Prisoners brought in say that the main body of the insurgents have little heart for a stand up fight with our advancing forces, declaring that after seeing our men come steadily on against a terrific fire, and having never seen them turn defeat, they conclude that they are not human, but devils. The officers brought in state that they have great difficulty in making their men stand against the "white devils." About a mile beyond Malolos the train comes to a standstill, for beyond there the line of track has been torn up and bridges destroyed by the insurgents in their retreat. A long train of freight cars serve as the headquarters of and field quarters of Major General MacArthur. Between the iron wheels of the cars, on the hard cinder roadbed, recline in every attitude, the headquarter guard enjoying a Sunday siesta after a hard campaign of the preceding week. The track extends to the iron bridge which spans the Bag-Bag River. It was at this bridge that the heroic Colonel Funston, with the brave Kansas and Montana boys, crossed the river on a small boat in the face of a hailstorm of bullets from the enemy's trenches.[39] The insurgents hurriedly removed all the flooring and iron girders in the central part of the bridge, but this was speedily repaired and our mule teams were being hauled over by hand. The horses and mules were led singly over the extemporized structure which replaces the span on the insurgent shore, which had been broken with sledges and dropped into the river. The banks on both shores are precipitous and heavily entrenched and fortified. The enemy had located here permanently, as they had not for an instant imagined that with the bridge partially destroyed our troops would dare to cross the stream in the face of an overpowering force supported by artillery, in bombproof trenches; but they did not know the American soldier. Our soldiers declare that these trenches are the strongest encountered since the outbreak of hostilities. They are sunk to a depth of six to eight feet, with a platform on which the infantry can stand without exposure. The heavy earthwork is backed with green bamboo and steel rails, loop holed, while overhead are heavy curved plates of iron. Our men believe in that maxim that the best protection against fire of the enemy is to keep up a better one. When our advance crossed the Bag-Bag River, it was under the cover of a terrific fire on the insurgent trenches of shrapnel, and shells, and Gatlings, Springfields and Krags poured such a hail of lead and steel on the crest of the enemy's trenches, that the "bolo men" were very loathe to raise their heads out of the gravel long enough to fire a shot. As soon as the assaulting party gained the base of the precipitous shore, they were sheltered from the insurgent fire. The insurgent "Old Guard" did not await the finale; a hand to hand encounter on the works, but departed unceremoniously. Had these same trenches been in the hands of a regiment of our troops, it would have taken a corps to dislodge them. The field pieces captured here were standing peacefully in the sunlight with typewritten inscription on the gun carriage stating the circumstance of their seizure. In the village, formerly occupied by the enemy, the ginger pop man, Sunday paper boy, and the pie vendor are doing a land office business. After crossing the river, the rails have been removed entirely; little spots of ashes mark the fate of the ties, while at intervals, great trenches cut the embankment in twain. The little iron bridges still stand; the flooring and some of the supports have been hurriedly removed. Coming in, on the embankment as far as the eye can see, were groups of "Amigos" or friends clad in their best raiment; the immaculate white shirt, the stiffly starched tails of which stood out and waved in the breeze, and the brightly colored heelless slippers. There would be sometimes as many as fifty in group; they claimed to be Macabebes, a friendly tribe who are endeavoring to drive the insurgents from their domain.[40] All were exceedingly polite, saluting and saying "Good morning." The soldier's opinion is that they are half-hearted *insurrectos* sneaking into our lines, taking good care to bring no arms with them. On the shirt of one, I noticed an ancient stain at the waist where formerly a belt had been worn. Hunger, fighting "white devils," wounds, and disease seem to quell the ardor of their martial spirits somewhat, and from present indications, any organized resistance will soon be a thing of the past.

Calumpit, on the banks of the Rio Grande[41] marks the last brief stand. On the south shore, our artillery was parked in a great meadow, the horses shaded by giant trees. The cavalry horses were picketed; the bulls and mules of the transportation outfit were quietly grazing; man and beast were taking a day's rest from the privations of war. In a great iron shed the sick and wounded were peacefully resting in hospital cots,[42] while in every shaded nook, the tired men were sprawled on the ground. In the clear waters of the river, many were enjoying a swim, others nude were "paddling their own canoes," or rather dugouts, or trying to steer unwieldy bamboo rafts. The bridge spanning this stream is so much larger than the former, and so sure had the insurgents been of holding this territory, that they, in their hurry, had been unable to destroy it. A few bolts, a few iron girders and all the flooring is gone, but our men soon put on a temporary floor and, practically, it is as useful as before. The entrenchments are even stronger than those met at the first river, in as much as triangles of railroad ties filled with hard clay cap the crest of the entrenchment. They are also more irregular in their alignments, making them much more difficult to take by flank attack, and are, furthermore, better protected with iron shields. The news of the speedy capture of the first line had evidently demoralized the enemy, as upon the approach of our men, they hastily vacated this impregnable trench without firing hardly a shot, leaving their clothing and accoutrements, with the exception of the much-prized rifle and ammunition in the trench. Even had they held these positions against MacArthur's advance, they would have been forced to retreat when Lawton's flying column had advanced far enough to the north to bear upon their flanks and rear.

The men in the ranks of the insurgent army are held there by ignorance and superstition; once the leaders [are] disposed of and they will surrender within a brief period. When insurgent officers are captured, the utmost difficulty is experienced in making them disclose their identity, as they have been led to believe from their higher officers that Americans immediately put to death all captured or wounded officers, and they, in turn, spread this among the insurgent soldiers. So it is with greatest difficulty that our generals can convince the enemy that surrender does not mean death, but peaceable return to better days than they have ever experienced before.

In the rear of these powerful earthworks on the Rio Grande is the town of Apalit, which is a single street of indefinite length; on either side are straggling banana trees and nipa huts of a Philippine village. Under the houses and amid the banana stalks, scurry lean pigs, fat pigs, little pigs, decrepit cats, shadowy dogs, and swarms of chickens. The pigs and chickens have but little rest, as the American soldier is always a good "grub rustler" whatever his other failings may be. In the better houses, reclining on mahogany bedstead, the canopy of which is deeply flounced with broad folds of lace, are bronzed and bearded conquerors; their general appearance would put the tramps of stage and cartoon lore to a blush. In front of the huge gilded mirrors, the Volunteer combs his tangled hair, while from the polished board, the Regular eats his pork and beans and drinks his coffee. Through the streets, enterprising Volunteers were carrying large double beds to their quarters, while in a secluded nook, others had a wheel of fortune which had been found in some grandee's house. The lucky owner was working it to its utmost capacity; however, his profits were not great, as the article, money, is a stranger to the boys in the field.[43] The church was doing service as a company mess and cookhouse. The only native I saw was a grizzled old veteran, carrying a white flag; he was marched through the streets by a grinning soldier who held a keen edged bolo to his prisoner's spine. Stepping out the back doors of their quarters, the boys were on the banks of the Rio Grande. The splashing, yelling, swimming and floating crowd were enjoying to their utmost, that rarity to a soldier in the field, a good bath. The men are as fine specimens physically as will be found outside the professional athletic ranks; their ruddy color could not be acquired in any gymnasium; such elastic muscles could only be gained by a hardy outdoor life. Those who could not swim had several of the big native water jars around their waists and floated about, secure from cramps, that calamity which has cost so many of our brave troops their lives while bathing in the Pasig.[44] Snorting water buffalo charged into crowds of bathers here and there, putting them to flight.

From the car windows as I returned to Manila, I saw everywhere the painful evidences of a destructive war. Amid the blackened ruins of one fireside, sat a yellow cat, the sole member of the family. The terrors of war could not drive the faithful animal from home; it was rather sad and yet suggestive incident. The return trip is rapid; the few stops made were to take on the wounded brought in from General Lawton's flying column. It is a very sad sight to see the dead, killed so far from home and friends, and the wounded, some cheerful, some despondent, some given up to their agony, and yet others in a state of utter nervous collapse. Humor everywhere is mixed with tragedy; the boys who are so gaily singing in the cars may be tomorrow among that sad list, the unknown dead. At one stop, an anxious soldier rushed out, and bearing a letter in his hand, said: "Which is the mail car?" A facetious individual in the armored

car remarked: "These are all 'male' cars." A soldier's wit does not spare his best friend, however serious the occasion. We slowly enter the outskirts of Manila about dusk. Across the wavy meadows to the westward, the white towers and roofs of Malabon are lighted by the last glints of the descending sun. Beyond, a crimson belt lingers on the horizon, although the stars are beginning to shine in the heavens. Along the muddy water's edge of the Bay, lighted by weird light, the squalid masses of the lower quarters of the city are gathering in their nets preparatory to returning to their reeking hovels."
Robert D. Carter

Reckless Driving and Army Politics

Carter retained his sense of humor, which was self-deprecating, as is evident from his telling of his mishap with the runaway *carrametta* that he and a colleague had hired one Sunday morning. Other than one's feet, the most common mode of transport throughout Manila and its environs was this small, covered, two-wheeled carriage, pulled by a single horse. Many soldiers' accounts refer to the use of this vehicle at some point during a tour of duty. It was a relatively inexpensive and efficient way to get around Manila.[45] According to Carter, the drivers could be reckless, as was borne out by his experience.

Carter was also a good observer. Attached to Lawton's headquarters, and obviously loyal to his father's old friend, he saw and heard things which he passed along to the family with an obvious bias. As a case in point, much has been made of the rift between Generals Otis and Lawton, implying that the latter was insubordinate and upset that the former had abruptly terminated offensive operations, thus thwarting his intention to carry the Santa Cruz operation to Calamba.[46] At this early juncture in their relations, nothing could be farther from the truth. In fact, on April 12 Otis had given Lawton permission to attack Calamba, at his discretion,[47] and only withdrew his approval three days later due to renewed concerns about the Northern Line, following a surprise attack by insurgents on some of MacArthur's troops guarding the Manila-Dagupan Railway on April 11. The fact is that he needed Lawton to help on the Northern Line to meet the current insurgent threat and to exploit MacArthur's previous gains.[48] Besides, there was no guaranty that Lawton would have actually continued on to Calamba, as he told Otis that "fatigue is beginning to tell upon the men."[49] An artillery officer who served with Lawton throughout his campaigns in Luzon was quite emphatic about the general's obedience to orders. While Lawton was not shy about expressing his views to Manila, "he demanded instant and implicit obedience of his subordinates [and] he gave the same to his superiors."[50] However, as time went on, Otis's reputation as an overly cautious leader persisted, perhaps fueled by the press who did not like him, and by his orders to Lawton, during the San Isidro Campaign, to pull back from San Rafael, one day after Aguinaldo asked for a truce, only to reverse himself the next, forcing his subordinate to re-take the village at the cost of additional casualties. It is more than likely that relations between the two generals soured over time.

In any event, Carter set the record straight, at least as far as the Santa Cruz story goes, when he described a conversation that General Lawton had with his adjutant general, Maj. Clarence R. Edwards,[51] aboard the *Maria*, one of the captured steam launches, then serving as Lawton's floating field office. The exchange took place just after Lawton received the telegram from Otis following the battle. It is clear that Lawton accepted his orders, and, moreover, recognized the simple fact that taking ground and holding it are two different propositions. Nevertheless, these private comments were taken out of context, perhaps by members of the press accompanying the expedition, and would later find their way into print, more than likely by some journalists as a way to push back against Otis's control of the telegraph line from Manila and his heavy-handed censorship of their dispatches.[52]

Carter's letters are full of all sorts of digs and gossip, as well as mentions of military men no doubt familiar to Carter's father, particularly Henry and Mary Lawton. He takes another swipe at Baker, hinting at his graft. Carter also discusses his health (as well as a home remedy for the very prevalent Dhobi Itch) which was always of concern, and we see the first hints of his dissatisfaction with his own situation.

May 7, 1899

My Dear Sister,

It is Sunday morning [at] 7:30. We arise here about daybreak sometime. I never know when. Leathe and I (Mr. L. is the other quartermaster clerk) started for *Aytumiento*, that [is] the palace where the Chief Quartermaster is.[53] He was dressed in his best white rig and was going to the races. I was going to draw my money. On a separate sheet, you will find our adventure, which luckily turned out for the very best. Had the right thing not happened at the right time, perhaps I would not be writing now. Sent papers home, and a letter to Helen yesterday, also [a] money order registered.

About the accident. We started to go as I stated above. The niggers drive like hell here. Any old way, and it is a wonder there are not 100 people killed a day. Well, up in a narrow street, we meet an orderly coming down the street riding pretty fast. Just as he got to us, his confounded nag jumped clean off the ground and shied in a lurch into our horse. I rather thought that there would be a crash, and that the horse and rider would hit the ground and we would go on. There was a crash, a most dreadful one, and in a second, we found ourselves upside down wedged into the cab. We couldn't get out. My first thought was [that] the horse will kick our harness out or run and drag us to death. But luckily, the very best thing happened—both shafts broke off close to the cart, the crazy harness parted, and our beast laid off up in a pike.[54] By this sudden parting, the other horse sustained a lessened shock, and, strange to say, did not cut or break his shoulder, nor stranger, hurt the rider. Our nigger hit on his face cut it somewhat. I didn't get a bump or even get dirty, although somewhat shaken and mauled. The cab was a wreck, and how we escaped a serious injury, being completely turned over, is a miracle. Leathe was going to the Horse Races. He is quite a sport and was dressed up in fine style. His pants were a total wreck. I laughed; he cursed. When we found the horse was gone, we sat in the cab and roared. It was a regular "Jap and Pad" time.[55] Do you remember? After getting out, I went to the Palace and drew my money, and then went to [the] P.O. in boiling sun and mailed you that bundle of papers. Leathe went to the tailors and bought a new pair of pants and got to the races after all, won $40.00 and won $60.00 the day before. He is an intimate friend of the starter, who gave him good tips. Had the shafts not broken, both horses would have met serious injury, or had the harness held, we would have been dragged and the flimsy top would have soon collapsed and the heavy axle and wheels would have maimed us. My very first thought was to get my head away from the direction of the horse, for I expected his heels to come crashing through in a second. So, what might have been heavy tragedy was a roaring farce. Tell Helen that she can see that we stand as good a chance to meet death in Manila as on the fighting line. She had a close shave to becoming a widow.

The heat now is at its utmost, yet I do not suffer; the humidity is what makes it so uncomfortable. The nights are far cooler than in Washington, a fine sea breeze. I believe that if one does not drink and takes care not to exercise severely in the sun, they can get along nicely. There is one thing which is very uncomfortable that is the "Itch."[56] Everyone has it, and it is something that will drive one distracted. I use the strongest carbolic soap and have not suffered hardly any. The two small patches which I contracted while on the Santa Cruz Expedition have not spread. An old resident told me about it.

I had some pictures to accompany the article which I sent father; also some that were taken of me sitting in the office, but with usual luck in this case, the entire roll of film was a failure. Unless Helen can come on a transport, advise her to stay, for she can save money, and the length of time she will be here, perhaps may not pay for the heavy money outlay, although one can live here in style dirt cheap.

Received my printed articles on "Gib" and transport O.K. Am very pleased with them as they appeared, and wish to thank Papa very much for his efforts toward correcting them and having them printed.[57] I shall send in all the good photos I can, in hopes they can be disposed of. If not, they are valuable to keep. Why [Manila] is run down is because a lot of homesick soldiers who have been having the hard side out here, [are] getting home and "knocking" it. You must be lenient on my newspaper stuff, as I have little time to prepare it. How do you think I worked the "Guide Book"—"figgers" pretty good? If at present I knew what Helen was going to do, I would like to help you financially, but not knowing, I must go easy. If you need any, touch Helen. She keeps her money as tight as Fagin.[58] She is a good banker. That first proof of her pictures she sent me was very fierce, although it was very much appreciated. Tell her no photo can do her justice. She must take that in a complimentary light, for that is a two-edged saying.

Gen. Lawton is engaged in chasing the niggers. Every time he gets them rounded up, old Otis telegraphs him to "suspend operations."[59] These niggers "negotiate" every time they are in a tight box. If Lawton can only crush them he will be a big man here, but Otis will see that he is nil in the U. S. [There is] great jealousy between [the] general officers. The troops all swear by Lawton.

The other evening I called on Mrs. Lawton. She showed me her entire house. At first glance it looks like the palaces we heard of in fairy tales. The walls of the parlor are covered with huge gilt-framed mirrors; the ceiling is gorgeous; the paintings magnificent; the furniture superb. In reality, the ceiling is painted canvas, above which sport rats and snakes, and the marble columns are of paper. The paintings are chromos[60] put together ingeniously, so that the figures and buildings project from the flat surface. At a distance, the deception is good. The furniture is curious and really handsome. We laughed long over the various tawdry ornaments. She can beat the young girls entertaining. Mrs. Lawton has treated me finely, in fact, from her I have received so many little kindnesses which she could have without effort left undone. She is a very smart and kind hearted woman. I shall never cease to remember her courtesy to me in my trip around the world.

The General I have seen little of since leaving the ship. Of course the dignity of his position behooves me not to be about him. For rank in the Army is nobility on a small scale. On the boat, I had several interviews with him in which he talked nicely to me, always noticed and spoke to me, gave me good advice and now when he sees me says, "Good morning, Carter. How are you today? Well?" and shakes my hand. He is a very busy man now, and he makes the officers stand around. One day a Volunteer officer argued some matter with him. Lawton said, "You heard what I said; now I don't wish to hear anything more about it. That is sufficient. You go and do what I say." And the Volunteer Officer moved when Lawton looked at him and spoke thus. He said it so quickly and quietly. Oh, he is a peach as a soldier, and when they go on a campaign with him, their bones stick out when they return. For in the field fighting, he has the energy of ten men. What do you think of that article on him May 5th in the *American* I sent?

I always look forward to your letters, as you tell me so much local news. Frequently you say Helen will write details of an event. I "rubber neck" her letters, and all I see is: "Don't die. Don't eat. Don't drink. Send for me. Come home." etc., etc. As soon as Kerr[61] comes back, [I] will go over and see him; also Major Leo Parker[62] in command of his regiment. The little photos of "Gib" which father said were overexposed, were just sent as souvenirs. They were taken during the stormy weather. My writing is bad, but the atmosphere here makes one very nervous. I always had a very steady hand, but somehow it shakes here. The newcomers are affected by insomnia, and I have had difficulty in sleeping regularly. I have a good appetite and am in splendid condition. One's blood is thinned out in the tropics.

I am glad old Baker's puff was left out, as he has all the puff he is entitled to, that is, his pockets puffing with Government funds.

Two cents brings a letter here alright. What does Helen put five cents on each for?

May 8

I must close this letter. I enclose a hurried manuscript on the RR line to the front. A photographer went with me, and all the views of bridges, trenches, etc. were a failure, although he also took some with a small camera. I cannot await their development, as he has got to fill his film before he will begin to develop.

[Your affectionate brother,
Tod]

May 13, 1899

My Dear Father,

Your letter of April 2nd received by *Hancock*. Things out here are going O.K. except they are trying to do Lawton [in]. Otis is jealous of him and some dirty work has been done in Washington, somewhere. I do not see why they are sending Gen. Grant[63] and Old Wheeler out here. If Wheeler does come, I guess if he goes into the field that the climate will do [in] the old devil, although I am afraid that he is too tough.[64]

There are too many generals here now, why do they send more? Why was not Lawton given supreme command in the field as he expected. Everyone is down on "Granny" Otis. MacArthur is a good man, but I believe that he is not entitled to the next Brig. Gen. in the Regular Service. Promotion is rapid.

The photos of battle scenes are hard to get. I sent you six the other day. Will send more as soon as I can get them. Unless I can sell some, I don't wish to go too heavy as they stand me 25¢ apiece. That was a fine picture of the dead nigger and MacArthur. After all poor Miles was censured, why don't they do this to Alger before Thanksgiving?

Lawton knows what is being done to him, as the following telegram he sent MacArthur while in the field shows: "I am dictated to in every detail, and I am far from being pleased." Mrs. Lawton feels very bitterly toward old "Otis." I talk with her frequently, but do not mention military affairs often. Have not seen the General for a month almost. In that list of 123 lieutenants, some rank "suckers" got in nevertheless. In sending me stuff, to Mell, I do not need letter paper or such stuff, as I handle all the stationary in this office for the entire division. Mrs. Lawton has General Anderson's old house,[65] a fine big establishment, has two carriages and a launch. Her back door fronts on the river.[66] She is not looking so well. This fearful heat tells in the women.

I do not walk out during the day, but as night approaches, I go to the *Luneta*. I mess with the soldier clerks and some civilians right at the Headquarters [for] $13.00 per month, [and it is] very poor grub compared with the *Grant*, but it is wholesome and good, better than I can get at any Spanish place. The meat we eat, outside of corned beef, is killed fresh, and inspected by [the] U.S. Commissary. My rooms cost nothing; am in with three soldiers, all are at the front now. Insects are thick, but I do not suffer from heat or bugs, bathe frequently, have gained flesh, and am now sleeping well. One becomes extremely nervous when they first live here—sweat, sweat, sweat, bugs, bugs, buggier. But the nights are cool, and we do have fresh breezes in the day. I have suffered more in Washington from heat. Why the people knock Manila when they return is that they are sick and disgusted with something, and in its brightest aspect, Manila is not equal to the States. Money can be made here, but it will take some capital.

May 14, 1899

It is very difficult to get any drawing materials here. Unluckily, I tipped over my only bottle of drawing ink the other day; have not been able to secure drawing ink yet. Received your letters with enclosures from publishers. I thank you very much for your efforts in that direction. I have but small hopes of getting written stuff in New York publications as their standard is too high for a rank outsider in the profession. It is very hard to concentrate one's mind or efforts here. At home, I could draw or stay at a gob of work for some time. Here you either feel like collapsing into a sleep, or your head aches and is so numb you can't think, or you get so nervous you want to smash the office. The climate has a curious effect on one doing much head work, all say so. I have a couple of good ideas for drawings, which, when I can get the material, will work up and send to *Judge*.[67] But as I have had previous experience with them and know from others how hard it is to get a drawing in on them, I have but little hope of their using them. You see for a new man to get in on a famous publication, he must do as good work or raise the standard. As each new man raises the standard, it is pretty hard to get it past their art critics. I have done work that I think is up to the standard of that published in the New York papers.

I shall try to send you all the photos I can. The fellows who take the best photos, however, are clever enough not to sell any until two weeks after a mail has gone, thus they send them in to the San Francisco papers. The first lot I sent you are O.K., none were sent to [the] U.S. by [the] taker. The second lot of big ones, I fear, were sent to San Francisco papers for examination.

My trip to Santa Cruz, which I sent you, has (the battle part) been covered in the newspapers, but their accounts were in many cases way off. At any rate, if it is not used, I have it for my own account, and someday may be able to use it.

I stick to the office so closely these hot days that I see or hear little, so have no news to write. The papers I send cover the fighting pretty well, but the reporters they have are fierce. One, a bedroom steward, was fired from the *Grant*. He showed up on Lawton's launch one day to interview the General. He went about it like a bull in a china closet. The General remembered him on the ship, and after a few cold drives, he vamoosed. I don't believe he will ever beard the lion again.

I have a box with my overcoats and heavy underwear, etc. I have been wondering how I could get it home. I could get it on the transport to Frisco, but it is losing them at Frisco that I am afraid of, then transfer to [the] Express Company. Some things are very high here now; others remain cheap. Clothing that cost $1.25 to $2.00 and $3.00 Mexican now brings $8.00 to $9.00 Mexican. Khaki is high. I work an order through Lt. Brooke[68] and get soldier's clothes at government rates. They wear the best and cost the least.[69]

As I write, a terrific old tropical rainstorm has come up. We have had a long spell of dry weather. The palms are withered; the banana leaves cracked. It won't be long before we have typhoons and rain galore. I have been endeavoring to get in a hook in the *Philippine Monthly Magazine*, the first copy of which was issued April 1st. Have written the editor, as I could not find him in. Have as yet received no reply. The mail system in the city is rank.

Unless Walcutt is killed or is mustered out of the Volunteer Service, I think my position good until July 1901. For he is one of the finest Quartermasters in the Army and will be retained to the last at his present position or a higher one. Leathe, the other clerk, expected to get married; his girl fell sick and did not come out. She, I think, has some money and is eternally nagging him to quit the Army and return to the U. S. or Honolulu to start in business. If she prevails, I will be with a Regular Quartermaster and will be fixed solid for a few years until I can save enough to cut loose.

I have been under fire at Calumpit and on the expedition at Santa Cruz. I am not anxious to get plugged and do not shove my nose into danger except when necessary. Lawton is now prosecuting an Apache warfare.[70] But old Otis neutralizes the whole effect by telegrams restraining Lawton when he gets them in the right place to pound them. The "nigs" are fighting desperately for "rainy season or Blucher." There is no country so admirably fixed by nature for defensive warfare. It is only the great fighting of our men, and supreme courage that keeps the coons from holding us in Manila. If they show themselves on shore, Dewey knocks them. Lawton is relentless. The niggers brought in say they had no idea "Americanos so warlike." Well after the islands have been dyed with our soldiers' blood, the whelps in the Senate will release the islands twice won and paid for. In talking with the English and foreigners they invariably say we have a weak form of government. And that if it were not for our high civilization, through flaws in our Constitution, a military dictator would or will arise and seize the power; that our mode of government is not good to run colonies; and the running of our army by politicians will eventually bring us ruin in war with foreign powers.

Mrs. Lawton gave me your letter to her to read, and the General mentioned that he received one from you on the *Grant*. Did Helen show you the pictures? Get the numbers of the *National Magazine*, Boston, commencing with April, "Grant Around the World Illustrated" [by] Peter McQueen.

May 15

Will send you some papers in a day or so. Some more transports have come in. Tell Helen I did not get her photo with her letters.

Love to all. I am your affectionate son,

Robert D. Carter

May 28, 1899

Dear Sister,

An unexpected pleasure for me came yesterday in a mail for which I was not on the lookout. Not expecting it, it came as a blessing, a roll of papers from Helen, your letter and two from her dated April 16 and 20. Your letter contained much news as did hers of the 16th.

The clipping from the *Times* is an unjustifiable assault on Lawton and as far as the editorial goes it didn't amount to salt. How easy for that man to write that in his office knowing nothing of [the] facts, when Lawton had been day and night working like a dog in the Philippines. The true circumstances of that was thus: Maj. Edwards got the dispatch of Otis telling him to return. Lawton read it; did not say a word, [and] came aboard the small launch to give orders for the return of the forces to Manila. While sitting chatting with Edwards, Edwards remarked, "General it is a shame to evacuate Santa Cruz. I would like to see it held." Lawton [said], "It would be impossible to garrison all these towns which we take. It would take a 100,000 men." This is not verbatim, just a gist. It *was not* said to a reporter; it was said in conversation to a fellow officer, and I do not recollect whether there was a reporter or reporters near at the time or not. He did not say it because he was angry at his recall, in fact, he did not say anything regarding the dispatch, possibly, "very well." I was near all the time and saw and heard. But what he did say was that, "he could take a brigade of picked men and go anywhere he chose, from one end of the island to the other. There were not enough insurgents in the Philippines to stop him." Lawton is the last man to give any encouragement to Aguinaldo or such curs as the Anti-Expansionists. A man who will live in the U. S. and earn U. S. Dollars and says that he hopes the American arms will meet with defeat should be boiled in hot oil then rolled in a barrel filled with nails. It is an outrageous thing to attack a[n] officer who is fighting like Hell in such a manner. That editorial is based on some attack of an enemy of his in Manila. As far as censorship goes, Otis did not desire to censor it. Anything that will ruin a brother officer old Otis is only too glad to let go. He [Lawton] never while I was near him ever expressed a word regarding orders, or superior officers and that to his own staff. How much less apt would he be to criticize them to reporters. The whole thing is a base libel.

I am very glad to know that you are getting some cash in. I would [have] liked to help you [and] also mother, but my salary is scanty and I am trying to save a little against my return. Congratulate Madame on attaining her 52 years. On April 18th I was just returning from Leguna de Bay.

I shall be on the lookout for the box. I have one here with my overcoats and winter clothes, which I want to return, but do not know how to make connections in Frisco between ship and rail.

Helen said that the *Post* kept my article on Port Said. I do not want to lose that because it will break the series which I may put in shape sometime, illustrate and use. I think my Colombo article was as good as any, and afraid that *Leslie's* will not accept, nor do I expect them [to]. Were the photos O.K.? Helen said the Colombo article was refused by [the] *Star*. I thought Harris said they would accept stuff. Remember, I wrote those between hours on deck, constantly interrupted, and could not prepare them on a typewriter or fix them up as I desired. Those who had nothing to do except write and sightsee had me beaten at the start.

Lamberton[71] was very nice to me, and I only regret I did not get out to the *Olympia*, but one could not get a small boat to go out to the warship, and my office hours prevented me from making the visit. I saw Dewey often. The steward on the *Grant* got a picture of Dewey and Grant together. I tried to buy a print, but the disagreeable cur refused. He was the most cordially detested man on the ship, and one of the lieutenants one night came very near to cleaning up the Salon with him. I believe Baker has since fired him. He is incompetent and owes his position to being some relation of Major Summerhayes, the Depot Quartermaster at New York.[72]

All is great here now that General Lawton and staff have returned last night. The troops are in quarters except that some new regiments which have been sent to the line. The U. S. has the most foolish way of dealing with the niggers. Now we have them well licked and they know it, and [they] are willing to come in if their officers will let them. The U. S. is paying $30 Mexican for every old gun they bring in paying them for old guns which are unserviceable and which a few more lickings would make them only too glad to throw away.

I have been sick but the doctor has righted my stomach, and if I can eliminate the malaria, I will feel much better. It is nothing, everyone has it. I am feeling so much stronger now.

Oh, if I could but get a job in Washington or New York which would pay me living money, what happiness life would be!

With much love to all, I am

Your Affectionate Brother,

Robert D. Carter

P.S. What do you think of my run-a-way?

Chapter Five

June—July 1899

"I am not homesick."

At this time, Carter displays an increasing sense of disappointment with his service, tinged with some self-pity. He feels somehow that he has "just missed" golden opportunities, particularly when he sees men that he considers less worthy receive commissions. He does not wish to fail his father or himself, but he has become disillusioned. It is also clear that Carter, the "army brat," has a chip on his shoulder, referring to junior officers as "snobs," "brats," "kids," and "young curs," taking offense at what he perceived to be petty slights. This is in sharp contrast to how he was treated by more senior officers, particularly those who had served with his father. The latter had sent his son a list of officers with whom he was acquainted, and who were already serving in the Philippines or on the way there. Carter even takes some small-minded pleasure when some of the junior officers are brought up short by more senior ones, or more perversely, when the 4th Infantry was attacked by the *insurrectos* near Imus that June. Moreover, he is somewhat standoffish and selective with whom he associates. He cannot be unaware of the fact that he is viewed as one who obtained his position by virtue of his father's influence with Lawton. It is somewhat ironic, if not disingenuous, when he complains about others who have done the same.

Despite the many kindnesses of Mary Lawton, he is lonely, and, although he would protest to his mother that he was not homesick, he clearly misses home. Nevertheless, his letters continue to be filled with news, particularly with regard to the doings of General Lawton, something that his father was always interested in hearing. He recounts tales of the inter-officer rivalries among Lawton, Otis, and MacArthur, and he feels that Lawton was totally misunderstood and misrepresented in print. Lawton must have felt this way, too, as we see a brief flash of his legendary temper in his encounter with a reporter. Carter blames Otis. Moreover, he was convinced that Lawton had somehow been led to believe that he, not Otis, would be in charge, and that this was a source of disappointment.

Although he received some complimentary comments, Carter struck out with the big name publications back home. He felt that with a full-time job, it was hard to compete with "those newspaper fellows." As a consolation prize, however, he did secure a position with a local Manila publication called the *Philippine Monthly*. Carter offers an opinion regarding the poor quality of the Army recruits, now that the first contingent of Volunteers were returning home, as well as a blistering attack on the anti-imperialists, whom he refers to as "American Filipinos." Civil Service was relatively new, but he sees it as an answer to his tenuous job prospects away and abroad.

Into Cavite Province

Following his return from the joint actions north of Manila, General Lawton conducted a campaign in the southern provinces, first, with a minor thrust into the Morong Peninsula,[1] and later from June 10 to June 22, a major campaign deep into Cavite, the home of Emilio Aguinaldo. Once again, the energetic Captain Walcutt handled the quartermaster duties. For the fighting men, wheeled transportation was deemed impracticable, nor were there any pack mules available. Instead, six coolies were assigned to each company, battery, and troop.[2] Walcutt assembled the supply train, with two-days' rations, at San Pedro Macati and awaited orders.[3] In addition to his many regular duties, Captain Walcutt was ordered to take a detail of two wagons to retrace the line of march and to retrieve the discarded uniforms, bedrolls, and other materiel.[4]

Two long columns of soldiers disembarked at San Pedro Macati and snaked their way south. Soon the heat (reported to be between 100° to 110°) became unbearable, and the troops began to shed their clothing, bedrolls, and other equipment along the trail. Their thirst was unslakable, as canteens ran dry. Worse yet, the men became scattered—nearly a quarter of the entire force. A skirmish at a stream crossing was soon followed by a major engagement outside of Las Piñas. On their own initiative, given the state of the troops and the need to regroup, the brigade commanders decided to give the weary men a rest, and Lawton had no choice but to encamp for the night. Division headquarters was established in the only stone structure in Las Piñas, the rectory of the Catholic church. However, from Carter's description, even this left much to be desired, referring to it as "a den of filth." The General was serenaded that night by local musicians.

Given the situation, Lawton ordered rations to be brought by wagon train along the main coast road through Parañaque. However, trouble soon developed when the bridge over the river at that point became impassable. Repairs proved fruitless, and supplies had to be brought down by casco along the shore of Manila Bay.[5]

The following day was, in Lawton's words, the "hottest scrap" he had ever been in, when his troops overcame fierce enemy resistance at Zapote Bridge. Always at his best in combat, Lawton was exuberant. "We are having a beautiful battle," he telegraphed Manila in the midst of the fight, "Hurry up the ammunition; we will need it."[6] Lawton pursued the retreating insurgents, and he engaged them in a sharp fight at Imus.[7]

Carter went along as a quartermaster clerk in Lawton's headquarters and endured some of the same hardships as the soldiers. Among his various responsibilities, at Las Piñas he disbursed food to Filipino refugees and made payments to those who had been hired as laborers. General Lawton ordered the distribution of 1,000 field rations to feed the hungry populace, and, in addition, he also asked for authorization to distribute 100 sacks of rice.[8] It was here that Carter learned firsthand the nature of guerilla warfare. Friendly by day, many natives either joined the *insurrectos* at night, or acted in sympathy with them. Carter found evidence that some American money and foodstuffs made their way to the insurgents.

On a personal level, at the start of the operation, Carter took his meals with the officers. This would have been an added expense for him, but he ate relatively well. However, when Lawton took his troops further south, Carter remained behind. Now separated from the officer's mess, Carter was like a man without a country and missed several meals. His reaching into the dying coals of an abandoned campfire in order to find a crust of charred bread to eat is poignant. At some point, Carter was taken by casco to Manila to replenish the cash box and returned to the field.

Army Medicine

Overall, Lawton's campaign was a success. Carter, however, now covered with sores and boils, made his way back to Paco, where he was temporarily in charge of the office. Like most men serving in the tropics, Carter had had a brush with the usual maladies, including malaria, accompanied by diarrhea, as well as the Dhobi Itch ("Itch"). However, his latest bout of illness, no doubt brought on by his field service, was with a serious blood disorder, for which he was hospitalized, and which lingered on and left him weak in body. It is likely this condition stemmed from boils or skin lesions on his legs and feet becoming septic from his scratching them amidst the filthy conditions. For him, and others similarly afflicted, the simple act of walking became excruciatingly painful.

Carter gives us an insight into the state of medical care, particularly for enlisted men. His experience, and that of some of his co-workers, left him with the impression that medical care was nothing short of incompetent. If nothing else, it was often inadequate.[9] Many senior officers maintained a low opinion of the Army doctors,[10] who were, in any case, in short supply.[11] At first, nurses were not assigned to care for enlisted personnel, who had to rely upon male orderlies or corpsmen and the kindness of army wives such as Mamie Lawton. In the case of the 1st North Dakota, a female nurse, Helen Penny, was hired by the homefolks just to tend to the sick and wounded of that state.[12] At some point during 1901, the Medical Department changed its policy and allowed more female nurses to treat the sick and wounded.[13] Carter's concerns for the prospect of a complete recovery were not unfounded, as his experience showed that many soldiers never fully recovered as long as they remained in the Philippines.[14]

U.S. Army, medical corpsmen in the field, Philippine Islands

On a daily basis, the Army Medical Department grappled with the vexing problem of how to accurately diagnose and effectively treat malaria, typhoid, and yellow fever then rampant among the troops serving in Cuba and the Philippines, though all too late for thousands.[15] In fact, disease accounted for the greatest number of casualties among the soldiers, by far.[16] Although the battle casualties were low in comparison with other wars, diseases contracted during a man's tour of duty could "shorten his life" even after he came home.[17] The Army established a number of hospitals in the Manila area, and as the war spread to the far reaches of the archipelago, smaller medical facilities were established, staffed by doctors and corpsmen. The wounded received effective medical treatment, and the Army developed a basic system to treat the sick and injured closer to their units and to evacuate the more serious cases.[18] It would build upon this model during the First World War.

Second Reserve Hospital, United States Army, Manila

Very common were the Itch, Dengue and other malarial fevers, tropical ulcers, and dysentery. Medical care, particularly in the more remote areas, was poor.[19] To some, the Itch was a minor inconvenience, something to be expected given the conditions.[20] Venereal disease accounted for 11% of all hospital admissions in 1899.[21] Carter also humorously alludes to this soldier's scourge, telling us that those so afflicted were placed in separate wards and were referred to as "Rough Riders."[22] In an attempt to regulate the spread of this disease, the Army adopted a policy of sanctioning prostitution, and, in fact, operated the largest brothel in the Philippines.[23]

"Fifth Wheel"

Job security was a large concern for Carter. The situation was fluid at this time, as the earlier contingent of Volunteers made their way home and were replaced by Regulars. This was the case with the quartermaster. As a temporary civilian clerk assigned to a Volunteer, Carter was concerned that if the Volunteer left, he would automatically lose his job. Being stranded in the Philippines without sufficient funds to find transport home was not a pleasant prospect. In Manila, he served first under Captain Charles C. Walcutt, Jr., whom he liked. However, on June 20, Walcutt was reassigned as assistant to the depot quartermaster, and his place was taken for a short time by Captain Abraham S. Bickham, a political appointment and a relative of the adjutant general, Maj. Gen. Henry C. Corbin. Thus, when he heard that Maj. Guy Howard, a Regular, and the son of famed Civil War general Oliver Otis Howard, had replaced Bickham, he was sure that he would lose his job.[24] After all, Howard already had four permanent clerks, so what would he do with a fifth? He still had Lawton's backing, and moreover, he had an education as well as a good work ethic. In addition, he had taught himself typing, a skill that was much in demand. He was, therefore, a cut above. Carter survived the change in command, and Howard came to rely upon him, something Carter was proud of.

June 1, 1899

Dear father,

This A.M., I went to the Palace to draw my pay. I got there safely this time. The last time I got dumped a la "Jap & Pad." I was very much surprised when one of the quartermaster clerks said there was some mail there for me: a paper from Mell, a letter which she wrote March 25 with an account of [the] Bolway wedding, and a letter of recent date (April 20th) from you. They were directed [to the] Quartermaster Department. Put "General Lawton's Headquarters" on them, then they are forwarded with Headquarters mail, otherwise, I would never know when I had mail and would have to make a long trip for it. Send Washington papers frequently, especially those that have much Army news, gossip, testimony or rumor. For the officers generally look to that gossip as being more authentic. They grab my papers from Washington eagerly. The papers we get here are Pacific Slope papers and deal with "John Smith's orange crop," or "Bill Jones was made mayor of Prairie Town." Eastern papers have the news strung out. I see all the illustrated papers and most of the magazines. The *Review of Reviews* has the leading cartoons, and *Judge's Quarterly* combines nearly all the best comic pictures, which are a godsend here. If you send any, send those.

In a day or so, Lawton moves on Parañaque. After cleaning them there the "hombres" will be many miles away from Manila. Helen is cool to this place now. I am feeling well again, and it was only by great care that I passed a dangerous crisis. My stomach has resumed, the malaria has been knocked, and better than all, the mess arose in wrath and fired the bum sergeant, and we now have a white cook who can cook fine. This morning we had good coffee, dry corned beef hash, and light cakes. The Filipino cook and son were fired. Now we expect the mess will be run right. Since the Captain returned, we have hustled with work; he is a fine Quartermaster, as he would have to be to suit Lawton.

Am sorry my articles were not published by [the] *Post*, even without the pictures, as Helen would have gotten some money out of it. I rather think my "Colombo" article the best. The newspaper fellows could beat me because I had to work nearly all the time on the *Grant* and used to write those articles on the fly, with little time to arrange them in a good manner or spend thought upon them. Am glad *Leslie's Weekly* expressed a favorable opinion. I hope when I have time, to try and do something in the newspaper line. With time, application, and thought, I may be able to write so that, with my drawing, I can do well.

I had no idea you knew Hall, and I would not have known unless he had volunteered the information. Captain Lamberton is indeed a man, and he treated me as a gentleman and did not snub me as the young curs did, some of whom had just received appointments from civil life. He with his rank and name, and before two generals shook my hand, and was very cordial and invited me "to be sure and call on him on the *Olympia*," which made the "brat" lieutenants eyes pop out. General Hall always spoke to me. General Lawton, when I first came off the ship and, for the first time, reported at his headquarters, shook my hand and said: "How are you, Carter. Well?" On the other hand, Lt. Halstead,[25] a tow-headed yap from civil life, who sat at the same table with me on the *Grant*, and spoke to me there, simply because common courtesy required it, cut me dead in Manila, or rather I did not allow him the chance to. While a young lady (whose sister is married to an Army officer) who had asked me to do several favors on the *Grant*, and who knew me there because General Lawton did, cut me on the *Luneta*, because she was riding in a carriage with a lieutenant fresh from West Point you know. One of the old officers gave one of those kid officers a dressing down about his bearing and conduct to his superiors, which made me swell with delight.

Old Birkhimer[26] wore a suit of overalls while in the field which the soldiers said had not been washed since Feb. 5th. While one of his sprouts complained because he had not been able to change his underclothes or wash for three weeks, Lawton don't even take his off. He pulls his boots off to prevent sore feet, eats beans and tack[27] and wears the liver out of the younger officers. They came

Carriages and strollers on the Luneta

back looking like old car horses with fierce whiskers, while Lawton looked just the same as when he started, had a leathery look, and managed to shave while in the field. He had a touch of old Cuban fever,[28] but stayed in the saddle. Walcutt worked day and night. For two days and two nights, he was without sleep. Oh, for a frail man, he has the sand! I remember Major Rodman.[29] Hope to see him when he comes out. Captain Lovering[30] I was thrown with daily while on the ship, he being regimental commander. I don't know whether he knows that I am your son or not. As I received your list after leaving ship, he is a double-sided case, all smiles while off duty, but with the men, he is a "tough nut," a regular tyrant, and they hate him all right.

That newspaper interview was a scandalous thing and Otis permitted it to go to damage Lawton. What every soldier in the Islands says [he] would [do] if he were given a sufficient force, [is to] clean every *insurrecto* off the map of Luzon. Lawton says if he is allowed, he can go anywhere with a Brigade. Mrs. Lawton is at white heat about old Otis hampering Lawton at every turn. It is always MacArthur, but old Lawton has been doing the work. These are about the way the two men telegraph. I saw the telegrams on file at Otis's Headquarters. *This is private.* MacArthur: "Enemy in big force in line of my advance, think it unwise with present force to advance." Lawton marches around on flank all night and day over rough country, and thus flanks the forces which MacArthur should have driven and says: "Number of Insurgents in my front unknown, will advance." About the 100,000, Lawton's meaning was misunderstood! He said "should the insurgents and populations of these islands resist to their utmost, it would require 100,000," and it would, but as far as applying it to the insurrection, it was a outrage, as only one tribe are fighting and are licked to a finish now. He also meant that a policy of garrisoning the towns taken would require a large number of men, which is also true.[31] He was never interviewed, and those opinions were private ones to brother officers, not to newspaper men. His whole meaning was changed. He is known as too reticent, and as far as allowing himself to be interviewed, a reporter might as well try to get an opinion from the Sphinx. He has been done a premeditated injury; he is the most tight-mouthed man in the Army. And he is the last man to attack his superior officer, which you know. And you know that whatever his private opinion of Shafter[32] as a soldier was, he would not even express to you. How much less then would he express them to newspaper men. It is an outrage. That is a soldier's reward for hardship and worry. He worked like a Trojan and kept his mouth shut to reporters, and now he is rewarded just the same as though he were one of those War Department "Brand of Strategy" or Eagan.[33]

The anti-expansionists ought to be jailed. The very men who would take the field that they might remain in wealth, health and ease are now being roasted by them. Our policy with the niggers was wrong to start with. They have been used to a kick and a good damning for everything from the Spanish. Our soldiers allowed them to insult them under the American rule previous to Feb. 5.[34] They came in the streets of Manila and taunted our men. "Americans no *combate*." They were treated well, were allowed to construct massive entrenchments right under our noses, which in February cost the loss of much life to take. They grew insolent in the belief of our timidity and laughed at the cowardly policy carried on. It was a North Dakota boy[35] who first opened their eyes. They assaulted him on guard and cut him with a bolo.[36] He then, in spite of his orders, turned to and killed the entire outfit, three I believe, "pronto" quick. Every day since they have learned about the American's "No *combate*." Those people at home do not understand that our men fought for their lives not for conquest. That they were dying to save the City of Manila from fire, murder and general slaughter; that a terrible plot was put down firmly just in time. Yet the cowardly curs think that a shot should not have been fired; that we should allow those fiendish devils to kill American women and children; loot the city and raise hell among themselves; and they would call that "self government." Now the right policy is being partly carried out. Kill everyone that a bead can be drawn on, which is pretty difficult due to their not being in sight most of the time. To issue proclamations is all wrong. It gives them the idea we are weak. It is very wrong to pay $30 Mexican, when they are licked into surrendering their arms. It is like giving pearls to swine. They do not know what it means, and tomorrow if it was not for the physical fear licked into them, they would knife every one. It is the pistol and fear of the powers of the Americanos now makes them say "*Americano mucho bueno*" (very good). It needs a firm policy.

When Lawton was in the field, I was in charge of the Quartermaster Department here. There is a pretty strong nigger with a tricky face who tends to the teams. For several days, I have tried to have certain carriages dusted, cleaned, and the horses properly cleaned and fed. He shirked the work, did not feed the horses, never cleaned them, and did not do what I told him, because I did not yell at him or kick him. In fact [I] was very easy with him and let him go off a good deal. Out of sheer spite one day, because I would not let him go off half a day for which he was paid to work, he took the harness of Mrs. Walcutt's carriage, which I used, apart, and would not put them together again. I told him several times, and after much trouble, found and collected the pieces and ordered him quietly to put them together. He gave me a villainous, crafty smile, as much as to say: "What are you going to do about it?" It made me hot. I just hooked him with all my might square and fair on the jaw, unexpected to him, and he dropped. I thought he started to pull a knife, but as I had a gun on him, he put the harness together pronto, and he hops now when I tell him. The change from American to Spanish treatment was beneficial.

I see Walcutt is retained under [a] new act of Congress with his Volunteer title, so I hope I am good for 1901.

I am the only Quartermaster clerk in Manila at $1,000.00. All others of low grade get $1,200.00. On July 16, I am entitled to a raise and, an order from Colonel Pope[37] from Schreiner to rank me at $1,200.00 would help me a great deal. Tell Schreiner I am married, that my expenses are big, as I have to mess at officer's mess while in the field, quite expensive, that our work while in the field is tremendous.

With much love to all, I will quit for "chow."

Your affectionate son,

Robert D. Carter

P.S. I believe I am now fairly well acclimated. Sent Helen a money order today, so she may look for registered letter. Tell her, should you receive this first. There is one affliction which nearly all have here [called] the Dhobi ["Dobi"] itch. It is on the legs and will drive a sane man to drink. The skin peels off, great circles like ring worms appear which itch terribly, turn into pus sacs, boils, [and] ulcers. The toes become small boils which burst. Use 20% carbolic soap which partly holds it down.

June 2, 1899

Dear Mell,

Your letter of Mar. 25 was rec'd yesterday, as you did not direct it in care of Gen. Lawton, it was held at the Chief Quartermaster and it was only by chance I got it. I received a paper also directed by the Dutch humorist. He is a warm hand. I suppose he finds it rather warm work this summer riding in cattle cars and "rustling" for pie on the road. I believe if I could get a newspaper job, I could do well, for I would have my drawing to fill in with. I am sorry I did not get my articles published, even without pictures, for then I would have gotten something out of it. The articles written from the *Sherman* and *Sheridan* for the illustrated papers were farces. If I had no more to do than Bengough[38] on *Harpers Weekly* and sent in such bum pictures, I would feel ashamed. It is the same old story, no matter how you can do a thing, unless you get the chance, you are not in it.

On the "QT" if ever there was a Hell of a trip for one, it was my trip on the *Grant*. They had it in for me from the start, [and] were down on me because I was assigned to the *Grant*. The clerks in the Army are first and last a pack of ignorant curs, not a man among them, not a gentleman. Not a thing pertaining to my duties has been voluntarily shown me since I have been in the Service. In fact, they have tried not to have me learn anything. I have stood it in silence until would endure it no more. I nearly broke one cur's head for him, since which time, I have been treated right for they dare not do otherwise. However, if I ever have a chance, I will do them up to the best of my ability. I would as soon jump into a living grave as stay in this Service all my life. For instance, a man who cannot write a letter, spell, and punctuate it correctly, would not allow me to do any work, simply because he was so conceited and filled with ignorance, that he would not entrust such work to me. They howl about work, swear and groan for days over [it]. I simply stick for the money, and because I am with a Quartermaster who is O.K., and I don't propose to let any jealous curs persecute me until in disgust, I quit. I feel like Grant. I sleep good, eat hearty, am cheerful, do my work satisfactorily, and propose to fight like Hell if pushed. They know that Lawton is behind me when it comes to a finish. So their ungentlemanly conduct only disgusts me. Of course, there are bright men in the Civil Service clerks, and there are nice fellows everywhere, so I pick my company. It is the men who never held a position above $10.00 per month and always shoveled coal that act thus, or soldiers whose faithful service chewing hardtack and cleaning mules are thus rewarded by a position which they are as much fitted as a monkey.

I am glad Hess has been settled with, as I do not know what I would do here with bad teeth. Have Helen square with you for what you paid Getner. I am sorry I could not send you something for your birthday, but my mess bill in [the] field, my headquarters mess bill, my clothing account, etc. have all come in upon me, and I want to give Helen as much as possible.

Even Lawton is not in the position he was sent to occupy and is being stabbed by "American Filipinos"[39] behind his back in the U. S. while he lives on soldier's grub and never sees a bed to sleep in. There does not seem to be justice in this world.

Our mess has just been changed. Last night we had fine hot biscuits. They were as fine as the best restaurant ones, and two kinds of fruit.

Give me the old soldiers for gentlemanly treatment. Of course, I write much here that is on the inside. It is between the lines. Unless one has a commission in the Army, he is much better in civil life, for there men treat each other as men.

You seem to think Helen writes the news; she don't. I get it all from you. She writes "Come home; I love you; Don't come home; I am coming; I am not coming; stay for me, etc., etc., etc." Well, I will close until the next mail. *Adios.*

Your affectionate brother,

Tod

June 12, 1899

Dear father,

I have not written for several days due to the pressure of work, and then I have been daily expecting the mail which has not come for two weeks and over. I am anxious to hear how my articles turned out, whether used, etc. At present we are overloaded with work, and the clerk, Leathe, has no business capacity and is the slowest man I ever saw. He was sending out bills at the rate of 10 a day. It made me nervous to see him labor over them. I made out bill forms and got 36 bills in an hour, which made him open his eyes.

Well, the last week has been eventful. In answer to a letter I wrote a long time ago, I received an answer. It was to the editor of the *Philippine Monthly*, a copy of which I will send you. He requested an interview, and I went to town to see him. Gave him [a] talk, showed him work, etc., and I am now an illustrator and have a story depicting the [attack] on Caloocan by MacArthur's division and Col. Funston. I am to draw a swell piece [showing] Mac and

Funston, the number I send by the Editor Furman. You can judge his ability as an illustrator [and] he looks upon finding me as a godsend. I propose to stick in hopes that he can get the thing going good in the future, and I may make easy money on the side. It's the only one here, and it can be put in good shape for local sale and well illustrated, I don't see but what I ought to get next to the editor being his right hand artiste. The magazine is pretty bum now, but it can be hustled up.

I think a great deal of the prices and [the] "American boom" here will collapse. It is like a stock bubble. Because things are new, when they grow stale, prices will go down, the soldiers will save their money, and wealth will not be easily acquired. In fact, I find that there are poorer wages here than at home, and smaller business openings without you have capital. A plantation here should be a gold mine properly worked.

The next important event was that on the 9th Walcutt was relieved and made Assistant Depot Quartermaster at Manila in charge of water supply. [Leathe] being his regular clerk will go with him and [I] will probably be transferred to the new Chief Quartermaster of the 1st Division on Walcutt's paper, so I will stay right in this office at these headquarters, only under another Quartermaster. I greatly regret that I could not stay with Walcutt. He's a very fine Quartermaster and a fine gentleman, and a man for whom I can work 100 years without a bit of trouble. Again, he [is the] ranking captain [and] will be [the] next major. [He] is in direct line of promotion. Again, he ranks high in the Line [and] will soon be Captain of Cavalry. [His replacement] was [the] Quartermaster of 2nd Brigade [and] will now be Chief Quartermaster. His name is Bickham,[40] a Volunteer, has a Regular clerk, appointed from Ohio, has Corbin as his pull, in fact is some relative, [and] is an able man from what I hear. His father was a prominent man from Ohio. This man is over forty, I should judge, and he is an editor of one of the principal papers in Columbus, Ohio. Well, I am going to get next to him solid, so when he is mustered out, perhaps I might get on his paper. His brother is now running it. He [is] good for 1901, I believe.

I hardly know whether I can stick it out here two years. This climate is something terrible, bugs, itch, constant bowel and stomach trouble is epidemic. Good food, well-cooked is hard to get. Thank God, we now have a cook who was chef in a big hotel, and he can cook and we now "chow" right. Sunday dinner (chicken soup, hot biscuits, tea, coffee, jam, fried chicken, potatoes, slivered beans, tomatoes, peach pie, [and] pineapple); Supper one night (beef steak, Lyonnais potatoes, hot biscuits, apple sauce, doughnuts and "trimmings"). Oh, the joy of such a sudden change has quite paralyzed me. I simply sit and think and dip my pen in ink, and sit and think of "chow" time.

Lawton has been down on the South Line as you will have seen. The niggers [are up to] their old trick of trying to ambuscade the column firing on both flanks. By the number of ambulances which passed by Headquarters all of two days, I judge it didn't work. Will close for dinner. Cannot write more as work is piled up.

Your affectionate son,
Robert D. Carter

June 20, 1899

Dear father,

If there are spells where you do not receive letters from me, know that I am in the field or no mail has left Manila for days. Yesterday the *Sherman* arrived. I got two letters from Helen [and] a "Mumsay" from Mamma for which [I] thank her. There is a 10 day mail due from Hong Kong and I should get whatever was mailed me between May 1st and 17th. The last ten days have been eventful ones, for I have been with Lawton's expedition on the South Line.

I have been in the field more than any other clerk at Headquarters. In fact, on the last trip had a hell of a time—no food for four meals at a time. In fact, the field is no place for a clerk anyhow, as he is neither officer or man, and has to rustle for grub. While I was with Lawton's Headquarters mess I got my chow; when [I] was not with them, I simply had to steal my grub, as I did not belong to any organization. I tell you, a man earns five thousand a year drinking such water, eating bread dug out of ashes as I did at Las Piñas, sleeping in foul dens, and carrying a haversack, extra from other load, filled with Mexican silver. Everything bad that has been said about Manila and climate should be doubled. I have landed in excellent health, in less than three months I am saturated with malaria, taking 28 grains of quinine at a dose, stomach & [digestive] track a constant fight to keep from having chronic diarrhea, and now boils, something I never had in my life—five boils on one leg. I am now much better than I was, because I am more acclimated and hope I will continue not to get prostrated. I will stay here until my time is up and I am ordered home. I hope when I get back, I can, by seeing hard service, get a good Quartermaster job in some large depot, so I can save a little money.

While down at Las Piñas, I was with a newspaperman quite a little. He says that at Denver, the newspapers had great difficulty in securing good newspaper artists. One who would cartoon, they would pay a man $30.00 or $40.00 per week. I believe my newspaper chances lie in the West.

We are now overwhelmed with work here, from 7 to 7, then again late at night. Captain Walcutt transferred [command] to Captain Bickham yesterday. I transferred to Bickham, so will stay at Headquarters. Have not seen enough of him to judge him, but would liked to have stayed with Walcutt. He was a fine Quartermaster and a gentleman. Just as soon as I can get a minute, I will tell you about my trip south and about things in general; also answer Helen's letters.

Love to all.

Your affectionate son,

Robert D. Carter

June 26, 1899

My dear father,

This is my first opportunity to write you for several days. The last mail although not the latest was the accumulated mail for ten days. I received a letter from Mell, Mama and one from you enclosing letters to Pope and Lawton. Sent the one to Pope at once. Have not seen the General yet. Am awaiting action of Pope. I understand he does not have the power to increase salaries but to recommend, and my temporary designation is the same as every other clerk, only the other "temporary" clerk in making up the payrolls, etc., signed himself "clerk" and termed me "temporary," but poor fool, he does not know that when he returns to [the] U. S., we will both be temporary clerks and be fired accordingly.

Where I have been sleeping turns out to be very unhealthful, and since I have moved, I feel better, although for four nights I have spent the greater part walking the floor in agony from Dhobi (Dobi) Itch and had painful boils filled with stringy poisonous pus from the itch. Last night I put on some "Itch Cure" which was in reality some powerful acid, I believe. At any rate it ate into my flesh and burned like hot coals. I was simply crazed. Water made it worse; in fact, it simply burned two holes in my legs and sizzled itself out [after] about 5 hours, and I still have the itch.

The new Quartermaster Bickham's uncle is General Corbin. He soon expects to be a major, is a very agreeable man, a regular country politician, full of tales of office-holding lore and political tricks, but he is not the quartermaster or man Walcutt was. I regret I did not get a chance to go with Walcutt. As I would have a pleasant, healthful job on the launches, constantly on the salt water, cool and comfortable.

The bundle containing the mackintosh which you so kindly bought me came through O.K. It is a very nice one, a perfect fit, and had I selected it, would not have been more satisfactory. It came wholly unexpected to me, a welcome surprise, in fact, a Godsend, as one could not be procured here for less than $20.00. As it rains daily, I found I had immediate use for it. In fact, ate dinner in it yesterday, as the tent fly leaks badly. It was very thoughtful and very kind of you to buy and send it to me, and there was nothing I needed more. I thank you many times.

I have a sharp lookout for *Hooker*. She was at Singapore June 22; should be here June 28. Saw General Grant[41] riding in his carriage. Think he looks exactly as the pictures of his famous father.

General Lawton looks remarkably well for one who has been in the field on such a hard campaign. While I was at Las Piñas at his Headquarters, he saw me out on the back porch, spoke very pleasantly to me, asked for news from home; sent his regards to you and all. I quoted what you said regarding him in a letter about the hard flank march, horse, etc. He said he had a big horse now, so he was carried along O.K. Otis handicaps him, but he gave the niggers an awful licking on the South Line, and they stood and fought there. MacArthur has reaped the benefits in the papers, and through Otis, of Lawton's fine work in the Northern Campaign. At Zapote River, near Bacoor, the niggers made a desperate stand, and it was a hard fight to drive the niggers from behind their solid entrenchments. Lawton fought all day. He said it was one of the hottest scraps he ever saw. Well, it finally got so warm the niggers raised a white flag. The officers ordered our troops to cease firing. As soon as our fire ceased, about 200 coons arose *en masse* and left their guns in the trenches and fled.

Our policy is wrong. We would have bagged the niggers to the north had Otis permitted Lawton to press forward upon the coons at Calumpit[42] instead of forcing him to remain inactive while [the] Filipino Commission were chewing the rag. They were whipped, and another 7 days continuous advance and fighting would have found every nigger glad to surrender. Now on the South Line a casco of rice and "Alger" 4 lb. cans [of] Roast Beef was sent to feed the *reconcentrados*[43] supposed to be suffering from hunger at Las Piñas. The meat cans have since been found in the insurgent trenches, so that is how we feed the enemy *a la* Otis.[44] I believe since they started the war and wanted it, to give it to them strong for the *amigos* (friends), who are allowed within our lines, on every occasion kill and mutilate our men, as the 4th Infantry fight at Imus testifies, also at Morong.

On June 14, I went on a launch and made a long trip up the winding river in a casco to Las Piñas, paid off some niggers and then started out in a casco and remained off the bar expecting a launch. No launch came. A storm did come. We could not get into Las Piñas on account of the tide being out, so I slept on the casco all night. I started with no breakfast, got nothing until the following day at 3 p.m. (five meals shy) and got a pitching around off the bar, which nearly broke every bone in my body. When the launch did come which took us back, it was loaded with sick. Mrs. Lawton came down with [the] General. She took me up to her house in [a] carriage and I staid to lunch, the first as I told her that I had taken since I used to dine with her at Falls Church [on] Sundays a long time ago. She certainly is good to me!

On my arrival at the office, I was greeted with a stack of work which the snail of a clerk had allowed to accumulate, and when the Quartermaster changed, it was boosted on me. Yet, by cleverly withholding work from me while the captain was in the office, he put himself in the light of a tireless worker and me in the light with nothing to do. When the captain was away, I was rushed. I saw through the game and loafed on the clerk and worked when the captain was there. So I checkmated that dirty deal. Well, I worked until 11, so you see I got one meal in two days and had a good bit of work.

Next morning, June 16, I again took to the field with a haversack filled with money to pay off [the] labor (the greater part of which was never performed), and these very men we paid were later found among the insurgent dead. Oh, the U. S. is a good thing! In the P.M., I paid 60 men. I [will] send paper. The article was written by a correspondent who came down on casco with me. He mentioned many of the scenes which I saw. Well, there was a boss contractor who "calculated" to receive the entire pay, a dollar apiece for each man. To simplify matters, I allowed him to sign vouchers, then compelled him, in my presence, to line up every man and pay each his dollar. Thus they got their money. He thought to pay the men about thirty cents a day Mexican and pocket the balance as a rake off. American methods paralyzed him, and he was mad, and the way he cussed me in Tagalog and bum Spanish was rich.

I ate that night with officer's mess. Got a fine meal. About dark, a Filipino orchestra hove in sight and proceeded to serenade the General. One of the officers remarked to Lawton that they had come to serenade him, but Lawton was not filled with musical sentiment that night. He remarked: "I wish they would put that much energy into covering up their damned manure, so a man could walk about without being offended with such an odor." That [is] how it struck the "Great Chieftain." Well, the niggers are natural musicians, and they put up a great article.[45] In fact, they played finely, all operatic music, heavy opera, and played quite late. I slept on a bench fanned by a cool breeze from a door by my feet. The house used by Headquarters was a den of filth. Under the kitchen, all the refuse, garbage etc., water, grease was dumped through holes in the floor. Beside the dining room, in a small passage in the main part of the house was the commode! In fact, filth was dumped directly under the dining room. Yet, this was the padre's house, the only stone residence in Las Piñas, and most pretentious. Connected to the house was the church, with a bamboo organ over 100 years old. Its tone was grand. In fact, it was one of the sweetest I ever heard. The chanting and singing was beautiful as those niggers have a peculiar sweetness yet wildness in their voice.

When I first came here the reporter walked up with me. I told him to beware of tackling Lawton as he was rather down on reporters. He scorned to listen [and] inquired which was [the] General's room, banged on the door and walked in on [the] "Lion." The old man, [who] was in his undershirt and was awakened from a snooze, was sore anyway. The reporter said, "I represent the *American*, etc., etc." Lawton said: "Now you can get right out of here. In five minutes, you will be writing Manila a big lot of rot about a private interview with Gen. Lawton in his room, alone, etc., private etc., he says 'this and that.' I want you to get right out and any information you desire, you can secure from Major Edwards,[46] the Adjutant General, etc. [string of expletives]." It seems there had been a drunken reporter camping in Lawton's trail for a week and had run against him that morning, so Lawton was primed for the next.

The next morning was when I had a talk with General Lawton, the first in months. On this day Lawton and staff left. I remained with the Assistant Quartermaster who was sick. As Lawton's outfit took all the grub, I was left at Las Piñas without grub or prospects of any. I did the work of the Quartermaster all that day and [the] day following. Got no lunch or supper; likewise breakfast. I managed to rustle a can of beans and filled my hide on those.

I also laid on to a can of clam juice & soup, but while I was away, they were stolen. In the middle of the day, I went to Bacoor, the scene of the big fight. The troops had been moving all night and were pushing forward to the next town. No one can have any idea what the men suffer here. A torrid heat, clouds of stifling dust, footsore men, mules, horses and bulls, exhausted from heat and overwork, lined the road. It was war; it was a glimpse of men on the march. No water fit to drink could be had here, and man and beast were parched. It is no play to carry equipment and 150 rounds of ammunition on a tropical day on a road cut up by ruts two to four feet deep. The church showed the effect of this severe shelling given it by the war ships the day before. It was knocked so full of holes, it resembled crumbling ruins rather than a church.

I saw the 4th Infantry outfit just advancing beyond Bacoor. They had not seen any severe service until they got on this trip. It did me good to see some of their snob officers covered with dirt and perspiration hoofing it. They had been howling about never getting a chance to get on a trip with Lawton. Well, they got on it this time. The following day, they ran into the insurgents, and the truth is, for a time were well licked, making a hasty retreat, but when more men came up, they dislodged the enemy and regained the lost ground. They lost 4 killed (mutilated) and 23 wounded in that scrap and have been getting it ever since. The hospitals are filling up with their sick. The best soldier they had in the Regiment, Gregg, was killed at Malolos.

Having to return to Manila for money, I compelled three natives to paddle me in a *banca* [for] a four-hour's trip across the Bay. Off and on, I was on the trip from Parañaque to Imus, and the way bullets whistled was a caution at Parañaque. And as to grub, I got [to] go hungry. I dug a piece of bread out of some ashes where a native had hidden it and ate it. I was in bad shape to take the field having 5 boils on one leg. And one day I was in the saddle seven [hours], though I could faint from pain and my whole leg was covered with blood.

Work goes by in fits and starts now that Bickham is in. He has an experienced clerk who tends to papers and I have my regular work assigned me, and the clerk is not boss but the captain. The other clerk I knew used to hold up work just through a stupid wish not to allow anything to go through my hands, as he was so self-conceited that he styled himself "Chief Clerk" by his own assumption. Finally, when work came in that I knew that I would have to do as soon as the captain was away, I would pick it up off the desk, present it to the captain, get his action, and do it then, right away, which used to make the swell-head mad. He never taught me one duty while I was in the office, but I picked it all up by working, the same way I learned the stock board, and it delighted me when Walcutt was rushed with work just before he left, to hear him say: "Where are those returns for the 3rd quarter, etc." and slowpoke would say: "Not made up," although it had been weeks, and although the captain was a good man, it was too much for him, and in the last few days, he fired the work at me because he found I could turn it out about twice as fast as the other. But the damaging work done by jealousy has only served to make me mad and determined to assume a different course, that is to ignore the feeling of such fellows and not to care whether they like it or not, but go ahead and do whatever is before me to the exclusion of their ideas upon it utterly. At last, I have work given me to tend to and I take pride in doing it, but sitting around being "done up" and put in a false position by one who was in the same plane as yourself, don't go.

I was pleased to learn that my letters got to Washington safely. I presume by this time you are well started for the North. How I would like to be by a cool lake, in fact I would not mind being in a good snow storm. I shall have a feeling of disappointment when the fall does not come here; no cool bracing weather; nothing to start the blood tingling. One is utterly nerveless here. Now that I have moved from that poison, fever hole, I feel better. I regret that I was so unfortunate as to so speedily lose all I had gained by my sea trip by getting into a foul sleeping place.

I have read Mr. MacQueen's article in the *National Magazine* on the *Grant*. He uses words, but if I do say it, I believe I covered the ground in detail better. If you get a chance, get those magazines & read what he says. If I knew that when I returned to [the] U. S., I would hold my job, I would feel better about holding out here in spite of the effects of climate upon me, but on $80.00 I cannot save much ahead, and my position may terminate tomorrow, and perhaps in New York, I might by hustling, combining both drawing and writing, get at least $75.00. What do you think? Even after putting in two years, I will not have gained a position in [the] U. S., and it is utterly out of the question for a man to remain here his life, for that would be a living death. So far as mingling with the natives, I might as well be in Mt. P.[47] for that I loathe the sight of them, and I very seldom go to Manila proper, except on business.

I am now illustrating stories for the *Filipino Magazine*, in fact, am "Chief of Staff." Went and dined with the Editor the other night. He used to be on [the] *New York Journal*, I guess as a reporter. His artwork is on the bum, as you may see from poor Funston's picture in [the] sample copy I send. My work will probably appear next month.

Personally, I have tried to persuade Helen to remain in Washington, as this is no place for her. And I still further urge upon her the absolute necessity for her health, but she wants to come. Unless things are more settled and she can come from New York or by transport, I believe it wiser for her to remain for two big main reasons: 1) Health— the women who came here on [the] *Grant* got sick and returned, and 2) uncertainty of my position. Of course, it is hard upon her to hold out such a long time, but it will be better for our future prospects, for then I can get some money ahead against my return.

As far as [the] war goes, one would never know that there was a war in progress from being in Manila. Things are the same as in Washington, only you get better news, and we see more soldiers and niggers. The mackintosh comes in mighty nice as it rains regularly every night now. The other day I ate dinner in it under the tent fly which leaked badly under the tropical downpour. I receive a good many letters, but few papers. Captain Bickham said the Post Office clerks at Chickamauga[48] got behind in work and burned up about eighteen days newspaper mail. I wonder if wise fellows here do away with any of it or it is opened and stolen from [the] wrapper!

I enclose [a] clipping of [the] *Grant*, [which] has [to be] the only picture I have seen of her. The fireman, John Kay, I remember well, because I had to order him out of the hold for stealing beer which was in cases there. He was a finely developed and [good] looking man about 35. A good many that made the beautiful trip on the *Grant* are now dead.

The General is looking remarkably well now for one who has been doing such hard service, dresses all in white and looks every inch a general. He is highly thought of by his soldiers. The old veterans who saw service with him in Arizona still call him by his army nickname, "Old Bean Belly," for they say he used to fast for two or three days, then go up against a lot of baked beans and fill his hide. He wears the liver out of the young officers. Right here there was a big excitement. The 12th Infantry was passing on their way to San Fernando, when a shot was fired. A wild rush was made outside, where it was found that it was caused by a drunken soldier of [the] 17th firing his revolver off in salute to the "passing regiment." He was seized, brought into Headquarters, charges preferred, and I guess that salute will "hold him for a while."

As to Lawton's assignment, he was sidetracked and a deal perpetrated somewhere. He lingered on the ship for many days, and it was nearly a month before they started him on active work. Old Otis favors MacArthur, also himself, to [the] exclusion of all others. I suppose as the fight had started, "military courtesy" forbade Lawton stepping into active military governorship while the strife was on. He will soon go back to brigadier general, and I suppose some old fossil like Joe Wheeler will come out here and rank him off the Island. Really, no one knows how it was done or why, but it was done!

As to the transport, they were not suspicions, they were facts of which I hold proofs, and I would never have spoken of them had I not been accused of being in a ring, which made me mad. Baker is alright as a man, but a bum, political Quartermaster, and his clerk, who I see has left at Frisco, was a rank cur, and his pockets are lined with money which he received from sale of liquor, which was brought on ship at "Gib" and sold contrary to Transport Regulations, and which was such vile stuff that even the sailors roared. He sold this for $1.25 per lot, so you see he made. I did not care to be a "Miles."[49] You see where he landed. It was only when I was dragged into it that I got hot. As to bribes, there was plenty of that, as I had occasion to see at Gibraltar.

I understand that *Grant* and *Hooker* have just arrived. I write this by snatches. Got a letter from Percy the other day. Will write Mama and Mell as soon as possible. Love to all. Give the dog some calomel.
Your affectionate son,
Robert D. Carter

July 10, 1899

My dear Mother,

It has not been through neglect that I have not written you, but work and illness have left me but little opportunity to write a small part of what I wish. Your long letter came by the *Sherman* over three weeks ago, but on the night of June 28, I had a severe attack of vomiting similar to the spell I suffered the worst previous. On June 29, I felt so badly and could not eat that I decided it was best for me to have treatment. In the morning, I fainted twice, and my whole system was run down. My lower limbs and feet were running sores, and I had many boils. My stomach refused to retain food. In the P.M., I went to the 2nd Reserve Hospital as it is near the sea and 3 stories high[50] and was anxious to get above the ground. I was assigned to a long corridor, under the care of Dr. Fogg, a contract surgeon,[51] who, it seems, comes from Waterville, Maine. We talked of the lakes, scenery, Bridgton, etc. He was much interested in talking with me. Well, when I struck that bed, a real spring bed, the first since I struck Manila, I felt I could rest and recover from my weakness. I was put on [a] liquid diet, soup and cow's milk. It seemed good to get something fit to put in my stomach. As my bowels got better, I got crackers and Wheaties and oatmeal. It was a treat. They fixed my stomach and bowels O.K., but my general system is reeking with poison which [the] doctor said would take weeks to eradicate.

On the 7th, although the doctor wished me to stay, I felt well enough to go over to Headquarters. He gave me blood tonic to take my last day or so in [the] hospital. I got [a] special diet and, oh my, it tasted good and the way I picked up—orange and peach tapioca, stewed chicken, soup & wine jelly and *blancmanges*. The Red Cross nurse treated me very nicely, and my stay was very beneficial, and I regret [that] I left quite so soon as my stomach had a slight set back due to the fierce grub. We have a good cook, but he is very lazy. [He] puts in more time making doughnuts than having good meals. I buy much separate at Paco Casino, a small Spanish hotel nearby, get toast, which I showed them how to make, also egg nog from condensed milk, which is fair. While I was at [the] hospital, Mrs. Lawton hunted me up. She is very nice to me in so many ways exceedingly kind. She went to Bickham while I was away and inquired for me, spoke with another lady, who was with her before Bickham, of my home, people, etc. to impress Bickham that I had "friends." Mrs. Lawton, wife of [a] major general, to voluntarily inquire for a poor Quartermaster clerk, she said she did the talking so as to put me on the right side of Bickham, as I had told her that I wanted to stand in with him. Now that he knows that I have some friends, he will place me on a better standard with him. Although now I stand in O.K., he is very pleasant, talkative, not exacting, and not so lofty as a Regular officer. In fact, he calls his clerk "Harry" and he places his clerks on the same standpoint as in civil life. It seems good to speak naturally and not continually on the ice house plane.

There is a rumor today that Roosevelt is Secretary of War. There is great joy among Army officers. I hope it is true. It rains now in bunches, torrents, such rain, and the mackintosh came just in time. One cannot go out without a rubber coat here for five minutes.

It seems the place I had been sleeping was over a drain and I got a good dose of rottenness in my system which the medicine is now driving out, though [there are] the big sores on my legs and the boils. In three weeks, [the] doctor said I would be better. Unless I get very ill and do not rally, I will not return.

Bickham, Walcutt, etc., in fact, nearly all Quartermasters here will remain until 1901, after which Bickham says they will probably be put in Regular establishment. Leathe, being Walcutt's clerk, will be permanent on return to [the] U.S. Bickham says he will not stay in [the] Army. He makes more money in [the] newspaper and is going to run for Congress. He is a big politician in Ohio—Dayton, [a] nephew to General Corbin.

General Lawton has been away most of the time, and I have not seen him. Big typhoon raging for the last few days, Bay very rough, cannot unload transports, shortage of everything in Manila in Commissary line (fresh stuff). Box is still on *Hooker*. When weather clears will hunt it up.

An orderly said here in conversation to me that he overheard General Lawton, in a private conversation with another officer, unburden his heart about the matter of his assignment. He said he spoke very bitterly, and said he has been outrageously sidetracked. And old Otis has hidden from the public you read at home. Otis, Otis, MacArthur, MacArthur, but it is Lawton who does the work, and yet not a word in the newspapers yet, because Otis oversees that the reports are censored.

A joke in the hospital: A great section is filled with beds of men with venereal diseases. In the Army they are called "Rough Riders." Ha! Ha! Woe to the "Rough Rider" who uses a [water] closet belonging to any other ward. I am now endeavoring to secure a room by the sea, but they change so much.

One of the porcelain teeth that Hess put in on right side is loose, not detached, but is held by a spike only. I am going to the dentist to have it recemented. I suppose they won't know how to do it, and will charge a mint.

There are no better business chances here than at home, except you have good capital. I never could endure this land over two years. Everything is against a white man, and it is foolish to struggle for a living here, which is no better than one can get by [the] same exertion in [the] U.S. A government position is the only thing that pays. If in the future, out of all this, I could but have a position in [the] U. S., I would feel repaid for the weeks of pain and sickness. But the boys in Washington have the cinch, I being a kind of hind leg, will be bounced. When General Lawton returns, I am coming home. Do not think of allowing Helen to come, she would die. Nearly all the women that came out have returned. Those that stayed have money and can buy every luxury, apples 25 cents apiece, etc., etc. In Helen's letters, I spoke of some flannel pajamas, which if you could make and mail, Helen will pay all expenses. They would be a Godsend. I need them very badly to sleep in, a dry covering from the deadly damp. The little photo of home which you enclosed was a surprise. I could not imagine so much snow.

The Lawtons do not live in the Palace, but in a fine house by the River. The Palace is an office building. I send some views. They were failures due to blotting paper sticking to them, but they will give an idea of Mrs. Lawton's house and view from her windows.

Also, Captain Walcutt was such a fine man. If I were his clerk, I would be O.K. permanent, as he is a Regular, but I got into the Service much too late.

Unless I feel much worse and do not improve, I will not return. I write this to let you know the exact state of my health. I am looking longingly for the next mail, which *Sheridan* will probably bring. *Grant* is now in harbor. May go out to her when sea quiets down. I have spells since I have been sick in which I seem to be home again, under your loving care. I am not despondent or downhearted, but when one gets sick among strangers, rough strangers in charge, where even money cannot buy a simple dish of milk toast, oh, then is the time youth, home, mother, [and] friends come to mind, and it is hard to gaily and cheerfully face these hardships when in pain and sickness. I am not homesick; not in any way changed in my determination to see this deal through to the letter "Z" and see what there is in it, but I must frankly acknowledge I am not as I was, because I believe illness makes me see the world in a little darker hue than when seen by one in the enjoyment of superb health.

General Lawton looks well, as does Mrs. Lawton. She has shown herself [that] she is true blue, one woman in a thousand. I do not believe I ever knew her or do you. She is an angel in the hospitals. Literally a thoughtful, courageous, kindhearted woman, and moreover a diplomat, who strengthens the General in every quarter. She has been very, very nice to me.

Give the dog castor oil and turpentine the cat. Love to all.

I am your affectionate son,
Robert Dexter Carter

July 27, 1899

My dear father,

Perhaps you may wonder at the long interval since I wrote you last. I received your short letter of May 27 just as I was going to the hospital. It cheered me up. I understand. I am OK here until 1901. I am no longer working with Walcutt. I am so sorry, but I am working with Bickham. In a few days Major Guy Howard ranks Bickham out of this place, and Bickham returns to the 3rd Brigade. As he cannot have two clerks as Brigade Quartermaster, I will probably be transferred to Howard and remain here. Howard brought four clerks with him, and they are all hanging around. When I am assigned to him, he will have five. I suppose he won't like my being put upon him, but General Lawton had me assigned to [the] Chief Quartermaster's Office at these Headquarters, and as my orders assign me to Lawton, what he says goes.

The General has been away up the Lake. Mrs. Lawton and Manley went on the launch with him. Tomorrow evening, I am going over to take Mrs. Lawton some photos and to see the General, and get his advice and counsel. One thing is certain; I cannot stay permanently in Manila. I will die or have my health ruined for life. So I am going to stick to the Army and am going to tell Lawton, so that I am not going to remain in Manila. I have conferred with many bright American businessmen, and they all say that unless one is making very good money from his business, it does not pay him to remain, as without a good capital, he is just the same as at home, an employee. Living is going beyond reason. I walked one-half mile at 5:00 A.M. to get a pint of milk (all I could buy) and was charged 25 cents American. My lunch, two eggs and some wretched toast cost one 40 cents American. $80.00 does not pay me to suffer physically what I have for the last two months. I do not write this to complain, but to face the situation, and speak the plain truth.

The climate now is terrible, clothes are wet, no washing can be done. I have broken down by degrees. I have put up the good fight. I never took such care of myself, and it seems the irony of fate that I, the one who totally abstains at Headquarters and am so careful, is the first to go under. But all are giving out. Nearly every clerk who has been here a year, no matter how good his position, has by reason of ill health had to quit. Without spending big money,

I cannot live in my present condition of health, for I cannot get or buy food (eggs, milk, etc.). I have stuck it out and intend to hold out longer. Now, what I am going to tell Lawton is that it would be foolish for me to leave a position at $1,000.00, where I get my transportation to [the] U.S., and government treatment in hospital, with a good chance of managing to get a transfer to the States, and thus retain a moneyed position. To accept a Civil position where if I am sick, I will get fired after thirty days and even an increase in salary to five or six hundred more, would only be what my fare back would be. Four to five hundred, and be bound forever to a country which would be in time, the utter ruin of my health.

If I can now rally, I will stick it out for some time until I can better myself. If I do not get better, I will have to return at once. The doctor told me that I was in a badly debilitated condition, my blood rank poison, and that it would take a long time in this country to clean my system out and restore me to full health. For a month I could do no work in [the] office, as I was in the hospital all that time with stomach trouble and could not walk because of boils and finally, an abscess in the ankle and feet. The hospitals are overflowing in the States. People do not know what havoc sickness and disease is playing with the soldiers. Oh, as Sherman says, "War is Hell." Three men died, two in fearful agony, within twenty feet of my bunk in the hospital. To my dying day, I will never forget the scenes of death and destruction I have seen here. I have faced death and its awfulness appalls me.

In a clipping from the *Star*, I see by the Civil Service ruling that the 700 clerks in the War Department will be installed permanently within the Civil Service. Could it be possible for me now that I am in and that part over, through an order be retained in the War Department or station anywhere in the U. S.? Schreiner[52] has the power if General Lawton advises me to return, and I am ordered to proceed to Washington to report to the Quartermaster General. Would it be possible if I brought a request or letter from Lawton to Ludington or Schreiner, that when I report, they will not discharge me, but put me to work in [the] War Department or some depot in New York, Philadelphia, Baltimore, or Washington, or any big station where extra clerks are required in [the] Quartermaster Department. I hate to be forced to give up when I am determined as ever to stick it out and have the grit and do not suffer from longing for home as so many. Mentally, I am cheerful as ever. Physically I cannot do the work for which I am sent, and thus my usefulness is gone, and perhaps I may be ordered home for discharge without my asking. Permanent stay in Manila is forever gone from my mind, as it would be my death by slow degrees of disease. Some men it hits hard; some seem to hold out well for a time then collapse.[53]

The ships that return carry many men who have the seeds of disease in their system for life. My life is before me. I believe that even now should I return, I could secure some position which would pay one at least $50.00, which is better than $80.00 here. As prices rise, my ability to live on my present salary decreases. All that I speak of here, I will tell General Lawton. I do not see why, with General Lawton's request or recommendation, that they would discharge me from Quartermaster Service on my return to Washington. I did the best I could. The climate conquered me. I have earned my salary, for since I have left New York, I have worked every day and many nights, excepting that period when I was in a cot, unable to move; the first spell of sickness that prevented me from performing my duties for years. If I will not be discharged, but put in any position of whatever description in [the] Quartermaster Department in [the] United States, cable Lawton, Manila "GOOD." I will tell him, so he will know who it is for and who sent it. "Good" will be the word that I am to understand things will not be an immediate discharge when I report. I will save an account ahead so at any rate I will not be busted when I return for some months. Thus I will have a chance to look myself up a job in New York or Philadelphia.

If I get very sick, will cable *Army-Navy Register*, Washington thus: "Register, Washington, return." Thus you will know that just as soon after that time as I can get an order and transport, I will be on my way home. I will write you at once what Lawton says, and if my health does not get very bad, I will be here for some months. And if I improve, will stay my entire time. I simply write this to tell you so that in any case you may know if in case I do return, whether I am returning to a discharge and a "look for work," or to another position however humble. It seems to me that when a man has rendered hard service abroad, and by reason of sickness, cannot live in that climate, and is obliged to return, he should not be the one dumped. When he returns, he might be given a chance at a position in [the] U. S. where he does not have every itch, humor, and disease in the calendar of ills. When you do get that cable to *Register*, you will know that it was a pretty sick boy who wrote it, for if I feel no worse than I do now, it will be some time before I return. Know from this that I will not quit the Army for a civil job which I will quit anyway within two years and have to give up $500.00 good money to get home with no chances. Whereas by sticking to the Army, I stand a show of being placed at work somewhere in [the] U. S., and if I don't, I am not at least out $500.00.

I returned July 26 from the Reserve Hospital. I was there from July 11,[54] had swellings of the veins in feet and ankles, groins [that] had to be reduced by poultices and hot water, and was, in the course of my stay, cleaned out of a bucket of hard puss through boils and running sores everywhere from my temples to my feet, which were the size of Jumbo's,[55] and a big sore [on] the right ankle, an abscess, coupled with diarrhea and weak stomach. My diarrhea is now checked, my stomach feels like a frail china dish, and the sores have been dried up by chloride solution.

At present, I do not know how I will land on this new major stepping in with four men and myself to fill two positions, but as Lawton is my direct boss, I expect I will remain in [the] office, as there is no other place for me to go, Bickham being allowed but his one clerk at Brigade Headquarters. I think tomorrow I will try to get over to Manila with Walcutt again. He said anything he could do for me, he would be glad to do for me. If I can get with him again, I will be with a Regular man, not an article of office furniture transferred under protest to each new cameo. Walcutt was glad to get me, so was Bickham, as they only had one clerk, but this new cuss with four won't like my being put upon him and have to part with one of his clerks. So, perhaps he may take it out on me as Captain Baker did. Well, *manaña* we will see. I will tell you where I land when their tinkering is over.

There is one thing of which I have not spoken, but in case I should get a favorable chance to reply, I would remain in the Philippines until I landed in Frisco, that is a commission in the Volunteers. Captain Birkhimer, was made a colonel and authorized to raise a regiment, well he has cabled to Washington requesting that Carpenter, [the] Chief Clerk at Headquarters,[56] be given a commission as captain in his regiment. He wants to make Carpenter adjutant of the regiment. Well, on that information, not knowing when Lawton would return from [the] Lake, I wrote Birkhimer a letter on the lines of the Marine Corps application, stating that I desired a commission in his regiment and wished to know if he would give a formal application, with endorsements, his consideration, and what chances, if any, there were for me in his regiment. I stated my school, my drill under Chase and French, my brother Captains Kerr (22nd Infantry), Smith (12th Infantry), [and] Leonard (Marine Corps),[57] and stated that Generals Lawton and Hall would endorse my application, as would many officers whom I named, have met, or who are friends of yours. I also spoke of your being his classmate and of often speaking of you to me. Now, I await his answer.

If he will consider a formal application, I will utilize my Marine Corps endorsements and get Lawton to talk to Birkhimer, who was on his staff for some months. I await his reply and will let you know what he says. He will have to return to [the] U. S. to raise his regiment. If he does, keep your eye on papers and write him a letter, unless in the meantime, I have written you he has sat upon the whole idea. I understand he does not have entire say, that at the War Department they will officer [the] regiment. If he is favorable, I will get him to cable request to Corbin for my commission, as he did for Carpenter's, and I will pay for cablegram. And in case you should cable me ever, I will pay for it. I am awaiting anxiously to hear how Carpenter will come out. If he gets it, I think, with Lawton's help, I stand a show. If not, I think that Birkhimer hasn't got the power with Corbin as lord of all, and I will quit trying to secure it. A cable from Lawton would get me a commission in one of the new regiments in case the appointments are made from [the] War Department. In my next letter I will let you know more definitely how everything turned out or is turning out. Be sure, that when I cable you, that the fight has passed endurance and to save my health for future life, I had to give up. But at present, I think I can hold out many months.

The Chief Quartermaster job is a holy terror. [When] Old Lawton takes the field, every officer has to hike, and the Chief Quartermaster has the hardest job of all. He is everywhere. This is no cinch here. War is pretty fierce and these niggers are not done for yet. My trip to Laguna[58] was a trip in Paradise [compared] to my deal at Las Piñas—one meal in two days and riding with five boils on one leg. I didn't feel much like a joke when I got done with that deal.

The mackintosh was a godsend. I even sleep in it during the heavy rains. Every time I look at it, [it] makes me think of the kindness and love of the people at home and your many kindnesses and efforts in my behalf since I left.

Helen will never see Manila if I can prevent it. I wrote her more from her urging and because the weather was good, prices more moderate, and my health was good. Now that I have had the experience, I honestly believe it would be her death to come here. Leathe was married at Captain Walcutt's house quietly last night. I understand the girl is an orphan worth $50,000.00. She tried every way to get him to leave Manila, but he knows that Walcutt has seen hard service here and will probably return to [the] States soon, and he being his regular clerk will have a permanent job in [the] U. S. whenever Walcutt goes. If I could get on the permanent list in [the] War Department, embraced by this new order, my very long struggle and scramble would be at an end. If I could live here, I would be contented, but to be an invalid comes pretty tough.

Mrs. Lawton has been so very nice to me. [She] came to see me right at [the] hospital [a] second time. She has just recovered from a severe attack of illness herself. On the quiet, it has not been made public, [but] Old Otis has been a very sick man at his home. People do not know the truth here—disease, death, and the whole army down on Otis and his methods. Insurgent officers are everywhere in the city. It is radically wrong, this policy of trying to overcome these whelps by kindness. They think it is because we fear them. I wish Lawton could get at them. They ought to be cut down tooth and nail, exterminated, houses and villages burned, until they begged for peace. The Spanish policy in the Philippine Islands was right, and now the U. S. is enforcing the very duties and taxes that Spain used and at which we roared. What a farce! Oh, the Philippine islands will be a wen[59] on Uncle Sam until he yells for mercy. There is but one way to do this, and that is to give them war, not a few scraps, and then allow them all to come inside our lines, get food, clothes, etc. and then sneak out to again fight us. Otis is very unpopular here, and the hope is that there will be another Governor.

July 28, 1899

I have just returned from a tramp for some milk. It cost me 20 cents a quart, but it will go good, and I will make a breakfast on it. I will give you full information how I progress and my expectations, [and] what Lawton says or advises me. The civil job is of no advantage to me, for it binds me here, and I will have to pay whatever increase in salary I get right out again to get home, and as I have said, my chances are preferable in the Army, for if I am made a Civil Service permanent clerk, I will have to be attached to some depot. I believe that a clerk engaged by an officer, even if he is his regular clerk, is not protected by Civil Service. But if I am made a Regular Quartermaster Clerk, then I am under orders of [the] War Department, who assigns me to a station and carries me on the roll as a War Department Clerk. Of course, I do not know.

I find my time so engaged and facilities are so bad, that I have no time to draw, and as I have had the bad luck getting my articles in, I will let up because I need a rest.

Last night I slept well [for] the first time in a long time, and today, I feel better, head, etc. It is impossible to describe the feeling one experiences here. One feels like a walking dead man. Energy is gone. It is an effort to think. The brain is in a cloud. I feel as though I was out for the first time from months in a sick bed. I am so weak. I have touched no liquor since I have been here, and even do not drink coffee or tea [but] rarely. Lemonade is not to be had, and oranges are worth their weight in gold. Curiously, an American has no desire for women here. For months and months, it seems as though [a] man's vitality, life, and spirit were eliminated.

The class of recruits filling up the regular army now are the worst men I ever saw. No words can portray their brutish aspect, fearful language, and a glance is enough to know that they are from the criminal quarters of [a] large city, with a sprinkling of green country boys. All the old soldiers have cleared out after the Cuban Campaign, and those that stayed in, and got a dose of this, which is even worse as far as [a] vet goes, curse the day they saw the army. Rheumatism and lumbago, consumption and dysentery are killing them off like flies. There were over 15 men in our ward out of a possible 40 stricken with typhoid and malarial fever. People at home do not know what this wretched land is costing us. I believe in conquering it and holding, but the present policy of fooling with these niggers, giving them self-government, etc., makes the Americans ridiculous in the eyes of the Filipinos.

I did not get the magazine of which Mell spoke of sending. I got my box from Lawton O.K. I will write you about it in my next. Thanks for the many little remembrances of home [and] the magazines. When I look [through] them, though, I will turn over to Mrs. Lawton to give to hospitals. There are now big shipments of magazines and San Francisco papers from San Francisco. So I see most of the illustrated papers and magazines, except comic papers. Send me New York papers or Washington papers for they have Eastern news in full, which Pacific papers never have. Am much gratified that the *Sun* was pleased with my article. It shows that the general rudiments of newspaper work were not so bad, and there is hope that with diligence I may learn to write the "King's English" which coupled with my pen work ought to secure me some job on a paper. Shall try New York and Philadelphia for newspaper jobs if there is nothing in sight when I return. I have small hopes at this distance from Washington of getting my Volunteer commission. It all depends on what Birkhimer answers to my letter. Old McKinley's prospects for the future are not as bright as they have been. It looks like the man from New York.[60] Even if my health continues bad, I will stay here some months yet. If I can get with Walcutt, I will try my best to do so. This constant changing of bosses is hard business, and unless Lawton fixes me by an order in this office, every Quartermaster who brings a bunch of clerks will try to oust me.

Well, it nears the time when I must be at work and wish this to leave in early mail. I will close with much love to all. I am not discouraged. The body is too weak for the will, and I have come to the conclusion that a residence in Manila is out of the question for me. And, accordingly, that I must stick to the Army. I would rather have $50.00 or $60.00 per month in [the] U. S. than $5,000.00 here for the reason that there I could work, eat, think, in fact keep good health. Here it is out of the question for me to be fully well. At this writing I wonder where you are. I suppose you are well out of Washington heat.

Your affectionate son,

Robert D. Carter

P.S. Do not direct letters to any particular Quartermaster, just Chief Quartermaster, 1st Division, 8th Army Corps, care of General Lawton. A clerk who is here of Howard said that the Naval clerks in [the] War Department were all retained in Civil Service, but there was no intention of retaining Army clerks, however good their service had been. Perhaps a letter or word from Lamberton to Long[61] might get me into [the] navy in case you find there is no show in [the] Army.

Chapter Six

August 1899

Dog Days

Carter's road to recovery was a slow process, and he continued to have significant issues with his digestion and with his feet, which made walking very painful. He details his afflictions, from his bowels to the suppurating sores on his legs and feet, often in graphic terms. His disability kept him from going into the field during the months of July and August to take part in what amounted to futile minor actions intended to disrupt and interdict a lively trade with the insurgents on the other side of Laguna de Bay.[1] In fact, things were slow enough for Lawton to take his family by launch to visit some hot springs in the same area.

At 1st Division headquarters in Paco, after some initial reservations, Carter found that he got along well with his new commanding officer, Major Guy Howard. He found him to be a demanding superior and a hard worker, and he respected him for that. With a change in command came new responsibilities, including work in the evening and on Sunday.

Life in the tropics continued to be a challenge, with cockroaches and other vermin, as well as heat, damp, mold, and disease, not to mention monsoons. One soldier told his daughter: "Everything in leather molds," and "clothes sour as soon as worn."[2] In addition, "typhus, malaria, dengue, and a dozen other diseases flourished in fouled sewers, stagnant backwashes, and public wells."[3] Large numbers of mosquitoes in combination with the overall filthy conditions, particularly in Manila, was a formula for the spread of disease. Carter compares the local variety of mosquito with its puny American cousin. He writes of damp bedclothes; frequent changes of clothing, particularly underwear; as well as the disintegration of his luggage due to the climate. Like all large cities, as Carter discovered, Manila could be a dangerous place. He

Escolta Street, Binondo District, Manila, P.I.

recounts the need to shoot a wild dog,[4] as well as a dinner out followed by an unwanted encounter at a "rough house" hotel. Moreover, the price of goods, especially food, remained high, no doubt due to local businesses taking advantage of the American soldier, flush with gold or silver come payday.[5]

On the positive side, Major Howard secured new quarters for Carter and the other clerks, with the added benefit that they were closer to the Lawtons' home. Carter's bedroom was airy, and he looked out over a paved street and not a muddy rice paddy. In addition, since he left the hospital in July, he had been particularly careful about his diet. As was the custom, he and his roommates pooled resources and hired a cook. They were able to purchase better food locally or at the Commissary in order to supplement their rations. In fact, at times they would barter away the Army ration.[6] Unless his system was really acting up, or he was visiting the Lawtons, he took his meals at his quarters.

The Lawton family continued to look out for Carter, and he was a frequent visitor at their home. In fact, Mamie Lawton carried on a regular correspondence with the senior Carter. During one memorable visit to the Lawtons' home, Carter was introduced to Brig. Gen. Frederick Dent Grant, the oldest son of the former president, who served briefly in the 4th Cavalry under Col. Ranald Mackenzie, along with Lawton and Carter's father. Moreover, Grant was a class behind Bob Carter at West Point. Grant never tired of telling stories of his early exploits and warmed to the occasion. No doubt with Manley Lawton in mind, he told tales of when his father took him to war during the Vicksburg Campaign.[7] General Grant would be involved in the pacification effort in Pampanga, Bataan, and Zambales Provinces later that year.[8] During another visit to the Lawton home, Carter witnessed evidence of Lawton's legendary temper in an exchange with Diaz the cook.[9]

Carter met another colleague and classmate of his father's when he unsuccessfully applied for a commission in a newly formed regiment commanded by Col. William Birkhimer. In addition to a letter explaining that all commissions had already been assigned in Washington, Birkhimer, himself, paid a visit to the young man. Although obviously disappointed, Carter takes this as another sign of the high regard for his father. Birkhimer's rise was relatively swift. Originally assigned to Lawton's staff, then-Captain Birkhimer became involved with Young's Scouts during the San Isidro Campaign; in fact, he briefly took charge when Young suffered what proved to be a fatal wound. Trained as a lawyer, his rigid insistence upon military courtesy upon assumption of command was not well received by the men of this unconventional unit. Despite his display of courage during the capture of San Ildefonso and San Miguel de Mayumo, his tenure in command was short.[10] Nevertheless, for that effort, he was awarded the Medal of Honor. Later, he was promoted to the rank of colonel in the Volunteers and charged with forming the 28th Volunteer Infantry Regiment. He was given temporary command of Southern Luzon Province, and he was succeeded by another friend of Carter's father, Brig. Gen. Robert H. Hall.[11]

Through it all, Carter remains concerned about his future. Will he stay in the Philippines? Will his health permit him to do so? Should he look for a secure Civil Service job in Washington? All questions he repeatedly poses to himself and to his family. He misses his family and the home cooking, and celebrated his 23rd birthday alone away from them. Although he is afraid to tell his father and mother, he confides to his sister Mell that he has reached the end of his tether.

August 1, 1899

My Dear Father,

If I do not write as often as I have in the past, you will know that it is because of illness and work. I endeavor to answer the letters I receive, but there are many at home writing and my time is limited. Last night I had fully intended to write. Tell Mama and Mell that a letter home is a family letter, and I am sorry I cannot write them nice long letters. Well, let me proceed to business. I did not write because I was taken with chill, which coupled with a bad cold on my lungs, so I could not speak [and] made me feel badly. I said I will fix it. Took a whole pot of hot, strong tea, a big glass of ginger brandy, and sixteen grains of quinine, wrapped in blankets and turned in with a temperature of 103. Well, I sweat, I spit up about a pint of hard matter from my lungs, and I thought my head would burst, but this morning, I felt better. My temperature is normal. It is very depressing to get a fresh disorder after coming from [the] hospital fairly well. However, I am much encouraged, as I have not lost the flesh I gained, my stomach is good, and my bowels are regular and the best since I have been here. On the whole, I feel better than any time for two months. For during that time there was not a night I did not suffer a fresh sore, pain, or sick turn. I believe I will now improve. The climax is past. My blood is better, no fresh sores; I have a fair appetite and look quite well in comparison. To what I did, I think that acclimation came harder for me than many, and unless I am very sick, I will not return very soon.

I still hold to my views concerning [a] civil position, and I do not think it wise to leave a position, which in two years may mean an assured position in [the] U. S., for a job at hardly any higher salary which will tie me to this fever hole. In my last, I spoke of my uncertain position due to illness, etc. Well, I was transferred O.K. to Major Guy Howard and am one of his five clerks. He assigned me to a hard job, the typewriter, and yesterday, from dawn to sunset, I wrote telegrams, letters, requisitions, etc. I have become quite proficient on this machine now. Maj. Howard is a peculiar man, a man of violent and quick temper, but a fine man when you know him, the clerks say. He treats me very nicely, and I think I have made a good impression on him. He is a very fine quartermaster, in fact, an authority, and things have taken a rustle in the division. Howard has cold, gray eyes, a hard face, smooth charm, in fact looks like the Sphinx. He is direct in statements, and every inch of him is business. He is one who cannot be approached familiarly, and in his conduct of the office, he is even more particular than Walcutt. No smoking, every desk clean, fixed just so, not a speck, and in dress, he is very neat and expects others to be so. He has not found a mistake in my work, and now dictates all letters to me. As he speaks slowly, I am going to brush up my shorthand and take his dictation in that way. Thus I will be the only stenographer and typewriter in his entire outfit. I may be retained with him. He is a Regular officer, and he is allowed several. I will have made quite a play. His chief clerk is the only one who is a superior fellow in education. He receives $1,800.00. He sees that I can write letters without being told every command, and that I catch on quick and am familiar with all the places, quartermasters, and duties pertaining to this office. When I heard of the five clerks, I thought I would get squeezed, so I wrote

Maj. Guy Howard, Chief Quartermaster, 1st Division, 8th Army Corps

Walcutt to try to work it to get me with him at Depot Quartermaster Manila. This was mostly for my health, as there is the main city, I could buy food and get a room. Have not heard from him yet.

Leathe was married at Captain Walcutt's house. Walcutt gave the bride away. Mrs. Walcutt made the wedding cake. $30.00 was spent on decorating the rooms by Leathe. The bride, I hear is worth $50,000.00, so Willie is alright.

Well, the other night, I went to Manila to get a dinner. A big storm came up and [I] could not return to Paco until [the] following morning. After going to every hotel, I finally managed to get in an open hall with four others, a horrible place, in a "rough house" hotel [at] seventy-five cents all night. Manila is pretty tough now. The soldiers and rough men of the West all carry the big 45's, and there is a killing every day or so. In one of the big saloons, there was a fist fight the other day, and an innocent man was killed. I steer clear of all places where many soldiers congregate. Well, at the hotel [the] night was made hideous until about 2:00 [A.M.] by fighting upstairs and drunken and disorderly sailors and soldiers being dragged out by the guard. The proprietor (A small, wizened, I don't know what nationality; he was malt colored.) gets the men full of bum liquor, and when they become disorderly and crazed (they have already paid for beds) has them taken to [the] police station. Thus he gets a bed paid for several times. Well, he went out to lodge [a] complaint against a prisoner and got fresh with the guard, and the guard cracked his head with a butt of a Krag. I was well pleased.

Well, I turned in, and as an officer had lost $300.00 a short time before, I rolled my clothes up, money, etc. and put them between me and the wall. I was in a long, dark passage, a pocket, only one entrance door. About 3:30 [A.M.], I sleep poorly, I heard a rustling [and] thought it was rats, listened intently, and heard the stealthy movements of a person. Then my mosquito net was raised slightly by an arm on the inside toward the wall, thus showing he was under the bed trying to slip my money belt and clothes out quietly. I yelled: "What are you doing here?" at the same time, making a jump to get out under the mosquito bar at the end of the bed and get to the door, thus having the fellow in the passage. Before I could clear myself of the bed, the fellow dashed out the door, and I saw the fellow dash around the corner of the courtyard and disappear among the numerous carriages. It was dark, but as he got in to the moonlit courtyard, I caught a glimpse of him, a rather tall, spare nigger in white pants and striped undershirt. I had awakened the fellow sleepers, who wished to know the trouble. I told them. They seemed to think that was to be expected, and as they had no money, I suppose, and were used to sleeping in such brothels, they deemed it a matter of course. But they all said that it was well I did not get to the door first, as the nigger, desperate at being caught, would have dashed out for liberty and probably stabbed me, as they all carry knives and cut without compunction. I was unarmed, as I have not carried my gun with me for some time. Henceforth, I shall always carry it.

I had been just in time, my clothes and money were alright, and I had lost nothing. I dressed, got a table leg and slept over in a dark alcove for the "next," but there were no more. Although in a distant section of the building, I saw a nigger stoop and sneak across a lighted space. I mentioned this matter to the proprietor and clerk in the A.M. The proprietor shrugged his shoulders, raised his crafty eyebrows, and the clerk did not even look up. So much for a night in Manila.

I went to Mrs. Lawton's and got my box and opened it. The caramels were not hard, but soft, very soft and green with mold, but I appreciate though the thought that prompted their sending. It really made me happy to see the numberless kindnesses of home, Mell's handiwork, my neckties, all so nicely washed and organized, I hate to disturb them, my pants so neatly mended by my dear mother, and numberless papers and magazines you so kindly sent me. I have not had a chance yet to even look them all through, for every minute of my time is now taken up, and I am so exhausted in my physical condition, that after my work is done, I drop on a cot and endure agony from my feet and veins of my ankles which I have again. These doctors cannot seem to cure them. Walking is agony, so I ride, more expense, and when I do walk, my feet swell, and although the sores are healed, the feet feel to the touch like stoves and are green, purplish red and pain and throb like I imagine gout does. I am out a side tooth, broken at [the] hospital, and last night, lost the ruby setting to my little ring. So I feel like cursing. If I have of late written despondent letters, it has been due to the depressing influence of this climate, coupled with natural depression following sleeplessness, pain, and sickness, away from every friend and the natural necessities of a sick person. I had to, at last, tell you at home how I was. I told Mrs. Lawton not to write of my sickness, and she said any way she had not intended to unless I was seriously sick. She said when she saw me in [the] hospital [for the] first time, that she would have had me at her house, but thought that I could receive better care at hospital.

Well, you know I spoke of going to [the] Lawton's night before last. I went down in [a] carriage [and] took a great number of papers I have accumulated to her to distribute in [the] hospital. They were eating dinner, and as there is no doorbell, and as I was unannounced, I sat in the hall. They had just got a new cook a short time before, a Filipino. I heard the General say: "Send for Diaz the interpreter." He came [and] the General said: "Ask this man if he is a cook."

A. Yes.

Q. Does he consider this a meal to place before a gentleman?

A. He does.

Q. Does he consider this properly cooked and served?

A. He does.

Q. Well, you tell him, God Damn it, that this is the same stuff we have had every day for two weeks, and I won't stand it. If he is a cook, I want him to cook and serve properly these meals. If not, he can get out, the sooner the better, and I will pay someone who can.

Exit Diaz and the cook.

Mrs. Lawton soon came out [and] was surprised to see my face had filled up so much since I left the hospital, [and] thought I was looking better than she had seen me for a long time. The General came in. He was looking fine after his trip to the Lake. His face is ruddy and his black eyes snapped and fairly beamed from the previous conversation I had heard. I was rather afraid he would be off color after his bum chow chow. He said: "'Sez he ter me,' how are you doing young man. How's the Dobi Itch coming on," and shook hands cordially with me and remarked, "You have fever filling my hand." Settling back in a chair, he said: "How's the Old Man?" He was in a better humor, more the Lawton of old than I have ever seen him. He seems to want to be nice to me. I had written some extracts from your letters about the Lawtons, which Mrs. Lawton read to the General, and he smiled.

Then an officer came in and had to drag out a similar roast as that outrageous libel in the *Post* editorial about the Zapote fight, his face flushed, and I never saw him so mad. He did not speak. At last, he said: "I never heard anything so far from the truth. There is not a true statement in it." It is strange how such a thing can be printed. He feels bitterly against Otis, because Otis allows untrue reports to go uncensored from Manila regarding Lawton, so he will be roasted in the U. S.—anything to keep Lawton from the just credit of an able campaign, and the rewards of his hard work. No wonder Lawton feels badly. He does the work, and then these fearful roasts reach him ("out-generaled," "all but licked," "saved by gunboats"). When in reality, the gunboats were firing at another place two miles away, and Lawton defeated and utterly routed the flower of the Insurgent army in Cavite Province, and effectually ending the organized fighting on that line. (Yet, after he accomplishes these important achievements, is credited at home with a licking, and Otis does not take the pains to discredit it.) Otis telegraphs Wheaton's brilliant move and energy, whereas in truth, Lawton had reprimanded him for his slowness and failure to move, thus defeating the accomplishment of an important movement.[12]

Lawton further remarked to this officer in a low, private conversation, that it was strange that these saloons were allowed to be running full blast. They should all be closed, as they demoralize the troops, and ruin their health, and relieve them of their money, and are the cause of fights and deaths. He also said that troops should be gotten out of the city, as they are no good while in there and are running about drinking, gambling, and getting diseased, filling the hospitals. He said he could not understand why artillery had not been gotten here before, and why Otis had not called for cavalry and mounted those that were here. Lawton: "I have seen the line several times here when if I had had one good regiment of cavalry, I could of finished this thing up right there. Very strange management." No wonder that the home papers are calling for a general. There is a general here if he had the chance, and that man is Lawton. In *Collier's Weekly* is the best photo I ever saw of Lawton. It is taken at his headquarters recently. In *Harper's* and *Leslie's* are some very good pictures of him in the field. They are in the June numbers. *Leslie's* has photos of [the] route taken by [the] *Grant*, and the pictures illustrate my descriptions of that voyage. Keep your eye on *Leslie's*, *Harper's*, and *Collier's*, for every issue I see here now commencing with the June numbers, are full of places and scenes of which I am familiar, or have been. The photos of Lawton in the field are true to life as they are characteristic.

After Mrs. Lawton read from your letter, "Give the General my sympathy, for I am afraid that is all he will get," he nodded his head and seemed to be in a deep study. He did not talk anymore and seemed to be in brown study. He is sensitive to the attacks of these newspapers [and] *Harper's* who are urged on by rotten politicians and jealous army officers. The U. S. does not know the truth. A rigid policy is needed to deal with these natives. The Insurgents will fight forever until they are cut to pieces by crushing blows. They are a class who have no homes, never worked, and follow blindly their officers.

Mrs. Lawton gave me your letter to read. I was very much interested in it. [I] am glad you appreciated the detail and humor of my sketches. Said it seemed strange that Bob and she were carrying on all the correspondence. I told her that Father appreciated the fact that it was impossible for [the] General to correspond, and Mrs. Lawton says, yes it was impossible. His mail is tremendous, and he has not begun to answer it, and Mrs. Lawton said hers was large. She has rheumatism in her hand, so she has Prichett, the General's secretary, do all the work. She simply dictates. Prichett is an incompetent, ignorant little cur, with the manners of a pig. I did not know until the other day that he cannot write a decent letter, so [he] has two clerks in the General's office doing his work for which he is paid $1,400.00 to do. And as the General is too busy to take up correspondence, the one who ought to don't (the secretary). Mrs. Lawton says she likes to get letters from 3218.[13] She reads all to [the] General, and he is much interested as was Mrs. Lawton. I showed him [a] picture of our house February 14 in a blizzard. He was much interested, as was Mrs. Lawton. They told me of the Hot Springs they visited while up the Lake. At present, the General is looking better than I have ever seen him. His face is full and he has picked up in flesh since the hard campaign is over.

I think my health, if it continues as it is, will [mean] I can stay here. My head, stomach, and bowels are better, as is my blood and skin, than for two months. My feet still are bad and I have some malaria, fever, flushes, and incipient chills and ache pretty badly at night. To take quinine in big doses is dangerous, for I now owe my severe cold in my lungs to quinine, open pores, the cold damp bed clothes and air. Many die in the hospital from pneumonia, and to allow a cold to stay on lungs may lead to the seeds of consumption common here. I have quit on milk because I am afraid of diseased cows, for they have a disease here which the very best cattle suddenly drop over and die, sometimes an entire herd. The niggers die of "Berns" or some such disease—too much rice, or rice in some way is the cause. It is as severe among them and as deadly as the plague in India.

I did not have a chance to speak to Lawton about my future desires and intentions. As my health, to my surprise, continues to grow better and I am gaining flesh. I thought I would say anything until I was on my back. As there are no prospects that Lawton will be in a position to deal out civil jobs for several moons, or as long as Otis lives, I guess I was worse in not telling him anything regarding my determination on that point. Old Otis is filling positions in civil life by the wholesale. Now nearly all ex-Volunteers, and Lawton has recommended orderlies, etc. at these Headquarters, and nearly every day, one who was here as a Volunteer mounted orderly returns as a civil messenger. The salaries are small in civil jobs here, as they are paid from private civil fund, and Otis is trying to cheese pare. It is much better for me to remain appointed from the War Department, rather than from a department headquarters; to be paid from a U. S. fund than a Mexican-Philippine fund, which depends on a fluctuating revenue, to have prospects of permanency against an uncertainty here, in case the niggers are given too much power in Civil Office or the U. S. turns over the Philippine Islands;[14] and last, to be able to return expenses paid to [the] U.S., against a permanent residence in [the] Philippine Islands, and [no allowance] to get home, without a job or prospects.

I am now familiar with Quartermaster work, and having friends in the War Department, I can do better by staying in Quartermaster service. As every quartermaster I have worked for [has] told me they would gladly do anything for me, and being in the Army where I have many officers as my friends, and being the son of an officer, I am sanguine that if I prove myself a good clerk, that Schreiner will not drop me. I was only greatly worried when I was sick, because I could not do the duties for which I was paid, and foresaw that if I continued in bad health, my usefulness in the Philippines would be gone, and I would be forced to return. The clerks with Howard get $150.00, $125.00, $100.00, and a messenger at $72 and rations. $100.00 per month would be a big item to me.

Mrs. Lawton and [the] General told me that their home was mine; I must always come when I am able, for they are glad always to see me. One reason that I did not go oftener was this, not because I stood on ceremony, for I never someway felt an awe of the General in his house, for I know him not to be like these cubs with shoulder straps, but like all the older officers and gentlemen, willing to greet a gentleman like one. But I worked until dusk and was tired, so would dine and slowly stroll over to [the] *Luneta* to get the salt air and music. It is quite a little walk, and when I returned, my evening was generally devoted to writing or reading in an endeavor to keep track of events, or to take a bath. I was generally exhausted and feeling badly and glad to go to bed. I knew Mrs. Lawton always went to [the] *Luneta*, then drove to her house and had a late supper (7:30 to 8:00, custom here to eat in cool of evening). As her house is a long walk from headquarters and carriages cannot be secured as 7 o'clock order is enforced, I had to walk both ways, tired after my day's work, through a section of native houses, and my return was challenged and held up by every sentry and nearly eaten by the packs of these mangy dogs. One I shot one night. So, it is not thoughtlessness, reserve, or laziness. It was simply hard for me with my hours and her hours to get over to see her. Had I felt better and had the energy, I would have gone oftener, but one feels like a dish rag here. Mrs. Lawton understands [that] all the night orders makes it hard, and I cannot go in [the] day.

I have worked every Sunday and have not been off an entire day since June 16, except when I lay in [a] cot in [a] hospital and prayed I might be working. The new bunch wanted to know what the hours were here. And now, being the only clerk who stays at Headquarters at night, Howard has started me doing the night work. Telephoning, telegrams, writing them on typewriter, etc. rather tough and as there are many papers, and Howard requires everything typewritten, you will see I handle every paper in this office, so I have the working job. If I brush up my shorthand and write fast on [the] typewriter, Schreiner (if I have to return to Washington) may put me in [the] War Department, as typewriters are in demand. Although I was slow on the machine, I started right [away] using both hands equally and learning to use fingers and with practice, I have gradually increased my speed, although I will never be fast, because my joints are large [and] my finger tops broad.

Now in regard to my commission, you know I wrote Birkhimer. Well, I had to laugh. Commissions are a hoodoo to me. I come so close to them. My trip to the hospital cost me the one, for while there, I heard nothing about Birkhimer being made a colonel. I got out on June 26; wrote Birkhimer June 27; and on June 31 received the following:

Corté Suprema de Justicia
de las Islas Filipinas, Audrmencia, Manila, P.I.
July 31, 1899
Robert D. Carter
Chief Clerk Chief Quartermaster
Headquarters 1st Division, 8th Army Corps
Manila, P.I.

Dear Sir:

Replying to yours of the 27th instant, I regret to say that on the 28th instant I received a dispatch from the Adjutant General U.S.A saying that all officers of my regiment had been commissioned; otherwise it would have given me great pleasure to second your news.

I am glad you wrote me. I will do anything I can at anytime for the son of my esteemed friend, your honored father.

Very truly yours,
Wm. Birkhimer
Col. 28th Regt. Inf. Vols.

So time and sickness made me just too late.

That evening, Col. Birkhimer came to Headquarters to see me, introduced himself, and asked me if I had received his letter, and said my father was a particular friend, a very warm friend, and to remember him to you; inquired where you lived and invited me to come and see him at his quarters anytime. You must have many warm friends among the old officers, for whenever I need one of the old friends who knew you, they seem more than glad to do anything for me. The cordial greeting given me by Col. Birkhimer, supposed to be an austere man, made me feel as though he had known me a long time, as did General Hall, and General Lawton always treats me nicely. I believe the friendships in the older Army days were the right sort. These men do not have a false bearing because one does not wear shoulder straps. One is continually subjected to unwarranted snubs by the young cubs and Volunteer satraps. I am now receiving the *Register* O.K. Thank Thompson. You must have been a popular man in the army from the high regard your brother officers have for you. Col. Birkhimer actually came all the way from Manila just to see me for fear his letter might not reach me promptly. Carter luck. Well, my heart was not set upon this commission. After that Treasury deal and the Marine Corps, I shall never hope until I find myself actually in the job.

Mrs. Lawton gave me a flutter after Birkhimer had gone. Lt. Brooke[15] came into the office and said, "Mrs. Lawton wants to see you in [the] General's office." I went; she was all alone. I thought, "she has some news." She asked me how I was feeling, and then told me she had a book for me to read: *Cyrano de Bergerac.*

I will try to write often. I await that Schreiner deal and questions regarding chance of holding Army job as Quartermaster in [the] States. I hope to get an answer in two months. Until then, when I will know better what to do, I will stay. I will return only in case I am so sick and cannot work, and am afraid to stay longer for fear of permanent effects. At present writing, I am sanguine. I have passed a crisis, and from henceforth hope to mend. Love to all.

Your affectionate son,
Robert D. Carter

August 2, 1899

My Dear Little Sister,[16]

Yesterday while at my desk I received a little mail six pictures from Helen, a *Judge*, a *Washington Times*, and a letter from Mrs. Thompson, but there was another letter of determined hand, a hand of regular proportions, and I thought what lawyer writes this. Imagine my surprise on opening it to find it from Powell Carter, and such a long letter and so artistically illustrated. It was as welcome as it was a surprise. It hardly seems possible that you are now writing such nice letters, and your spelling and expression is very effective. I am afraid, in time, you will rival Mell as a letter writer. At this writing you are no doubt in Portland by the sad sea waves. I also am by the sea, a sad sea indeed for many. I am glad next year will find you in the 8th grade. Possibly, when I return, you will be a high school graduate.

Tell Mamma and all that I am now feeling better, and with the exception of my feet, am quite well. Major Howard has succeeded in having an entire house assigned for Division Clerks to sleep and eat. All will have much room and the place has been cleaned. I have entered a new mess over there which, at present, is very nice, and [I] get side edibles at my option. In [the] course of time, I think, the five new clerks and myself will rent a house, hire a Chinese cook, and buy the best Commissary stores. Thus, we will be able to live nicely at a moderate rate per man. I could not have entered a scheme of that sort with the former bunch of civilian clerks, as they were all at swords points with each other. But these new men are all quartermaster clerks and can afford to pay for what soldiers cannot, and the other civilian clerks would not.

As our health depends largely on good food and a good bed and dry room, it is good to have them at any price. I have advertised and then could not secure a room, for now prices are beyond reason. I will take your love in a secure box to General Lawton and the family. I am sure they will be glad to receive it.

When I get into my new quarters and have more leisure, I will write Mama and Mell, and endeavor to answer a few letters I have been unable to. I hope I am on the mend.

With much love, I am your affectionate brother,
Robert Dexter Carter.

August 3, 1899

My Dear Mother,

Your letter of June 27 is before me. I received it in the Hospital and have not had a minute in which I could answer it since I left the Hospital. I am now looking and feeling better than I have for two months. My stomach works and my bowels for the first time since I have been here are fairly regular, and as that old complaint seems to have been conquered somewhat, I am filled with hope for the future. When this reaches you, you will be home. Mell will have a little surprise from me for you when you get home. Guess? Your letters, my dear mother, are never dry to me. I am glad now that you have seen more of Helen and know her better, [and] that you think much of her. I find she has a very fine character. Mrs. W.[17] kind of depresses Helen. Helen must not mope, and I am glad to hear she is bright and happy.

I cannot understand about my letter to B.[18] Answered her first letter. She seems not to have even received it. I now have another which I will answer right away.

Mrs. Lawton and I are on the finest terms. Whenever my poor, sore, swollen feet will permit and I can secure a carriage, I go down and see her. At night is the only time I can go, and as the night order is in effect, I have to walk home, a rather hard walk after a day's work and with sore feet. [The] General is very nice to me. An account of my last visit in full I wrote Papa. In the box many little things I found brought me back to your loving kindness to me. I have not mended a sock since I left and am shy a few buttons, otherwise my wardrobe is fair. When I got back from my sick spell, [I] felt rather blue to find every linen shirt I had in my trunk was hopelessly mildewed, collars ruined, rats ate up my heavy shoes, and my transport cap (uniform which I wished to keep as souvenir). In fact, when I return to [the] U. S. I will have to buy all new shirts and collars and new clothes, as that old black suit was all I had for heavy, and a light pair of pants. They were torn up in [the] hold of [the] *Grant*, and as I wear white here, I am cleaned out of everything by rats, giant cockroaches, and damp. My two overcoats, by constant care, I have kept. I hope to sell the military one. My trunk will never come home with me. Damp has warped it, so it will not lock or close. Rats have gnawed holes through it right and left, and the [frame] and woodwork are rust and decay. I bought a small camphor wood chest made by Chinese—very neat and nice, like a trunk, and it holds all my stuff. When I return, [I] will buy a small steamer trunk.

When I feel my very best here, I do not feel as I did in the States. I do not feel the same person.

Natalie's letter was immense. I enjoyed it hugely and was greatly fooled when I opened it.

In the June numbers of the illustrated papers are pictures of Lawton [on] the *Grant* and places where I have been—Singapore, Suez, etc. Keep all photos I send home, for when I return, I shall want them. Papa's mackintosh has caused much remark. I have received big offers for it. It is [a] good fit and now it rains all the time, I carry it all the time. I believe now I would have rather stored my wheel than sold it for $10.00. Many have bought theirs out here. $1.50 to clean bearings and tighten it up, and it would have ridden like a new wheel. The saddle $5.00, and tires worth about $5.00, covered the $10.00 alone. Too bad $50.00 sacrificed. Tell Helen I have abandoned the camera idea. I find the fellows have a hell of a time. The dampness swells the frame, shutters, etc., will not work. Rats and damp destroy leather, and ants eat wood.

Love to Papa and Nat, much for yourself, from your affectionate son, a kiss,

Robert D. Carter

August 6, 1899

My Dear Sister,

As usual, it rains and Sundays all "look alike" for here it is every day. I have not noticed a Sunday since January 16. I sometimes long with a great longing for a Sunday dinner at home. Since I left the Hospital, the few events of importance I have written in letters to Papa and Helen. I have been struggling to catch up with back work and have just got around to some letters from you I hitherto have not answered. I am now under Major Howard. There are three other clerks and a messenger in the office besides yours truly. It has eased the work on me, but they have assigned a working job to me at the typewriter, as everything, telegrams and all, are typewritten. You can see I write some "few" each day.

Last night a typhoon, not very hard, was blowing. I went over to the *Luneta* [and] was about the only one there. It blew great guns and the beach was whitened by the heavy surf and spray. Coming home, a great rain descended. It never touched the parts covered by the mackintosh, but wet my feet and legs.

I sent Helen a photo I had taken on the impulse of the temporary fat they got in my face at the Hospital. It was taken July 26. For a Manila job, I think it puts Stalee[19] in the shade. You can judge for yourself as to [the] likeness. I had just been barbered for the occasion. Hair looks pretty slick, don't it? I was pleasantly surprised when I got the proof photo, which I sent Helen. I hear you had the house to yourself all summer. Great times. Natalie wrote me an "Essay," illustrated and which I was very glad to get. Will show it to Mrs. Lawton.

Well, I missed another commission, but I don't care much, as my health is so wretched, I do not believe I could have done much in the field. This climate is down on me tooth and nail, and I am afraid I shall have to give up or ruin my health. My stomach remains so weak that I can now eat little or nothing, and to buy myself suitable food takes about all my salary. It cost me nearly $15.00 on food from July 25th to August 2nd. I tried the experiment of buying milk and separate meals and was not in the mess. I feel rather down now that I find I cannot stay, and look to my return home with anxiety, for I do not know what awaits me. I have done my best, and now find myself with feet I can hardly walk [on], so swollen and sore that I cannot wear any shoes, except some very large soft leather ones I got off a Chinaman, with a weak stomach, and, in fact, to describe it, I have felt sick and like hell, (a dead man) for two months, and in spite of Hospital, I feel no better.

I tried to get transferred to Walcutt in Manila, but my authority in letter ties me to Lawton's Headquarters. I wanted to get in town where I could get a room and good food. Howard has just got a big house, formerly [the] quarters of Idaho officers, for clerks' quarters and for the mess. I have a nice room with four others, a very large room, for things are immense here. It is in the sea-breeze side and overlooks [the] road, so will get fresh, pure air and can dry my musty clothes during the day.

Mrs. Lawton knows about my marriage. [She] saw it in [the] *Register* [on the] *Grant*. Said she did not ask me about it, as I never mentioned it.

[Your affectionate son,
Robert Dexter Carter]

August 9, 1899

My Dear Father,

It has been some time since I have received a bunch of letters from home, but by the end of the week I think mail will be in. From Natalie's letter I suppose at this date you are enjoying the salt air of Portland.

Last night I went down to Mrs. Lawton's. I went to get some books which she seemed anxious for me to have to read. I had not had minute to read, hardly to write, but now that the weight of work is lifted somewhat, and I have made up back work, I will have leisure to do some reading. When I arrived, I saw Mrs. Lawton alone in the hall. I found that General Grant was in there and a chaplain, some relative of Lawton. I, at first, demurred against staying, but she urged [and] wanted to know if I would not like to meet General Grant. I said so many generals were a little heavy for my weight, but as I was arrayed in a brand new white suit, I felt I could hold my end down, so went in. General Grant was there alone with the chaplain. Lawton was in a side room having a conversation on "Biz" with some officer. Mrs. Lawton said: "General Grant, permit me to present to you Mr. Carter, a son of a very old and intimate friend of General Lawton's. Captain Carter has been in many campaigns with the General. He is now living in Washington." General Grant pricked up his ears somewhat at the name, arose and shook my hand very cordially, gave me a warm greeting which immediately placed me at ease. He turned his chair so as to address his conversation to me. General Lawton soon came in [and] said: "Well, Carter how are you? How's the feet? I see you can walk now. Any news from home? How's the old man?" He was in a very genial mood, but there was a vast difference, I noted, in his appearance since my last visit, when he had just returned from Laguna de Bay. Then his face was a healthy flush and well filled out. Last night, I noted his face was thin, and the deep lines from the inside corner of the eye and around the mouth were deeply marked and drawn. He did not look as well as hitherto.

Manley wears a khaki suit with miniature captain's straps. The General says he is on his staff. He takes him everywhere with him and seems to think so much of him. Manley is delicate, and I believe if he died, it would be the severest blow that could befall the General. While General Lawton was in the side room, we were talking about Manley. Mrs. Lawton said he was "such a comfort to the General." General Grant spoke up and said, "Yes," smiled and said, "I was on my father's staff during the war, and from what he often said, I believe (he grinned) the campaign could not have succeeded without me. Manley is going on my staff tomorrow." He is going to take Manley with him for a few days to Bacoor.

General Grant is rather heavy in the neck and [has] a very ruddy complexion. He has small, roving, smiling "pig" eyes—a peculiar way of describing them. In appearance, he greatly resembles the pictures of his father—the heavy jaw, close-cropped head, and general contour and setting of the neck. He constantly smokes cigars. To resume, he said, "yes, when I was twelve, I was on a campaign, a real campaign, if you will pardon me for saying it, the Vicksburg Campaign." He said, "in seventeen days, 200 and some, I forget, miles were marched, five great battles fought," and, he mentioned, "results accomplished." He said, "I was the first of the Union Army to be in Jackson, Mississippi, in fact, I was in there before the Confederates left, and, Mrs. Lawton, I was there as close as I am to you and saw the columns of Confederates marching out of the town." He added: "Had they known I was there and had taken me, I would have been quite a prize, for taking the son of the commanding general, would have caused him much anxiety."

"However, I was taken prisoner twice during the war, but that was by our own men. The way I happened to go into Jackson was thus: Father had got in between of the main bodies of the Confederates and was in a position to hit out on all sides and was doing so thus (he made a drawing). There was some heavy fighting, and father and I went with Sherman's Corps to the left. All day there was cannonading and bullets were thick. A move was made on the works (to be sure I cannot say whether this was the works of Jackson or not)," and he said, "Dodge's Brigade or Division carried the works, which they intended to try the strength of rather than occupy. I went in with them. Father immediately saw, after they were inside, the thing to do was to turn and go down the works thus. (he made another drawing) I got lost and did not turn, but kept straight ahead and found myself in the town amidst the confusion of departure." He laughed and said: "We found the Governor's table strewn with papers where a consultation had been held. They left in such hot haste, that the Governor's corncob pipe, partly smoked, lay at his place on the table." "Yes, I was a great help to father," [he] said sarcastically, "and I seriously doubt the successful termination of that campaign except for me."

He is a very easy and interesting talker, jolly. Deep within him, I think, he has a swelling of conceit, as he is not adverse to referring to the "old man," but is modest in statement and is not obtrusive in bringing up his "daddy," the great Grant. What reference he made to the Vicksburg Campaign led one to believe, as he expressed it, "a great campaign," for I think (and rightly) he worships everything that pertains to Grant or his campaigns. He addressed most of this talk to me. Really, I could have sat all night, he is such an easy and interesting talker, and heard him talk of the Great War, or at least of his impressions derived as a small boy, and his references to the great general were more than interesting coming from his son.

After Lawton came back, they had a great confab about the present situation on the South Line where Grant commands. Grant said the civil officers down there (niggers) were remarkably able and efficient, and a great surprise to him. In fact, he would rather have that outfit to manage than the peasants he had seen in Italy or some other place he mentioned. In the course of conversation with Lawton, he said, "Well, it don't look as though the war would be over until you (Lawton) and I are mustered out." General Lawton said, "No, nor for some time afterwards." General Lawton was in the best of moods and joked. General Grant spoke of having some conveyance for some move. Lawton said, "What's the matter with swimming, wading, seizing boats, any old way," and grinned. His rough and ready tactics kind of dumfounded General Grant, who reported seeing about 75 niggers at some place, which he kept gradually increasing until he said that there were reported 500 at a certain place. To every number, Lawton grinned and said, "That's not many." Speaking of the termination of the war, Lawton said: "I will tell them to take prisoners with arms. I don't want them bringing in a lot of men who have run and hidden their guns, and then surrender to be well fed." He said: "We get plenty of prisoners, but not a gun. Guns are what we want." He also ridiculed the present idea of Otis not to fire on niggers not dressed in uniform. It is as absurd as to say that the niggers would not fire on our men, unless dressed in khaki. He also said the present pass system of allowing "*amigos*" going to and from Manila was foolish. He believed in letting them all come in who wanted to see conditions for themselves, or to confiscate all insurgent property and utterly exclude them altogether. The unanimous opinion of the soldiers is that Lawton would be a great military governor, and that the scrap wouldn't last long if he were "turned loose," instead of kept muzzled and chained by Otis. I venture to say that Lawton would make good his statement that if he had some mounted cavalry, he would end this thing up.

I gave Nat's letter to Mrs. Lawton to read. She was astonished by the writing, as were all (for a little girl they considered it very nice) as also the letter. Mrs. Lawton thought the expression remarkable. She don't know what an "old headed kid wrote it." I think a great deal of that letter from little sister and am proud to show it to people. Mrs. Lawton and all were much amused with the drawings.

Just as I was leaving and had shaken hands with General Grant, Lawton remarked, "you know his father, Bob Carter, who used to be in the 4th Cavalry." "Of course," remarked General Grant, "we were at West Point together." [He] was glad to meet me, impressed about you, and when I left, Lawton and he were speaking of Bob Carter. I was sorry that came out just at the last, because I would have liked to [have] heard what he said, after he found out who my father was. I said I had often heard you speak of him (General Grant) and had seen a photo of him in his West Point clothes and days. I like General Grant very much, and I enjoyed my evening, for I felt absolutely at home, even if I was with two generals, for they were gentlemen, and men. I felt as easy in conversation with Generals Grant and Lawton as I would at home. I listened much, and talked little, but kept up a good conversation on the subjects with which I was familiar, as General Grant talked most of the time to me.

I owe it all to Mrs. Lawton, that by her manner of introducing me at her house, that I felt at home and at ease. General Lawton greets me very cordially and seems glad to see me. I have explained why I have not gone oftener. It is not because I do not enjoy it or feel at ease, but because the distance is long to walk both ways and carriages have to be in at 8:30. They have dinner late, and I have only the evening in which to read or write, and the twilight to take exercise. If I exercise, I cannot take the walk to Mrs. Lawton's. Our new quarters are much nearer her residence, so I will see more of her in the future. When I left, she gave me five lemons, something money cannot buy—about 25 cents apiece for Hong Kong lemons which have no taste. They were sent her from home.

I showed Mrs. Lawton my pictures taken in Manila. She has not spoken to you of my illness, as I particularly requested her not to, and would not have written myself until the time came when I foresaw that I was unable to perform my duties. I am now feeling better than I have for some months. I believe it is due to a blood purifier which the English druggist put up for me. Every old sore is discharging at a great rate, and I feel decent now. My head has cleared, the deadly weakness is going, I can work, walk, etc. without prostration from exhaustion. I have managed to retain most of the flesh I got in the Hospital. My feet will not heal and still remain sore. They discharge pus and swell every time I use them. I am almost cured of the Dhobi Itch. Once my system [is] purged of this filth due to the Dhobi Itch being driven into my blood by that jackass of an Army doctor, I will regain my good health and be able to hold on.

If I ever cable, or you do, it will be in the Adams Code cypher. A word stands for a sentence and a glance at the key and all is clear.[20]

I had to spend more money than I wished this month a new chest (little) and some khaki and white suits. My blue suit is good. It does not pay to keep more than one [you] can wear from day to day here. A man got a new suit here, wore it that day, hung up the pants and the rats ate up the seat of the pants that night—quick work, and we all laughed, but the owner felt it was no joke.

I mailed you a rough draft (1st draft) of Lawton's report of the North trip. This was made entirely under the Adjutant's[21] direction by the chief clerk. Lawton had not laid eyes on it probably. Some way Bickham got hold of it. I made a corrected copy of part of it for him, but he, in [the] great haste with which he was kicked out by Howard, left it and has forgotten it. At any rate, I send it to give you an inside view of that trip and how, at the end, Otis defeated its purpose. You will see several [digs] at Otis among its pages, and as it is a report to [the] Adjutant General's Department, it will come direct to Otis, so he will read what Lawton thinks. I do not know how the amended copy reads, but it was fuller. At any rate, I send it, otherwise it would get lost or end in the waste basket.

With much love to all, I will close

Your Affectionate Son,

Robert Dexter Carter

P. S. Howard is alright, and I am well fixed. He is a very nice man to clerks and an "A No. 1" quartermaster. A Regular, thank God.

August 10, 1899

My Dear Mother,

I could not let this day go by without writing you or someone in the family. How strange, one year ago how little thought I would spend my twenty-third birthday in the Orient. It is the first birthday that I have ever spent outside the U. S. What a guess it would be, whether my next will be in the U. S. or here, or dead. I anxiously await the mail which is expected daily. I do not know whether you have forgotten that the 10th is my birthday or not. At any rate, I am twenty-three. And I am well and about. The 10th did not find me in bed as the "Glorious 4th" did. I have been making up back work and answering a number of letters. My visits to Mrs. Lawton I described in the letters to Papa, so you will see them, and I need not repeat. I am feeling very much better in general health and strength. My feet give me great trouble, and for the last day have been very painful, discharging pus, etc. I long for a good home meal, some waffles, in fact, anything at your table. As Papa has so often said, "You will see the day when you will be glad to eat this and that." Yes, I have seen many days when it seemed as though I could have eaten the table cloth on the home table, because it was American and smelt of American grub. Oh, for a Sunday dinner! When I do return, I believe I will die of joy, everything is so depressing to one sick here. He can get absolutely nothing, and the more sores and boils one has, the harder becomes the bed, which is devoid of anything like American bed clothes or mattress, just a plain woven mat.

Mrs. Lawton has taken your place. I find in her a friend who is more than good and kind to me. I can never forget the many, many kindnesses she has done for me and still does. General Lawton is also very nice to me.

I am now in new quarters and have fixed up pretty nicely. Nice airy, dry room, as dry as one can get here. I have been sleeping for two months on a canvas stretcher, which I carried up into the office, my wicker bed downstairs being too heavy to carry. I fear that I cannot hold out much longer here. I feel so badly all the time. When I say I feel well, it is well for what has been and is. I am going to stick to Quartermaster Department. For me to remain and live in Manila is to ruin my health for life. For the climate is down on me, and yet I take and have taken better care of myself than one at these headquarters. Not a drop of drink, very particular about food, yet my blood becomes liquid poison and my stomach a mere bag which will not hold anything without prolonged growling. Others at these headquarters eat meat swimming in grease, bread soaked in gravy, smoke cigarettes constantly, and swill ice cold slop and booze night and day, and, except spells of diarrhea, are apparently stout as mules. I cannot understand why this climate is so hard on me.

I often hear of Teddy eating, but little of his doings. I suppose he is among the unemployed—just eats and loafs at 3218 16th. Well, a few days out here could give him enough mange to hold him for ten years.

Mrs. Lawton gave me *Cyrano de Bergerac* to read. I have just finished it. It is so very fine. She has also given me *Hero Worship* by Thomas Carlyle which I will read. Now that I am over in a room where I can get at my stuff, I shall read and look through all the papers you sent me. There is a fellow, Schwentenham whose father is very wealthy. He sent [his son] every illustrated paper, [the] latest books, and all magazines. I see many of them, but [he] has now been mustered out, so I shall miss the illustrated papers and magazines. I was very much pleased with my box. I could not eat Helen's caramels, but the tin box was a Godsend to keep postage stamps in, as cockroaches eat the stamp for the mucilage.

I hope you will like my picture. The eyes are bum, and I look very solemn, so Mrs. Lawton says. But I had just been fatted in the Hospital, so concluded to grasp the golden opportunity and have my pictures taken. I got an extra one, as there were spots on one, so I got seven for my ½ dozen. If you think them good enough to get more, I can get more printed for not a large expenditure.

Well, Mama, I must cut this short. I wonder where my 24th year will find me. Many kisses and love to all,
I am your only affectionate son,
Robert Dexter Carter

August 16, 1899

My Dear Mother,

Now that I have more time and have less to do, I will write oftener again. Writing came hard when I felt so badly and could not seem to think. I feel very badly to hear father has suffered so much from his legs this summer and was in such poor health when he left for Portland. By the time you get this, I suppose you will be again at home and I hope he will be much improved by the cool, bracing salt air of Casco Bay. I shall never forget my trip to Harpswell,[22] the beautiful little isles, the cold ocean breeze, and the delicious fish dinner in the big hotel. Sometime again in my life, I want to go up through Maine, and, strangely enough, in this hot land, my thoughts have often reverted to our days in Maine.

I am feeling as well as I can hope to here, and at last, it seems as though my feet will heal. Last night, I went over to the *Luneta*, and it seemed good to be again able to enjoy the salt breeze.

The clerks who are now here are all civilians and seem very pleasant gentlemanly fellows. One in particular seems to have a great liking for me, as he is much interested in drawing. Two of them are married, so altogether, I am very pleased with the way things are situated. I believe I will no longer have to take the field, as Howard has a civilian orderly who accompanies him in all his trips. My work, when Howard is not in the office, amounts to very little now the first pressure of business is over. When Howard is in, he dictates letters, telegrams, etc. to me which I write on [the] typewriter. Formerly, I did everything except keep the quartermaster papers and money accounts. Now they have a property clerk, and a clerk who tends to all papers and books, and the chief clerk, who draws $150.00 per [month], does the quartermaster papers and money.

Bickham was an easygoing man, the last man on earth for a quartermaster, and both Walcutt and Howard, who are Regular quartermaster's, made him and his work look like two cents. Of the seven weeks "Bick" was in, I served in the office about 14 days, the remainder I was in the field or Hospital. The cooking at the mess and stealing of funds by the manager was a howling outrage. It became "slum"[23] three times a day, nothing more or less than a Hell of grease.

I spoke to the Chief Quartermaster Clerk about the cook, and the chief clerk got over there and ate [there] about three days. This morning, I heard him ask Howard to have the cook returned to his regiment, and to secure someone who could cook, so I got my work in on the greasy scoundrel. I laid in a supply of Commissary's "goodies" etc. through an officer, otherwise I would have had to pay 10% extra. This a.m. they had a bum breakfast, so I go to my store, open a can of brown bread and a can of butter, walk out to the stove and lay slices of brown bread on the top—make toast—hot buttered toast and ate. And I was the one who escaped dyspepsia this a.m. So now am commencing to live. What joy to sleep in dry clothes, to have a fresh breeze free from stench blow through the room all night. I am sleeping, eating, gaining flesh, no diarrhea, a good stomach. In fact, I am existing. My feet have troubled me greatly the last week. The sores opened and discharged, the whole foot and ankle assumed a purple hue, and the pain I endured made me sympathize with the accounts I have read of the old devils afflicted with gout. Of course, it costs me something more to live and buy decent "chow," but I found the expense pays.

Helen sent me a clothes bag for a birthday gift, which arrived August 11th. It was my greatest need and is very useful. Thank Mell for the underclothes and say that we are now able to buy things of that sort here. Although they came in just right, as I badly needed them.

I often think of your home table, mother, and of the nice meals of nice meat, of waffles, of "real dark brown" beans, of brown bread hot, and I could go on for pages. The eating out here is the worst feature of life. The heat does not make one uncomfortable. It is damp and vermin coupled with vile food.

There is wealth out here for those who secure government contracts. The contractors are waxing fat, but [for] one to start a good business must have a little stake.

I do not believe these niggers will be speedily conquered with Otis at the helm. It needs a Lawton or Miles or someone with a killing spirit. Old McKinley's policy is all wrong. I think he will not get in a second term.[24]

Lawton's children have fine health and look well. Mrs. Lawton lends me nice books and is very cordial. She is my nearest friend here. I wrote of my two recent calls. Will go again when I can stand the walk and so many generals are not there, as I kind of shrink from meeting so many high officers. It smacks of presumption. Both Lawton and Mrs. Lawton treat me just the same as in the days when I rode to Falls Church and took my Sunday dinner.

Peter MacQueen is a great fraud and liar.[25] For a minister he is pretty rank. He is a fake minister, [and] acknowledges he is a backslider. He has now returned to [the] U. S., [and he] is in Frisco editing *Campaigning in the Philippines*.

I am glad, so glad that you like my Helen, not for my sake, but for her own dear self. She is a very kind-hearted, generous girl, and I hope, in time, she will be loved as one of the family.

Well, mother dear, with many kisses, I close.

Your affectionate son,

Robert Dexter Carter

August 20, 1899

My Dear Father,

This is a Sunday morning and I try to generally make the day seem a little different from the others, for memory's sake, and also [to] write a letter home. I have not written you for some days, but [I] have written Mama, Natalie, and Mellie. The last letter I got from you was dated before your start to Portland. I was sorry to hear of your poor health and trust the bracing air of Casco Bay will invigorate you against your return to Washington. I should judge that you could not have selected a better locality for a summer sojourn than Great Diamond.[26] How different the air is there from here. I should like to be there with you this summer.

The rain by day has now let up, but every night it pours. It seems as though the roof would be crushed. My health does not seem very good—a constant battle to keep my stomach and bowels from throwing me back in the Hospital. I get so mad. Something new tending toward my misery pops forth each day. [The] day before yesterday, I had a severe turn with my stomach, although for breakfast that a.m. I ate but tea and toast. Well, the stomach trouble caused me a mean attack of diarrhea, which is so difficult to check here. Now I am much worried by a peculiar thing for which I cannot account. Every morning when I awake, I have such severe pains in [my] back, not in the small but higher up, that I cannot lay flat on my back, and I find movements simply take my breath away. At first, I laid it to cold or stiffness due to dampness, but it seems inside. Yet, when I arise, it is gone, and I am not troubled until awakening the next morning, when I have the severe "crick" again. In fact, sometimes it feels as though my entire diaphragm had [to] be pounded or a brick wall had fallen on my back while I slept. These doctors would put an Army mule under ground by their treatment. In fact, I owe my six weeks of blood poisoning in my feet to ignorant treatment. One leg, thank God, at last seems well. The other is gradually coming down to a finish at last. It has ceased in the ankle and concentrated all the swelling in the last two toes. I had a nice night with those toes last night, but I think it is the end of six weeks or more being a semi-cripple.

Since my best possible chance remains in the Quartermaster Department, as I could not stand a permanent residence here without physical breakdown, I hope to better myself in that department. I believe I made a very bad move when I came off the *Grant*. A transport quartermaster clerk is considered the best position in Quartermaster Service, and I would give much to get back, for there you get good food, a bed, and have superb health. Your room and board cost nothing. For me to remain here at my present salary, with prices increasing, is nothing gained, and I will be only able to live from hand to mouth.

Crosby Miller[27] comes on next transport to be Chief Quartermaster out here.

Lawton has gone up on the Lake to stir the niggers up.[28] I think the old man is pretty well disgusted with the present policy, and I guess before the U. S. is done with the Philippine problem, they will have something to look back upon which will cause a "dark brown" feeling.

The mail, which is daily expected, is a late one, and I am very anxious to hear from you all.

With much love to all, I close
Your affectionate son,
Robert Dexter Carter

August 25, 1899

My Dear Sister Mell,

Yesterday, a mail came in on the *Newport*, and I did not know anything about it, hence it was an unexpected pleasure when a letter from Helen and you came (with inclosures from Great Diamond Island), also two rolls of papers from you. The *Journal* is a great item out here. It has so much news and is interesting by reason of pictures. I am glad you managed to get enough cash together for a trip to Ocean City. I would have helped you, but I need every cent, and sickness has cost me what little I saved over the end of the month.

I am now as well as I will ever be here, but I cannot shake off my despondency. I cannot eat, and, at best, I do not feel myself. I may quit and come home. I am sick of the rough end all the time. I long to enjoy a little of life while I still am young. Lawton is not thinking about me, and my trip here to Manila has cost me the opportunities of my life. I see dozens of other Washington boys who are lieutenants awaiting orders. It would be equal to killing me to live here forever.

I hate this country as does every American. It is very well for those to hold out here, who have life positions and are sure of a good salary when they return. I risk my health and future life for the strong probability of a "bounce" as my reward when I return. I believe those who got in on these Volunteer Commissions until 1901 are good for the Regular Army after that time. I am not even in the Quartermaster Service, being unattached as a regular clerk to army officers and not drawing clerk's pay, although I have done field work, [and] every day, not a day off, to the cost of my health, of two clerks. I am very blue when I read [that] all my old friends and classmates [are] fixed for life, fellows who I stood ahead of at school. Lyman, who was quite a dunce, and here I am with the prospect ahead of accepting a civil position if Lawton ever has the power to give it. In other words, life imprisonment in a place where every breath is dead against my constitution, a place where Helen can never live. Consequently, I cannot accept it again, if I am sick and am obliged to return, I would have to pay my way, and living as a civilian would take all my salary. I only manage to scrape along now because I force myself to eat at this mess, wear soldier's clothes, and live a soldier's life, something for which I will never get credit in a Civil Service exam.

Do not read this to Papa and Mama. It is just a wrench from my heart. I have got to get my work in the Quartermaster Department. Does papa know Miller [the] Chief Quartermaster here now? If so, perhaps he might by a letter get Miller to assign me as a clerk on some transport, where I could get good food, etc. Again, I am very anxious to know if Schreiner, if I return now, will discharge me. He could assign me to some station in [the] U. S. My health is giving out. That is why I am desperate. I won't come home, if I die, to be out of a job, for I know what that means. Oh, what a Hell life is! Will I never know what rest is? Now that I have salary, I cannot live in the place where I am obliged to work for it. What fate! I have not howled to the Lawtons about my health, but I tell you, I have felt and do feel miserable beyond expression all the time. I have to drink black coffee, quantities of strong tea or keep full of quinine to keep malaria down. Sores have driven me crazy at night with pain. And my stomach won't digest anything except very light food. What enjoyment is there in such a life for me. I foresee no permanent position in [the] U.S. to urge me to hold out here. On the other hand, I see myself out of work, [and] in poor health. I feel heartbroken. Lawton might write Schreiner or General Ludington[29] to give me an assignment in [the] U. S., but I hate to ask him, he is so hard to approach, is seldom alone, and has his whole mind on military matters. If I foresee my immediate return, I will get a letter from him.

The family seems to be having a great time at Portland Harbor. When I read of the good times and good things to eat [you] all have, I feel like dying. If I had been home this summer, what a good time we could have had. If I could strike any job at $50.00 at home, I would quit. With General Lawton behind me, I ought to land somewhere, but I am afraid not, for he does not think of me at all.

People imagine that they can get an answer to their letters to Manila in about 2 weeks instead of 2 ½ months. Now I have more leisure [and] will clean up all side correspondence. Have not heard from Pap for a long time. I guess [the] high life is too much for him. Well, I too, quit for dinner, if we can call it such. Well, I have a little can hidden, so if it is very bum, I can manage to chow.

Much love,
Your only and affectionate brother,
Tod

Chapter Seven

September 1899

"Every letter here is a goldmine"

For a young man obsessed with his salary, Carter was very optimistic about saving for his scheme to settle on a ranch in western Canada. He is clearly a young man conflicted. On the one hand he is emphatic that he'll stick to the assignment, while on the other, he emphasizes his iffy health and uncertain prospects. When he started having dental problems, he tells his sister that he is "going to pieces in chunks." From his comments, it would appear that his days of going into the field are over, although he does make reference to another short trip to Las Piñas, where Mrs. Lawton had to assist him back to Manila due to an undisclosed health problem.[1]

Health in the tropics was a relative thing. According to Carter, everyone, even Mrs. Lawton, was afflicted with something, most commonly malaria or the "Itch," or both. Diarrhea and other ailments were prevalent, and the trick was to keep everything under control, or you might die. Carter's litany of ailments are a preview of the same or similar conditions that later generations of American soldiers would experience in the Pacific Theater in World War II and in Vietnam. Previously, he had told his sister that he had had it, but not to tell that to their father and mother. However, as his health improved, so did his mood.

In addition, he is becoming, by choice, increasingly isolated from many of his co-workers, some of whom he describes as the "dregs," and he remains very selective with his choice of companions. Like all soldiers he looks forward to the mail, so he was particularly upset when the steamship *Morgan City* sank, thereby losing the bulk of the letters and packages she was carrying. The turnaround between correspondences could be as much as three months, so one can just imagine the disappointment. However, when mail did come, it often came in batches, bringing with it packages and magazines. The *Ladies Home Journal*, with its scenes of home, particularly food, was very popular. On the bright side, Carter was able to get an article published in the *Philippine Magazine*, where he had been hired to write and to draw.

"I'll make any heroes"

Carter also gives us a further insight into Lawton's strained relationship with Otis and with some members of the press. Mamie Lawton is clearly in her husband's corner. Otis comes across as stuffy and full of hubris when he states, "I'll make any heroes that are made out here!" For all the bad blood between Otis and Lawton, there is surprisingly little apparent animosity between Lawton and MacArthur. Carter is also skeptical about whether the cautious Otis will impede an upcoming offensive into Central and Northern Luzon to, once again, try to seize the elusive Aguinaldo.

This operation, although similar to the spring offensive, would be more complicated, with Lawton and MacArthur driving north on a parallel course in an attempt to push Aguinaldo into the arms of Loyd Wheaton, who would land a force from the Lingayan Gulf well to the north and drive inland. Carter would not accompany Howard into the field, and since the chief clerk, Stedman, was gravely ill, it is likely that another permanent clerk did so. This time, the Chief Quartermaster was ordered by General Lawton to establish a headquarters at San Fernando de Pampanga some forty miles north of Manila in order to support the offensive.

At the start of the campaign, Major Howard had developed a plan whereby supplies would be sent by rail and water to Calumpit on the Rio Grande de Pampanga. Lighter supplies would be loaded on cascos and towed upriver, while the heavy or bulky items would continue by rail to San Fernando, where they would be loaded on wagons and carts and transported overland to Arayat. By the end of October, General Lawton had reached the end of his supply line, and he was holding his position near San Isidro. Supply was still a problem, in particular, a shortage of pack animals and carts, which was impeding the progress of the division. Prior to the offensive, Howard had repeatedly pestered Otis, who relented and finally forwarded a request for 3,000 mules.

Not wishing to lose their quarry, Lawton sent Brig. Gen. Samuel S. B. Young ahead with a flying column, while he awaited the bulk of rations and supplies to catch up with the main body. Complicating the quartermaster's problems was the extreme length of Lawton's force from head to tail. In addition to the shortages in animals and carts, Lawton felt that the cascos were not arriving quickly enough. Howard left his assistant quartermaster, Captain William E. Horton, in charge at San Isidro, and he set out to fix the problem.[2]

Maj. Gen. Lawton briefs Lt. Col. Howard, Central Luzon

According to reports, on October 22, Major Howard and his civilian clerk had been traveling south on the Rio Grande de Pampanga aboard the steam launch *Oceania*. As the craft approached the confluence of that river with the Rio Chico near Arayat, insurgents, concealed by the jungle lining the banks, suddenly opened fire, killing Howard and wounding his clerk and another passenger.[3] Howard's place was taken by Major John T. Knight.[4] Carter's reaction is not known, as his correspondence had stopped three weeks earlier.

September 1, 1899

My Dear Father,

I inclose herewith a little scheme which I have been rolling about in my mind for some little time. It is a little start in life when I shake clear of the Army in 1901 or thereabouts. A young man's future lies in the West, I believe. Conditions are such that a man, to command a good living in the East, must be skilled or highly educated or have a pull. I hope by rigid economy, to have in a year and a half from now about $1,000.00 saved at the present rate. I am laying by, and if my salary increases more, I give a liberal estimate, and $2,000.00, I believe, will about cover a start. I can get on to someone who [will] help out to [the] extent $500.00 and labor. I believe I can make an independent start in life in the West with strong hopes that, as the country fills up, etc., natural profit will accrue. And as those who started 20 years ago on the plains of the West ranching are now well off financially and independent of all, so far as they live on the production of their own land. I have been thrown in with many western men, raised in Montana, North Dakota, [and] Idaho.[5]

Mamie Thompson sent me some *New York Journals* with some Davenport cartoons[6] which were simply immense. The officers at Headquarters roared.

The ranch project is one which I am thinking of at the expiration of my time here, in case I cannot get a good thing in [the] States. Get a pamphlet from Canadian Pacific Railroad office and consider this from every point of view, and advise me what you think about it on the whole. I will not go it alone, as to working the claim, but if I raise the necessary cash, [I] will own the place at the end of three years, and will hold it then for its value in years to come. I cannot settle in Manila. [O]wn your grant and your returns come in after that and is simply a case of steady increase in value, stock accumulation, with game, hogs, sheep and lots of poultry and truck garden, and for Hudson Bay Company stores selling provisions fairly reasonable, living should be almost nothing. A man must work and work hard in any line. How much harder will he work when he knows it is for himself; that it is for a future independence from the worry of business and office holding. A clear brain, healthful country air, outdoor life, a simple life I believe preferable for Helen if I [were] to make a start for our home, rather than the scramble in the East at dog's wages, [with] nothing after years of hard work to show [for it].

Sunday Morning, September 2, 1899

It is seldom one can finish a letter on the day started, as constant interruptions preclude. I am anxious to get this in today's mail to you. I am feeling very much better, and unless I can be transferred to [the] States, will remain in Manila for now. The worst is over and the good weather is coming. I will stay. I have not, since leaving the hospital July 26, once had a return of the old weakness.

I will write again soon. I got a letter from Mama yesterday in mail. Love to all.

Your affectionate son,

Robert Dexter Carter

September 6, 1899

My Dear Mother,

Last night I put on my white suit, very best new bonnet, and white socks, in fact, felt white all over, and went to call on Mrs. Lawton. They had just finished dinner. A Mrs. Nelson was staying with them, a very pleasant lady. As they came out of the dining room, the General's face beamed and he remarked,

"Here is one of your fellows, Mamie, or rather admirers." I said, "the very same thought occurred to me, as I was walking over, that I was going to see my only lady friend in Manila, the only one I had gone to see or had gone to see since I have been in Manila." We all went into the parlor and sat down to a fine evening's chat. I brought the *New York Journals* down with cartoons, the same [ones] Mrs. Thompson sent me. They were great. The General simply shouted, thought them immense. All thought them very good. In conversation, they often referred "to your friend in the Palace"[7] to the General, and he made some pretty hot [remarks] at him himself. He was in a fine mood and talkative.

I drew about 50 paper dolls for the kids and a picture of Manley, a quick sketch in his military clothes, with which the General and Mrs. Lawton were so pleased, that she said it should go in her scrapbook. I also brought down a lot of particularly complementary clippings I had seen in [the] Washington and New York papers about Lawton. One, after reading, he said with a grin, "that sounds like some of Bob Carter's work." I assured him it was not. "Well," he said, "they (U.S.) will find out in time," referring to his 100,000 deal.[8] The paper had remarked in the paragraph that that opinion of Lawton's was the first dawning of the truth the American people had. Also, said General Lawton, "by saying that and no more, showed he was no book or magazine soldier, and that expression was worth whole volumes, etc., as it told the truth almost in a word, etc., etc." It kind of tickled him after some of the roasts in the past.

I never take any articles which are not of a complimentary nature, as I once showed him a clipping about the Zapote fight, which after reading, seemed to worry him and put him in a bad mood. He has load enough to bear, not to add the extra stings of ignorant newspaper writers in the States. He hates Otis like hell, and I don't blame him, after doing the work he has, to have Otis cut him out of all the credit. Otis once remarked to a newspaper man I know of the Associated Press, when he was putting through some pretty strong praise of Lawton, that he (Otis) "would make any heroes that were made out here." The sooner the old goat is fired, the better. The soldiers are all howling—Miles, Lawton, Wheeler.

Howard, by simply hammering requests into the Palace, has forced Otis to send to the States for 3,000 mules. There is no transportation to move into the field a division for a campaign, and Otis will do nothing on [the] grounds of economy. He is a regular "Holman"[9] and cripples everything. I remarked last night to General Lawton that Otis had at last been forced to send for mules. Lawton said, "a pretty time to be sending for them now." Mrs. Lawton said she would write oftener, but her hands are crippled with rheumatism. They waded into the newspapers in great shape. Lawton being on to the *Post*, I blue-penciled all remarks bearing on the situation pretty well before I took them down. I am pleased that the knocking has commenced on the right man at last, and I think it tickled him to death to know old Otis is getting some real stiff roasts himself now. For he so misrepresented the campaign on the South Line, Zapote fight, that the papers knocked Lawton, and he was so damned mad over it he could hardly contain himself.

My health is so much better, leaving my stomach out of the question, that I think I shall hold on. I try to save clear $50.00 per month out of my $83.00, but it is hard work. I wear soldier clothes, eat bum grub, etc., and deny spending a cent outside of actual necessities, so that if I am forced to return, I will have a little account, or if I stay in service for some time, that when I do leave and branch forth, it will be with the little sum to start with. What do you think of my starting on a ranch, not necessarily in Canada, but as a start with the prospect that 15 to 20 years will see my holdings so increase that when I am 40, I will be on a sound basis for the rest of my days.

The *Morgan City*[10] has been wrecked we hear, and I am afraid our mail is gone. I hope not. Every letter here is a gold mine, and one would prefer to lose money rather than his mail. We now have a new manager to the mess and am living better. My room is a pleasure to me, so cool and dry. My old trunk which was so warped that I could not get it together, and the bottom full of rat holes, I traded for a brand new chest, double back, brass bound, larger, and keeps insects out, which ate up my clothes, also partly the damp. A returning volunteer wanted a trunk and thought he could repair mine. He had just bought the chest and found it too large for his belongings. My trunk would have never got across the U. S. on my return. When I do go back, I will sell the chest and buy a trunk. While I stay here, the chest is what I want. The old trunk was a goner, and as it would not lock or close, was no good. The fellow partially succeeded in fixing it, but I doubt if it will hold against one or two good falls.

My old military coat, well honeycombed by moths inside, I sold for $5.00. I could not have kept it and was well pleased to get rid of it. I now am able to buy extra Commissaries which help out very much. I often think of you and the good table at home. I shall surprise 3218 when I get back. Am glad you like my Helen and am so much pleased to know that all is well at home, for it would worry me to know she was not free to go to see my family. As it is now, she feels one of the family. I hope when I return, that the other side of the house will welcome me in the same way. Doubtless they will. Do not worry about me whatsoever, for if I am ill again, since I shall return. But I think I am now another person in health, at least I feel like one. My feet are well, and I take my long walks every evening, and almost nightly sit on the *Luneta* and hear the roar of the surf and the fading light in the mountains to the West. It is sometimes very beautiful. The leaden sky is lifting at intervals, and the rainy spells are not so prolonged.

The campaign will soon begin, and I will not have to go in the field again, I think. If I could get up at Otis's Headquarters in the Palace where Bickham's[11] clerk was ordered, and could secure me good rooms, and find health remains good, and there are strong prospects of my prolonged stay, and I get my drawing in on the side, and get my $100.00, Mrs. Helen F. Carter might come on, and being thus comfortably fixed, after her first sick spell natural to acclimation, live here and return to [the] U. S. when I go. All this is very remote—nothing definite. I would prefer she remain.

There were fellows who sneered at my first attack of sickness and pointed to me as an example of one who was particularly careful of his health becoming sick right away. Well, two of those pikers are now doing a little turn with bloody dysentery, and one, if he doesn't stop drinking on the sly will be buried. I have pulled through and have my natural strength and clear nerves in hand, filling myself with stimulants, drugs, narcotics, etc. Everyone's liver gives them a bad turn here. Sometimes mine feels like a paving stone and aches "real fierce," but I keep up my exercise though it rain torrents. They often ask me what I find all alone on the *Luneta* [on] a rainy night. I say nothing, but keep sawing wood. I have no companionship; desire none. The dregs of humanity, the worthless of worthless do not attract me. Their vulgarity and filth sickens me, yet I do not show it to them unless absolutely necessary. Some of them hate and detest me because they have found that I am in their class. Especially because (not through me) they have found I am the son of an officer. I never turn on one unless it becomes necessary, which has been seldom. I have some very fine friends, valuable friends among young men of education, higher thoughts and purposes, and who have the refinement, which goes with the bearing of a gentleman. Men who grossly insulted me, have come to borrow $5.00 at the end of the month of me, because they know I do not spend every cent on booze and am not strapped at the end of the month. Sometimes I do a man a favor to show them I bear them no malice. I shoot the ice house into them very good and strong and disagreeable to show there is a two-edged sword. I write this just to show some of the conditions which are the natural sequence of a big change in my life and surroundings at the present.

Keep me posted concerning father's health, as I am anxious to know how the summer at Diamond Island fixed him up. I distinctly recall my beautiful trip up in that region—Cape Elizabeth, Harpswell, etc. and the breezy Bay.

Well, I must close this as I have much to do.

Your affectionate son,
Robert Dexter Carter

September 19, 1899

My Dear Mother,

The weeks roll on until it is now nearly a month since I received a line from home. All our mail for 10 days dated from July 26th to about August 8th went down on the *Morgan City*, only 25 bags being saved, and those in horrible condition, registered mail I should judge. When one goes a month without a letter here, life becomes monotonous, and one becomes nervous. Last night, it rained in torrents, and today a steady downpour follows. Yesterday, I had to work hard. Today, I have but little to do. The chief clerk, Mr. Stedman from New York, is at the 2nd Reserve Hospital, and his condition is such that his recovery is doubtful. The ignorant Army doctor here at Headquarters, the one who after I fainted away, did not come near me and allowed me to lie a day unnoticed, alone in a room and did not take the trouble to write an order admitting me to the Hospital, pronounced it Dengue Fever,[12] and allowed Stedman to lie over at the house for seven days without suitable food or medical attendance until his temperature reached 102 [degrees]. A man dies here when his temperature reaches 105 [degrees]. I believe he has typhoid, and as he is a weak, puny fellow of nervous temperament, his death would not be remarkable after such a bad start. We now enjoy distilled water which, after much difficulty, Howard has secured for our quarters and has compelled the lazy whelps, who tend to getting it—get it.[13] He found they would get a can about every eight days, [and] did not cover it up. Consequently, filthy Chinamen dipped into it, and it soon became corrupt and foul to drink. The ignorance among human animals one feels in the Army is remarkable. A soldier will gorge himself on our fried meat, twice of gravy, three times of bread soaked in gravy, then wonder why he has chronic diarrhea come on him in time. Yet, very strange, there are some of them who can stand that. I suppose it is because they came from a hog pen and always ate garbage all their life, and never tasted properly cooked food in their life.

I am feeling so much better, yet am disgusted at fresh sores breaking out. My left arm has a huge boil, a small ruby-colored abscess on my ankle, and numerous small eruptions which never heal, showing a rotten, corrupt condition of the blood. I do not understand, as I eat but little, and that the simplest, absolutely no grease whatever. It does seem so bad to me to be thus. While some soak themselves in liquor and drugs and tobacco, and are apparently enjoying the best health of their life.

My greatest comfort is being able to take my long walk every night. Last night, although raining and blowing heavily, I went and sat by the seashore and watched the breakers and driving clouds and absolutely enjoyed being alone where I would no longer hear, "you lie," "you s. o. b.," and cursing and swearing and blasphemy constantly. Every night in the next room, they call each other every name in the category of vileness, any one of which would cause a gentleman to fight or leave. And it apparently runs off their blunted intellects like water off a duck. I speak of soldiers. The civilian clerks of the Quartermaster Department are educated and gentlemanly with one exception. The civilian clerks who came on the *Grant* were ex-soldiers, and, including General Lawton's secretary, are ignorant and ungentlemanly curs, always ready to borrow anything from him when they need it. The rest of the time, they offer scant courtesy. Knowing that I am the son of an officer is sufficient to make some of these brute soldiers delight in small, contemptible ways be mean to me. I never notice them unless they go too far, and then, generally call the man down in a way he generally remembers. No wonder Father loathes cards. I never touched once since leaving the *Grant*, and only played cards twice in the evening while on her. I could not sit in a game with such people.

I hope old Otis will have a pain in the liver. He seems to be about the only man who holds out, although he has been pretty sick, but they kept it quiet. Lawton looks exceedingly well, and looks very handsome in his white uniform. He perhaps, as Mrs. Lawton, I think, watches him, and he is after the head place here for which he was sent. Creelman[14] in the *Journal* hit the nail on the head and spoke the truth. We are approaching the typhoon season, season of hurricanes.

Helen seems to be quite a homemaker, since she ran her mother's house all summer in grand style. Well, she will have to do good work when I come home in 1901, for I mean to eat melons, peaches, strawberries, everything good.

I contemplated sending some stuff home Christmas, something that I could fold in a small parcel and send by mail, Japanese or Chinese curios, but I find that they nail everything in Frisco at the Custom House and charge big duties, more than they are worth. However, I will see. I can get almost anything now in the American line of goods and clothing, by paying the prices, but I wear the soldiers's stuff, as I go nowhere, see only soldiers and officers, and have no desire to be a Manila sport. I have some white suits, so when I spruce up, I look like the "Lady in White,"[15] white shoes, hat, socks, etc.

Well, I will bring this to an end, with much love to all, I am

Your affectionate son,

Robert Dexter Carter

September 20, 1899

My Dear Sister,

Yesterday after many, many days of severe waiting, the long looked for mail came. It was such a small mail reported, sixty-five sacks, that I thought I would receive nothing, as I only got two papers in a much bigger mail about the first of the month. Imagine my joy when I received three big fat letters, yours dated August 12, and one each from Mamma and Helen dated August 11. My mail you sent dated July 26th to August 8th or 9th went down with the *Morgan City*. Some medicine, which Helen says she sent July 30, is feeding fishes, and you say in your letter to look out for some shirts that Bess had sent. So, alas, I am afraid they too are lost if sent before August 10th or about the 1st of August. Hard luck indeed. That was a big mail of nearly 300 sacks of which only 31 got in yesterday, a mass of pulp. I do not expect to get a letter out [of] that lot. If the shirts are lost, I will be more than mad, for I needed them badly.

We are now having a hurricane or semi-one. It rains in torrents, no let up. The water in the streets is nearly to the knees in many places. When it starts to rain here, it rains, that is hour after hour at the same pace, no stopping.

I am quite well now, am getting on alright, the food is better, and when it is not good, I go out and buy meals, which takes up about $20.00 a month. So altogether, my grub costs me nearly $31.00 per month, and as I have $33.33 and a little over made by exchange, you can see it is living "close to home."

The letter of Mrs. Lawton's telling of bringing me home from Las Piñas was on a one day trip I made there and was done up.[16]

Well, misery seems to come in chunks. I lost one tooth whole, a false one in the hospital, [and] now one of the gold fillings in my front tooth came out and was lost. That means about $10.00 or $15.00 gold. I never got the other tooth replaced, as I do not believe they could do it here, and bridge work would take a month's salary. I am dropping to pieces in chunks.

I guess you gave Mrs. Wright a job, which will hold her for while, namely the fleas which Ted[17] left behind in Mamie's room. I had a Hell of a time getting them out of the house last summer. It would be fine if Helen came and stayed north long enough to come home with Papa and Mama. As I am a little rushed today, I will have to cut this short now to go to work. I will write Mamma and Helen. I await Helen's next letters from the north with interest, especially if she visits Gramp. With many kisses and love to all, I am

Your affectionate brother,

Tod

September 20, 1899

My Dear Father

Your letter dated August 4th went down on the *Morgan City* off the Japan coast, but luckily, was in one of the 31 sacks of mail rescued from the briny, as was also one from Helen. They (the letters) were hard looking customers after their sea bath, but I was doubly glad to get them after nearly a month without any mail. I had not received a letter from you since I left the Hospital July 26th so was very much pleased. I shall send you the envelopes to keep as a curio. All of Choate's medicine which Helen sent July 30 and August 4th was lost. Both of the letters which I received were dated August 11 and 12 from Mell, Helen, and Mama. Mellie gave quite spirited descriptions of the movements of the "hunde"[18] on his summer outing.

Everyone is ill now; dengue fever is prevalent. Our chief clerk, Mr. Stedman from New York, is at the 2nd Reserve Hospital, and I believe will die, as he was a very frail man to start with. I believe my troubles took the best course through the hide rather than culminating in a fever. I feel well, have picked up in weight, am still breaking out in eruptions all the time, my Itch has gone except in small patches. My stomach is bad, and I eat lightly and carefully, but still have to go some pretty bad stuff for a weak stomach, since I cannot afford the prices asked for such simple luxuries as peaches, eggs, or milk toast made of condensed milk. We now have a genuine nigger cook, an old Southern darkey, a regular Hercules in build and always singing the old familiar melodies, which I have so often heard the coons sing about Washington. He puts up much better grub than the former drunken slob we had. Each night I take a long walk to jolt my liver. The liver is the bane of life here. Everyone is sick, sick, some light, others hard. I no longer have that awful weakness, so am much more certain I can hold out.

I like Col. Howard. He is a fine quartermaster, and tends to business strictly, very courteous to his clerks and is not unreasonable. I have been fortunate to be with such men as Walcutt and Howard. I hope I can stay with him as a regular clerk, then I will be permanently with a regular quartermaster of sufficient rank to insure high assignments. When I have saved enough ahead, I will quit the Army and have my own row. I favor a sheep herd for a rapid increase on a small outlay. It will not even be necessary to build buildings, make hay, keep farm implements, etc., as with cattle. Of course, the Western idea is in case I find it absolutely impossible, when I quit the Army, to get work in my line East or West at a good salary, $1,200.00 or more. If I get in with Howard as one of his authorized clerks, I will get my $100.00 in spite of Schreiner or any of them, as he is authorized to pay that.

I am so pleased to learn that you gained in health by your trip to Diamond Isle. I rather think Mell missed it bad. It makes my mouth water reading about lobster and fish dinners, such fish dinners as one gets on the Maine shore.

I would have liked to [have] made a Volunteer commission out here, for I believe could stand a show for the Regular Army. I conclude that it's damned bad here, but I hear the soldiers tell of worse, and as I feel better now that my U. S. blood has been parboiled out of me, I conclude to see this deal through or be put on the boat on a stretcher. Everyone knows here that the niggers would have surrendered with two weeks more campaign on the North Line after Lawton's long flank move, had not that infernal ass, Old Otis, just to thwart Lawton, and insanely jealous of him, recalled him. Otis is rotten. Shafter would be aggressive. Otis won't even be that, will cheese pare his Army bills, will not get transportation ready, yet will OK and pay niggers, insurgents turned friends for five minutes, enormous rents for house or property for which they can show no title. He (Otis) made one nigger mayor of Imus. He has since become a general in the Insurgent Army. Another collector, and he worked for the interests of the Insurgents. Nothing done or doing toward aggressive action, and still the farce goes on. Lawton is wild; says little. He has the backing (moral) of the entire army, but what is that against the political ring in Washington. Old Bill and Uncle Mark[19] are "doing this."

One does not eat very much meat here, as good meat is not to be had very often at a moderate price. And rice gags a man after eating it, as much as one has to here. I have long since quit trying to regulate my bowels. It is impossible here. All Americans, even on boiled grub, have a chronic diarrhea more or less bad. One has to take the grub as it is doled out to them, full of grease or not. Ignorance of hygiene and cookery and everything else here are at the fore. A more ignorant lot of whelps than these new recruits is hard to find. When I ache and I have a touch of the dengue, I drink some good whiskey and quinine and roll in a blanket to sweat the ache out.

Today and yesterday and the day before that, etc., we are enjoying torrents upon torrents of rain. The water in the streets is nearly to the knees. In going from quarters to the office and for meals, we have to roll up our pants above the knees and wade. A regular old typhoon.

I was quite delighted to get $17.50 out of *Colliers*. Am afraid I can send no more good photos, however. Those were taken by Volunteers who have gone home and the regulars are such a herd, that I don't believe they ever saw a camera.[20]

Well, as tomorrow the mail goes, and it is now dinner time, I will close this, with love to all I am

Your affectionate son,

Robert Dexter Carter

September 23, 1899

My Dear Sister,

Mail has been so scarce of late that owing to the loss of so much on the *Morgan City*, I have not had much information from your end on the line. In your last letter, you were by the rolling deep, you and the hound, and from the tragedies, hair-breadth escapes of the hound, etc., I judge things were lively enough for you. I rack my head for news. Every day is like its predecessor, the only change being in the inches of rain, if all. There is a new copy of the *Philippine Magazine* out, with one timely article by your humble servant, done when he was in the agonies of pain between the period when he came out of the hospital and again went back. Some other pictures I drew have not been printed. I suppose they will appear about December, as these paper things are done here. The picture printed is pretty fierce. It was not my idea, but as ordered.

Say, Hess's job on my teeth is proving pretty bum. I lost one of the porcelain teeth in the hospital a few weeks ago, lost entire front filling, gold, out of my front tooth, and last night (damn) I lost a filling in one of the big eye teeth, the sharp tusks you know.

I was sure surprised in reading Helen's letter saying she started for the north on the morrow. She showed a great head. I am glad she went north. Am only sorry I could not go with her. Hope she will not miss Grandpa, for I want him to see and talk with my "Leedle Baby." I sometimes call her "Babwee," the Tagalog for pig, quite a joke on her. I send her drawings and comics in my letters. You get a bell and ring it when it's time for her to see the point.

I walked to town last night and regaled my inwards with a genuine American lemonade and the Chinese waiters stretched their necks when, after drinking, I fished out the peels and ate them too. Oh, I got my money's worth!

Our chief clerk is near death. They think he has typhoid now. I suppose they will know when he is dead.

Old Lawton's staff officers fixed themselves OK, OK. King[21] was 2nd lieutenant, he is now captain [in the] Volunteers; Brooke[22] was a 1st lieutenant, he now is a major [in the] Volunteers; Starr[23] was a major [in the] Volunteers, he is now lieutenant colonel; and Sewell,[24] son of Senator Sewell, a big, fat, brainless slob was a captain [in the] Volunteers, is now made captain and quartermaster in [the] Regulars, [a] permanent, life position.[25] Poor Walcutt, after sleepless nights and tremendous work, is a captain and quartermaster of Volunteers, and Sewell is a Regular quartermaster, ranks him, and is on the General's staff for life. Such is the irony of Fate.

I contemplated sending some Japanese stuff, etc. back home, but find I cannot get it by the San Francisco Customs House.

Well, this is but a short note. The Lawtons are all well. The General looks fine. They treat me great when I go down there.

A kiss, love to all, tell Natalie to write, I enjoy her letters.
Your affectionate brother,
Tod

P.S. During the illness of our Chief, I am doing quite responsible work. I make out all money vouchers, and keep the books, likewise beat the typewriter, and am generally good [I] think. I am going to stand in with Howard or bust. I stood in with Walcutt, for when he left, he said he would do anything he could for me at any time.

September 27, 1899

My Darling Mother,

Yesterday was a day of great joy before the transport *Puebla* came in with a large mail, the first large mail in a month. In the first batch, I got some Boston papers from Helen, a novel she sent, a magazine and the *Ladies Home Journal.* The latter is very welcome here, and when I finish with it, there are many eager to read it, and after they look it through, I take it down to Mrs. Lawton. The photos in the back of each number depicting strawberry glacé, Banana Charlotte, Peach Mousse, etc., etc., nearly drive me wild. Such exquisite torture could not better be invented than a real hard look at this page, yet, I like to linger over it. Sunday nights, the swell Manila restaurant makes a cut price reduction, and for $1.00 American, puts up a very fine dinner, better than one could get for three dollars during the week. It is as an add and the boss claims he makes nothing on his Sunday layouts. An orchestra of niggers play while you eat, and the meal is excellent.

In the second lot of mail, I got two or three hours later, I received eight letters, five from Helen, and one each from Papa, Mellie, and yourself. Yours was dated August 14, and inclosed a letter from Helen. Papa's was August 17, and Mell's August 20. My but I was glad to hear from all, as for a month I had not received hardly any mail.

I am now well, very well, have regained my flesh and can walk. My stomach is erratic, but I have got used to it, and let her go. I feel in physical strength 100% better than I did. I feel now some vigor, and almost as well as my first months here. Some sores, but they come and go. It's a hell of a land on health, but as all suffer and I am now in health above the average, I have no kick.

Unless a clerk gets sick, I will not again have to take the field. Howard and his messenger and one clerk leave in a few days with the General for another campaign. The whole Manila headquarters, Lawton's, may have to move up to San Fernando within a few months and take up a regular headquarters about 40 miles from Manila.

Now while the Chief Clerk is sick, Howard has moved me up into the most important and hardest job in the office, and I hold it down. The work on the jump in a stock broker's makes even a rush here a cinch for me. Talk little with Howard, but do much and think the old boy rather takes a shine to me. For I want to stick with him.

Our grub is fair, now the coon cook went off on a drunk the other day. So it was rather bum until he got sober. Then he atoned by making some pies and extras.

I would not go to [the] trouble of getting me novels to read. I can get plenty from Mrs. Lawton, as she handles most of the reading matter for the hospitals now. Send me illustrated papers. They tell the whole story here, and are so eagerly looked for.

The other day, the messenger was down to Lawton's house and said the General was arrayed in blue overhauls, and he and Mrs. Lawton were hard at work with a bottling press bottling wine, a keg of which he received, I suppose, from Redlands on the Pinabla.[26] Every time I go down there, the kids make me draw them paper dolls, so I now cut fashion figures out of papers, which relieves my work somewhat and pleases the kids.

There is quite a change in the weather now. It does not rain often, and, at night, a stiff sea breeze blows and is so refreshing after the long heated day.

Several admirers have taken my picture in the office at the desk, "but there is something rotten in Denmark," for the films are always a failure.

Say, those fish dinners around Portland Harbor, with ginger bread and trimming make my vitals roll around in despair. I believe the worst of life is over for me now. I have little patches of the Dhobi break out, even after several times disappearing from the surface, but, in general, all around health, mentally, etc., I feel better. Now that the sun shines and the sky is blue and the rain has quit, my spirits lift, and each night rain or shine, blow hard or easy, I do a long tramp all alone. I feel good, and my greatest enjoyment is to sit alone and see the grand sunsets, which are again appearing, and [to] get away from the foul-mouthed gang which populate the Army—the left over bits of humanity which now fill the ranks of our Army.

Well, work has piled up on me, so that I must quit. I wrote this in scraps. Will write and answer them all when I have leisure. Do not spend a thought about me, I am well; am going to stay. Many kisses from
Your affectionate son,
Robert Dexter Carter

September 28, 1899

My dear Father,

Yesterday was such a rush that I did not get a chance to read over my letters or to answer them. We are now doing big work in this office, moving troops, etc. for the Rio Grande River Expeditions. I think, in general plan, it will be like the one old Otis sported last spring, by ordering Lawton back at the very time success was possible.[27] The weather is now very nice, of course, very hot in the day, but at night a real cool breeze blows from off the Bay, and it is simply immense, after a long day at the desk, to go over and sit by the seashore and have a howling breeze, with a good band accompaniment, cool you off. The sunsets are getting grander each evening. The clouds no longer seem on top of the trees, a black pall so depressing to the spirits. Yet, I can hardly imagine it [is] September, that next month the cool breezes will blow, the leaves fall, and chestnuts be ripe. Here, the banana trees are always glossy, and the everlasting green and perpetual bloom is sickening to the sight.

I feel very well, even my stomach is picking up. I have some sores, but they don't count, as I can walk and sleep now, both of which I could not do formerly.

I have a day to write in today as Colonel Howard has gone out on the railroad to Calumpit to inspect his storehouses, and, consequently, there will not be the business as when he is here. Owing to the illness of the Chief Clerk, I am doing double work and have the hardest job now in the office. Will be glad to resign it to the Kanuck[28] when the Chief Clerk comes back. I make out all vouchers, keep the books, both letters sent and received, and write the endorsements and telegrams. The Kanuck now writes official letters and renders returns and keeps money books. Formerly, I simply was the corresponding clerk, doing all telegrams, letters, and endorsements, copies, etc. on [the] typewriter. I have been using my shorthand of late and picking it up, as Howard dictates to me so much. He seems pleased that I am now writing shorthand for him.

Your letter was dated August 17. I was so glad to know that you are spending such a pleasant summer and your health had improved. Sometime, I want to again visit Casco Bay and indulge in the lobsters, etc. If my letters were rather doleful this summer, it was due to my continued illness and the dreadfully gloomy weather, nothing but rain and no sun. I told Mrs. Lawton not to mention that I was sick, so if she did not write about it, that was the reason. I preferred, if I got very bad, to let you know the true state of affairs myself.

Our food is pretty fair now, and when it's bum, my feet no longer being sore, I can get out and get something to eat which formerly I could not. The malaria never got me bad. I think the Dhobi overpowered it. I seldom take quinine, and that in small doses when I ache severely. The Itch I did not get on [the] Santa Cruz trip, as I was sleeping on [a] launch. It first broke out on that trip [Las Piñas] because I sweat [and] I could not change my clothes, and slept in them. It affects all. Mrs. Lawton has had it. [It] appears in a small patch and itches terribly; it rapidly grows like a ring worm. And so on a small, raised red and ridge and the skin falls off in scales and scratching it makes it raw, and some doctors claim it is due to the natives never boiling the clothes and drying them upon grass that a parasite is in the clothes which attacks the pores of the skin at points where there is profuse perspiration, under the arms or chafing as between the legs.

Cleanliness has nothing to do with it. Much bathing makes it much worse. When I first came, I took a shower every day. Now, I take one once or twice or three times a week, and a half sponge off in the morning. People imagine that plenty of washing and soap and absolute cleanliness will stop it. Water, most times, makes it worse. All have it, some immediately, some after a prolonged stay, some severe, some slightly. Riding provokes it. It takes five or six forms. When it leaves the skin and gets in the blood, it is very bad, as I had it, but it is still worse, as in cases which I saw, where the glands and pouches inside fill with this stringy, thick white poisonous pus and have to be opened. My glands in the groin, when I went to the hospital in July, were swollen like bubo and so painful, I could hardly walk. A few days and I would have had to be opened and cleaned. One fellow I saw in the hospital had a great hole under his arm which the nurse daily cleaned of pus and sprayed out. Grease, Vaseline, and ointments do more to check it on the surface than any medicines, acids, and things to dry it up, make scabs and drive it into the blood, and does not keep it from spreading. I never would have had the bad sores I had and painful swelling, had not my damn fool doctors in the Army hospital painted my small exterior patches with iodine, which drove oil clean off the surface. By hot water application, they reduced the buboes and swelling, so I did not have to be cut, but my what pain and scalding I did endure.

The green swelling in my feet is peculiar to here. It is Dhobi settling in the feet, and the doctor's don't understand it and do not attempt to treat it. They simply kept mine cleaned (the pus) in a wet packing of [a] cloudy solution and application to reduce swelling and fever. They did not cure me, and my feet were bad when, in desperation, I left the hospital and broke out in a final spell weeks afterwards. My ankles now are a dark red and greenish purple color, but no swelling and only one or two small sores, my feet are well. The numerous boils, all have, some worse than others. The Dhobi in connection with those seem to prevent the discharge, so your blood is corruption and your hide is a mess of sore, painful, partly (come to a head) swellings and sores and life is hell. The Dhobi boil discharges puss like rope, tough, elastic, solid white and yellow and are slow in healing. I had two on my temples which, even now, the marks show. The pain nearly drove me wild at night, and it was that which sent me to the hospital.

To sum it up, Dhobi here is as sure as death or taxes to those who are in any way exposed to privation or do not take in hand at the onset. As I said, some have boils because one's blood has to become thin and watery, and it becomes so by boils, diarrhea, or fever. I slipped the fever, thank God, which so many have, and it literally cleaned my blood, but through the holes in my hide. It is contagious, for if you scratch yourself in many places, it spreads and takes root. I was very careful about this at the outset, so all of mine was confined in one or two localities. Boric acid ointment was the best thing I struck, a box of which I got just as I left the hospital. It has the germ killing qualities of acids, and yet does not aggravate the sore, as it is an ointment, and, again, it burns the itch into surface sores, full of pus which, when they discharge themselves until tired, dry up, and quit. And that is how I finally managed to end up my siege. I still have several small patches which are "still with me," but after the big trouble, I do not notice them. The doctors do not know anything about it, and have it themselves as bad as any.[29]

All natives are a walking bunch of sores, small pox, and leprosy [and are] seen in the streets. The majority of the niggers have sores on their legs and feet. I believe it comes from moisture, water, damp. For absolute dryness of the skin all the time, especially after bathing, is the best preventative. I hate the sight of the niggers and, although they are always bathing and are cleanly as a people as far as washing goes, in other ways they are filthy. I avoid them like the plague, and have never been near one or a nigger joint since I have been here, nor have I any desire to. Too much bathing is as bad or worse than too little for aggravating the Itch. And this curse stays with you alright, you can't lose it. The niggers are always scratching. They perpetually itch. Soldiers all have the Itch. The hospitals are filled with severe cases, some serious, some die when combined with their other troubles. I was in fine trim when I landed, and it was the natural cleaning up of the blood by boils and by the stupid treatment of the doctor drove it in to my system and caused my sickness.

The reason I got left on eating on the South Line was because I was to eat with the headquarters. They left, and as the companies constantly changed, and I was up and down the line for five miles on the jump. I got what I could scrape, which was little. As long as you are near organizations, all is well. [It] is when you are by yourself, as I was, the lack of grub comes in.[30]

I seldom get a chance to talk with Lawton, and I have never talked with him alone since I left the *Grant*. If I get my $100.00, I am satisfied where I am. Don't want any Manila civil jobs out in this rotten, disease-breeding hole for life. I prefer to get steady with some Regular Quartermaster, and then I have a permanent job and, in two or three years, can return to [the] U. S., still having my job. If I can stay with Howard, I will be well pleased. I will not have to go in the field again, except in case of illness of his messenger or other clerk.

Ward in Second Reserve Hospital, Manila

I keep up good spirits. Helen writes cheerful letters, and Mell's please me so much. She is so cheering and always tells me all the news. I long to hear from her. She braces me up and I feel so cheerful after reading her letters. I have about seven suits of underclothes now, and change constantly, live in white clothes.

About my bowels, Ha! Ha! It is not to keep them open; it would take an Edison[31] to keep them closed or even moderate here. I have long since ceased, as all run here, and as it is a natural condition found in all, except the old, I let her rip, using ginger brandy to check any cramp symptoms. No liver pills are needed here. I run every night and am never normal. The main thing is to be careful not to let it become severe, weakening or chronic. For once chronic, it is death here.

I never was anxious for Helen to come here and have positively taken a stand against it. I much prefer for her to remain in Washington. I never worry about it. When conditions are changed, and I have a better and more permanent standing, it will be time enough to see about her joining me. I never want her to come here. It would kill her. She never worries me by writing or pleading for me to return or to let her come out. She accepts the situation and all is serene. I have never worried over pay. Life is too short to worry much, so I take things as they are, yet believe in sawing wood when [it] comes to getting pay, as that is what I am out for, enough money to get a start. The General looks fine, as do all the Lawtons.

With love to all, I close.

Your affectionate son,

Robert Dexter Carter

Epilogue

Carter's correspondence abruptly stops with a letter to his father dated September 28, 1899, just as General Lawton was preparing for his second campaign into Central and Northern Luzon. While he could not have known it at that time, the subsequent death of Lt. Col. Howard and the wounding of his civilian clerk on October 22, 1899, near Arayat during that expedition, followed by the death of Carter's patron, Henry Lawton, at San Mateo on December 19,[1] must have removed any remaining luster from a job that was becoming increasingly unrewarding. Despite his troubles, he would finally tell his parents that he intended to "stick it out," provided his health remained good. Stay he did, and on January 1, 1900, he accepted a commission as a second lieutenant in the 12th Infantry Regiment and continued his service in the Philippines.[2] Afterward, he made the Army his career, and, in retirement from active duty, he served as Professor of Military Science and Tactics at the Bingham Military School in Asheville, North Carolina.[3] At the time of his death, he had attained the rank of lieutenant colonel. Carter died on January 22, 1926, and he is buried at Arlington National Cemetery. Helen Wright Carter survived him by many years, and after her death on September 16, 1961, she, too, was buried in Arlington at his side.[4]

Robert Goldthwaite Carter, aged 90, would survive his son by a decade, dying on January 4, 1936, at Washington, D.C.[5] In addition to the Medal of Honor, which he received on January 23, 1900, the senior Carter went on to write about his days as a soldier, his most well known books being *Four Brothers in Blue* (1913)[6] and *On the Border with Mackenzie* (1935).[7] Young Carter's mother died in 1923. Both she and his father are also buried at Arlington National Cemetery. Nothing is known of what became of Carter's sister Mell, although there is a good chance that she may well have saved her brother's correspondence, and it is through her that his writings actually see the light of day. It would be nice to think so.

Henry Ware Lawton died a hero's death, and the nation mourned along with Mamie and the children. The fallen soldier's final journey home was, fittingly, aboard the U.S. Army Transport *Thomas*.[8] His body lay in state, first in his former hometown of Fort Wayne, Indiana, and later in Indianapolis, where fellow Hoosier James Whitcomb Riley eulogized him with a poem called the "Home Voyage." "Bear with us, O Great Captain, if our pride show equal measure with our grief's excess. . . . ," Riley wrote.[9] Lawton was given a large funeral in the Nation's Capital, followed by burial at Arlington National Cemetery with much pomp and pageantry.[10] Soon after, the public erected statues to him in both Fort Wayne and Indianapolis, Indiana, and later in Lawton, Oklahoma, as well. In a Memorial Day ceremony at Indianapolis in 1907, his statue was dedicated by his old comrade in arms from their "crowded hour" together at Kettle Hill and El Caney, President Theodore Roosevelt.[11]

Mamie Lawton and the children came home. Ordinary citizens were so moved that they contributed $100,000 to a fund for their benefit.[12] Lawton's adjutant, Lt. Col. Clarence Edwards (later major general and commander of the 26th Division in the First World War) remained close throughout his long, successful career. As a boy, Manley served for a time as an aide to General Grant in the Philippines; however, outside of his father's long, protective shadow, Manley Lawton would live a quiet life outside of the limelight. He died at Washington, D.C., on January 11, 1960. One can only speculate if things would have been different had Lawton survived. Would he have succeeded the cautious Otis? While he definitely took the fight to the enemy, he also recognized the value of President McKinley's policy of benevolent assimilation. In the short time Lawton was in the Philippines, at Baliuag he oversaw the election of the first native Filipino as a mayor[13] and distributed foodstuffs to hungry Filipinos.[14] Mary Craig Lawton would follow her husband in death on January 5, 1934, and she is also buried at Arlington.[15]

Lawton's death paved the way for Maj. Gen. Arthur MacArthur, who would succeed Maj. Gen. Elwell Otis several months later, and, as well, for Samuel

Young, who would succeed Lawton, and in 1903 he became the first Army Chief of Staff following the reforms implemented by Secretary of War Elihu Root. MacArthur would soon clash repeatedly with the then-civilian head of the Second Philippine Commission, William Howard Taft, and he would eventually be the loser.

Brigadier General Robert Henry Hall retired from the Army in November 1901, following a long and distinguished career, including his service during the Civil War and as Commandant of Cadets at his *Alma Mater*, the United States Military Academy. He was also the author of several works on military history. Hall, well regarded for his kind manner and devotion to his troops, died at Chicago, Illinois, on December 29, 1914, at the age of 77.[16] William Edward Birkhimer died at Washington, D.C., on June 10, 1914. During his career, he taught at West Point, earned a law degree from the University of Oregon, and served as Judge Advocate for the Department of the Columbia. Though of slight build, he was known to be earnest in his devotion to duty and aggressive in a fight. He was awarded the Medal of Honor for his actions at San Miguel de Mayumo, Luzon, while serving with Lawton, and later given command of the 28th Infantry Regiment.[17] He is buried at Arlington National Cemetery.[18] Brigadier General Charles Carroll Walcutt, Jr., a classmate of John Joseph Pershing at West Point, also enjoyed a long Army career, including his service as Acting Chief of the Bureau of Insular Affairs (1918-1920). He died at the Fort Hayes Hospital (formerly Columbus Barracks), Columbus, Ohio, on December 17, 1946, at the age of 85. He is also buried at Arlington.[19]

About the time that Carter's letters stopped, the war was taking an uglier turn, and it would continue so for nearly two more years. As Aguinaldo watched his army disperse, he came to realize that the war needed to become a guerrilla contest, island by island, province by province, village by village. Moreover, Manila, a city of 30,000 people, had no real strategic significance aside from its obvious symbolic value. So he let it be known that the contest would now be a guerrilla war—*amigos* by day and fighters by night. The Filipino leaders, along with sympathetic journalists, published stories of outrageous atrocities by American troops, in the vain hope of swaying the American electorate in the presidential election of 1900. Perennial candidate William Jennings Bryan, an anti-imperialist, lost as usual, thus tamping down the hopes of the Filipino military. Most stories were either false or blown way out of proportion. Sadly, however, many were true, and the image of America, particularly its Army, would be tarnished by some incidents of brutality and the use of the "water cure." It reached a point where President Roosevelt himself stepped up and imposed discipline on Brig. Gen. Jacob H. Smith and others for abuses on Samar.[20]

Charles Carroll Walcutt, Jr. as a Cadet at the U.S.M.A.

Aguinaldo remained on the run until March 1901, when Frederick Funston, with a small mixed force of American soldiers and Philippine Scouts, tracked him down and captured him in a daring, if not controversial, operation. Thus, he accomplished something a large part of the American Army could not. Thereafter, the Filipino leader, once burned, accepted the inevitable and urged cooperation with his captors. Aguinaldo's dream of a free Philippines, united under his leadership, would have to wait. Frederick Funston would continue to serve his country. A seasoned soldier, on the eve of World War I, he was thought by many to be the logical man who would lead the American Army in France. Fate took a hand, as he died of a sudden, massive heart attack in February 1917, at the age of fifty-one.[21]

Although Fred Grant would never achieve the pinnacle of success that his father did, his service within and without the army proved that he was a capable military man and a valuable public servant. Upon his graduation from West Point in 1871, he served briefly in the 4th Cavalry in Texas. He would

Brig. Gen. Frederick Funston captures Emilio Aguinaldo

later serve as Minister to Austria and Police Commissioner of New York City. He, too, died suddenly on April 12, 1912. The immediate cause of death may have been a heart attack, but Major General Grant suffered from a number of health problems. At the time of his death, he held the prestigious command of the Department of the East.[22] He is buried at West Point.

On September 6, 1901, President McKinley was felled by an assassin's bullet. Thus the ever cautious chief executive was succeeded by Theodore Roosevelt, his ever combative vice president. President Roosevelt, tired of the distraction, declared the war over on July 4, 1902. While the war itself took a tougher turn, McKinley's policy of benevolent assimilation was carried on by his immediate successors, Roosevelt and Taft, as well as Brig. Gen. Clarence R. Edwards (Lawton's former adjutant general), as the chief of the Bureau of Insular Affairs. The seemingly slow process, what we today would call "nation-building," actually bore fruit relatively quickly in the overall context of history. While the American policy toward the Philippine peoples often demonstrated both ignorance and hubris, America ultimately kept her promise. The Philippines achieved independence on July 4, 1946, somewhat later than planned due to the intervening Japanese occupation.[23] Ultimately, Aguinaldo lived to see that day, and, in fact, passed away in Manila in 1964, at the ripe old age of 95.[24]

Notes

Editor's Note

1. For Taft quote, see Stuart Creighton Miller, *"Benevolent Assimilation": The American Conquest of the Philippines, 1899–1903*, 182–89.

Introduction

1. Jerry Golway, *Washington's General: Nathanael Greene and the Triumph of the American Revolution*, 164–67.
2. George Washington, "Address to the Continental Congress," June 16, 1775. In George Washington and John Rhodehamel, ed., *George Washington: Writings*, 167.
3. Thomas Paine, "The Crisis," December 23, 1776.
4. George Washington to Joseph Jones, August 13, 1780, Washington and Rhodehamel, ed., *Washington: Writings*, 382–85.
5. George C. Marshall, *Memoirs of My Services in the World War, 1917–1918*, 138.
6. David F. Trask, *The War with Spain in 1898*, 146–48.
7. Miller, *"Benevolent Assimilation,"* 251.
8. Walter Zimmermann, *The First Great Triumph: How Five Americans Made Their Country a World Power*, 7–8, 240, and 283.
9. Ivan Musicant, *Empire by Default: The Spanish-American War and the Dawn of the American Century*, 656–58; D. W. Meinig, *The Shaping of America: A Geographical Perspective on 500 Years of History, Vol. 3, Transcontinental America, 1850–1915*, 365.
10. Charles M. Robinson, III, "Forward" to Robert Goldthwaite Carter, *On the Border with Mackenzie; or, Winning West Texas from the Comanches*, x–xi.
11. *Sixty-seventh Annual Report of the Association of Graduates of the United States Military Academy at West Point, New York, June 11, 1936*, 78–81.
12. *Washington Post*, June 15, 1894, 5.
13. Ibid., January 17, 1899.
14. 1900 U.S. Census, District of Columbia (Series T623, Roll 158, Page 264).
15. Mamie Lawton suffered from rheumatism. See letter of Carter to his father dated September 1, 1899.

16. Louis Kraft, *Gatewood & Geronimo*, 127.

17. Frank Freidel, *The Splendid Little War: The Dramatic Story of the Spanish-American War*, 96–106.

18. Steven L. Ossad, "Henry Ware Lawton: Flawed Giant and Hero of Four Wars," 4–25.

19. H. Wayne Morgan, *William McKinley and His America*, 219.

20. Ibid., 274.

21. Trask, *War with Spain*, 33–34. The so-called "Fifty Million Bill" became law on March 8, 1898. Edmund Morris, *The Rise of Theodore Roosevelt*, 632.

22. Musicant, *Empire by Default*, 186.

23. Morgan, *William McKinley*, 341; Evan Thomas, *The War Lovers: Roosevelt, Lodge, Hearst, and the Rush to Empire*, 1898, 394.

24. Wake Island was seized on January 17, 1899. Trask, *War with Spain*, 468.

25. Zimmermann, *First Great Triumph*, 330.

26. H. W. Brands, *Bound to Empire: The United States and the Philippines*, 72.

27. Thomas, *War Lovers*, 178.

28. Trask, *War with Spain*, 454.

29. Ibid., 145–46.

30. Musicant, *Empire by Default*, 247–48.

31. John Durand, *The Boys: 1st North Dakota Volunteers in the Philippines*, 127–28 and 310.

32. Carter to father, July 27/28, 1899, Robert Dexter Carter Papers.

33. Formerly S. S. Mohawk; rechristened USAT *Grant* following its purchase by the Quartermaster Department, along with four other vessels, in July 1898. See http://www.atlantictransportline/22Mohawk.htm; Durand, *The Boys*, 191n14; Erna Risch, *Quartermaster Support of the Army: A History of the Corps*, 1775-1939, 566.

34. The 4th Infantry had been transported by train from Fort Sheridan, Illinois, and the battalion of the17th Infantry had been transported from their barracks at Columbus, Ohio.

35. *New York Times*, January 18, 1898.

Chapter One The Diary

1. Carter's wife, Helen F. Wright.

2. Maj. Gen. Henry C. Corbin, adjutant general of the Army. Corbin was born in Fremont County, Ohio, in 1842. Following his service during the Civil War and a brief stint as a lawyer, he made a career of military service. He served on the staff of Gen. Miles during the Geronimo Campaign. Known for his diplomatic and political savvy, he became a trusted advisor to presidents Hayes, Garfield, Harrison, and McKinley, and he moved in the best

circles. McKinley appointed him as adjutant general in 1898. Corbin retired in 1906 and died suddenly on September 8, 1909. Information available at http://www.arlingtoncemetery.net/hcorbin.htm.

3. Cortlandt Street. At that time, the street, located on the west side of lower Manhattan, ran from Broadway to the Hudson River, where there was a ferry to New Jersey. The present street is substantially shorter, the land having been taken in the mid-nineteen sixties for the construction of the World Trade Center.

4. Most likely Assistant Quartermaster Captain Charles T. Baker who served as quartermaster/commissary on the *Grant*. Carter refers to him as "Captain Baker." The Quartermaster Department had a chief quartermaster, Major Chauncey B. Baker, but I doubt that one of his rank would be assigned to one ship alone. Adjutant General, *Register of General Officers and Officers of the General Staff, U. S. Volunteers, 1899*, 7.

5. Mary Craig Lawton, wife of General Lawton.

6. Gibraltar.

7. An Annapolis Class, U.S. Navy gunboat on her way to her duty station in the Pacific.

8. To take on coal.

9. HMS *Devastation*, a 2nd Class British battleship.

10. Brig. Gen. Robert H. Hall.

11. Royal Artillery.

12. Mediterranean.

13. Ceuta. Enclave of Spain in northern Morocco.

14. "on account."

15. Port Said, Egypt.

16. A Cincinnati Class, U.S. Navy–protected cruiser. Unlike an armored cruiser, a protected cruiser only has armor protecting its decks, and not the hull. The Raleigh was part of Dewey's squadron at Manila Bay in May 1898, so she must have been on her way back to join the Atlantic Fleet at this time.

17. Ismailia, Egypt.

18. Mt. Sinai, now Gebel Mûsa ("Mountain of Moses").

19. Island belonging to South Yemen lying in the Bab el Mandeb Strait at the entrance to the Red Sea.

20. Somalis (pl. natives of Somalia).

21. Post Office.

22. Manila, Philippine Islands.

23. Tanjungpinang, Indonesia. An island opposite Singapore.

24. Carter taught himself typing, a skill he would put to good use as the corresponding clerk in the division quartermaster's office in Manila. See letter to his father dated September 28, 1899.

25. USS *Monterey*, a monitor originally designed for coastal and harbor defense, sent to strengthen Dewey's fleet following the battle of Manila Bay.

26. A casco (plural "cascos") was a long, wooden, canoe-like native vessel. At this time, the Port of Manila had no docks or wharves capable of handling ships of this size, and ships were slowly loaded and unloaded by means of lighters and cascos. Edward M. Coffman, *The Regulars: The American Army, 1898-1941*, 61.

27. Rear Admiral George Dewey.

28. Capt. Benjamin P. Lamberton, commander of Dewey's flagship Olympia, an Olympia Class, U.S. Navy–protected cruiser.

29. A Baltimore Class, U.S. Navy–protected cruiser.

30. U. S. Navy battleship.

31. More than likely the section of Manila called Binondo, which is located north of the Pasig River. It was mainly populated by immigrant Chinese, and it, along with the section called the Escolta, was the principal commercial and shopping area of Manila.

32. Located at 38 Calle Nozaleda, Paco. Carter refers to Paco as part of Manila; however, it was then a separate town or suburb. It was, however, well within the Southern Line designated by the American forces. Durand, *The Boys*, 142.

33. Maj. Clarence Ransom Edwards.

34. The Casa del Ayuntamiento (literally "house of the city council"), a palace in the old, walled city of Manila, was the former city hall, which was used as U.S. Army Headquarters, including the chief quartermaster. It should not be confused with the Malacañan Palace (sometimes spelled Malacañang), a former summer residence built on the north bank of the Pasig River in the suburb of San Miguel. The latter would be used by generals Merritt, Otis, and MacArthur as their residence, and thereafter, by the civilian governors, commencing with William Howard Taft in July 1901, all of whom commuted to their office in the Ayuntamiento until much later. Otis may have conducted some business from Malacañan, since there is evidence that some documents originated there. At present, it is the residence of the Philippine president. Clearly, when Carter refers to the "Palace," he is referring to Quartermaster Headquarters at the Ayuntamiento.

35. Captain Charles Carroll Walcutt, Jr. (U.S.M.A. 1886), chief quartermaster, 1st Division, 8th Army Corps.

36. 8th Army Corps.

37. "money order."

38. A captured Spanish steam launch used by General Lawton as his floating headquarters during the Santa Cruz Expedition.

39. Pasig River, which rises in Laguna de Bay and flows into Manila Bay, bisecting the City of Manila.

40. Most likely a brand of bottled water.

41. Laguna de Bay. Large inland lake and source of the Pasig River.

42. For a more complete description of the Santa Cruz Expedition, see Chapter Four.

43. For a complete description of the incident, see letter of Carter to his sister Mell dated May 7, 1899.

Chapter Two January–February 1899

1. Risch, *Quartermaster Support*, 565–66.

2. Morris, *Rise of Theodore Roosevelt*, 632–33.

3. Trask, *War with Spain*, 184–85.

4. Thomas, *War Lovers*, 280; Theodore Roosevelt, *The Rough Riders*, 43. According to Roosevelt, three hundred of the original nine-hundred-man regiment was left behind.

5. Risch, *Quartermaster Support*, 567.

6. Secretary of War Russell A. Alger (1836–1907). He enlisted in the Army during the Civil War, rising through the ranks to become a general officer. Alger became a successful lumberman, and he later entered politics, becoming the Governor of Michigan. His inexperience and difficulty dealing with the Army's bureau system resulted in a failure to arm, equip, and transport troops to Cuba in a timely and efficient manner. At the time of his death, he was serving as a U. S. Senator from Michigan.

7. Joseph Earle Stevens, Yesterdays in the Philippines (New York: Scribners, 1898). On the title page, Stevens referred to himself as an "ex-resident of Manila."

8. A bitter General Nelson A. Miles, commanding general of the army, told the Dodge Commission, which was looking into the overall supply situation during the expedition to Cuba, that he had heard complaints that the men were eating tainted or "embalmed" canned beef. Although the charges ultimately proved false, the controversy caused quite a sensation in the press, and it virtually ruined the career of Brig. Gen. Charles P. Eagan, commissary general of subsistence, who was forced to defend his actions and that of his department. Miles was later censured. Musicant, *Empire by Default*, 353–54 and 639–40; Risch, *Quartermaster Support*, 353–54. In some Army circles, Miles was considered a "self-promoting schemer." Robert Wooster, *Nelson A. Miles and the Twilight of the Frontier Army*, 161.

9. Captain Charles T. Baker was quartermaster on the *Grant*. Adjutant General, *Register of General Officers and Officers of the General Staff, U. S. Volunteers*, 7.

10. Baksheesh (var. bakshish, backsheesh, or backshish) in Eastern or Middle Eastern countries, a small payment, such as a tip or gratuity or gift of alms, or, in some instances, a bribe. In this instance, Carter is undoubtedly referring to young beggars.

Chapter Three March 1899

1. Trask, *War with Spain*, 159 and 385–87.
2. David Traxel, *1898: The Tumultuous Year of Victory, Invention, Internal Strife, and Industrial Expansion that Saw the Birth of the American Century*, 218, and 223–24; Trask, *The War with Spain*, 370, 376, and 384–85.
3. John M. Gates, *Schoolbooks and Krags: The United States Army in the Philippines*, 1898–1902, 148.
4. Brian McAllister Linn, *The U.S. Army and Counterinsurgency in the Philippine War,*
1899-1902, 6–7.
5. Musicant, *Empire by Default*, 197–98; Trask, *War with Spain*, 400–404.
6. Trask, *War with Spain*, 409–10.
7. Morgan, *William McKinley and His America*, 295; Trask, *War with Spain*, 437–38.
8. Brian McAllister Linn, *The Philippine War, 1899-1902*, 24.
9. George F. Telfer and Sara Bunnett, ed. *Manila Envelopes: Oregon Volunteer Lt. George F. Telfer's Spanish-American War Letters*, 38–39.
10. Trask, *War with Spain*, 400, 404; Morgan, *William McKinley*, 306–7.
11. Zimmerman, *First Great Triumph*, 388–89.
12. Miller, "*Benevolent Assimilation*," 46; Frederick Funston, *Memories of Two Wars: Cuban and Philippine Experiences*, 159.
13. Linn, *Philippine War*, 27–31.
14. Durand, *The Boys*, 190.
15. Linn, *Philippine War*, 27.
16. Ernest D. Scott, "*Gunner in Luzon*," Part 1, 517.
17. Telfer, *Manila Envelopes*, 134; Durand, *The Boys*, 220–21.
18. Miller, "*Benevolent Assimilation*," 172–73.
19. Durand, *The Boys*, 41.
20. Carl Anthony Sferrazza, *Nellie Taft: The Unconventional First Lady of the Ragtime Era*, 157; Musicant, *Empire by Default*, 196 and 207.
21. Regarding Carter's use of such terms, see "Editor's Note" above.
22. Miller, "*Benevolent Assimilation*," 58.
23. Durand, *The Boys*, 152; Telfer, *Manila Envelopes*, 102, 122–23; Risch, *Quartermaster Support*, 528.

24. Brig. Gen. Robert H. Hall (U.S.M.A. 1860) was in command of the 4th Infantry Regiment, and he was one of several senior officers that Carter met during his Philippine tour who had served with his father. Hall knew Carter's father and mother from his service days in San Antonio, Texas. George W. Cullum, *Biographical Register of the Officers and Graduates of the U.S. Military Academy at West Point, New York Since Its Establishment in 1802, vol. 4*, 121; Adjutant General, *Official Army Register for 1899*, 121.

25. The USS *Oregon* was an Indiana Class battleship built in San Francisco. Commissioned in 1896, it sailed around the Horn to join the Atlantic Fleet in 1898, and was ordered back to the Pacific to bolster Admiral George Dewey's squadron in Manila. According to Carter, it must have arrived there on or about March 19, 1899. The two-ocean deployments of the ship lent support for the military necessity for an Isthmian canal. Kenneth Wimmel, *Theodore Roosevelt and the Great White Fleet: American Sea Power Comes of Age*, 105–9; Musicant, *Empire by Default*, 329–30; Edward W. Eberle, "The 'Oregon's' Great Voyage," 912–24, available at http://digital.library.cornell.edu; The HMS *Pauncefote* was a British warship named for Sir Julian Pauncefote (1828-1902), a diplomat who negotiated the Hay-Pauncefote Treaty (1901) which gave the United States the exclusive right to build and operate what would become the Panama Canal.

26. Shortly after taking command, General Otis concluded that gunboats would be of great assistance to the Army. As a result, six captured steam river vessels were purchased from Spain and re-fitted with armor and armament. His decision to follow through with his idea proved to be an invaluable one. A. B. Feuer, *America at War: The Philippines, 1898*, 121.

27. In addition to letters and stories, Carter sends photographs home, perhaps with the camera he found on the *Grant*.

28. Captain Charles Carroll Walcutt, Jr. (U.S.M.A. 1886) served as chief quartermaster, 1st Division, 8th Army Corps from October 24, 1898, to June 19, 1899, at which time he became assistant to the depot quartermaster at Manila. Cullum, *Biographical Register, vol. 4*, 421.Walcutt was the son of Bvt. Maj. Gen. Charles C. Walcutt, Sr., who served with distinction during the Civil War, first in the 46th Ohio Infantry, and later as a division commander in the Fourteenth Army Corps. Twice-wounded, he was mentioned several times in the Memoirs of General W. T. Sherman (New York: Library of America, 1990), 261, 403, 412, 568, 664, and 823.

29. Chief Commissary Major Harry E. Wilkins. Adjutant General, *Register of General Officers*, 7.

30. Carter does not say which member of the crew gave him the gun.

31. Slang for Filipino, a native of the Philippines.

32. Slang for jailed.

33. "brown man" (e.g. "little brown brother").

34. Capt. Benjamin P. Lamberton, commander of Dewey's flagship *Olympia*, an Olympia Class, U.S. Navy–protected cruiser. Available at http://arlingtoncemetery.net/bplamberton.htm.

35. First Lieut. John Caldwell Gregg (U.S.M.A. 1887), 4th Infantry Regiment, aide-de-camp to Brig. Gen. Hall, killed in action in the Mariquina Valley on March 31, 1899. Heitman, *Historical Register, vol. 2*, 23; Cullum, *Biographical Register, vol. 4*, 449–50; Adjutant General, *Official Army Register for 1899*, 122.

36. Undoubtedly a reference to Allyn K. Capron, Sr. (U.S.M.A. 1867), who was in command of the Light Artillery battery in Cuba, particularly at El Caney and the siege of Santiago. He died on September 17, 1898, at Fort Myer, Virginia, shortly after returning to the U.S. Cullum, *Biographical Register, vol. 4*, 421. Coincidently, Capron's son, Capt. Allyn Capron, Jr., was killed at Las Guasimas, "gunshot lungs" on June 24, 1899. Roosevelt, *Rough Riders*, 58 and 186.

37. Another insensitive reference to the Filipino insurgents or *insurrectos*.

38. The Krag-Jørgensen ("Krag"), a 30-caliber, bolt-action rifle, was standard issue for Regular Army units and was later issued to some Volunteers. The standard issue for the latter was the Springfield Model 1873, a 45-caliber, breech-loading rifle. Trask, *War with Spain*, 145–46. The Spanish and the *insurrectos* used the Mauser, which was very effective in the hands of a trained rifleman. The significant issue was the use of smokeless powder, which the Spanish used but not the U.S. Later in the war, American soldiers used a version that helped somewhat. Brian Linn, *Philippine War*, 100.

39. Lt. Col. James Worden Pope (U.S.M.A.1868), chief quartermaster with headquarters at the Casa del Ayuntamiento, referred to as the "Palace," or town hall in the old walled city of Manila. Cullum, *Biographical Register, vol. 4*, 184–85; Adjutant General, *Official Army Register for 1899*, 14.

40. Maj. Francis M. Schreiner, Chief Quartermaster in Washington, D.C., Adjutant General, *Register of General Officers*, 7.

Chapter Four April–May 1899

1. Gates, *Schoolbooks and Krags*, 6–7 and 92–94; David J. Silbey, *A War of Frontier and Empire: The Philippine-American War, 1899-1902*, 13–16.

2. Funston, *Memories of Two Wars*, 279–83.

3. Linn, *Philippine War*, 95 and 101.

4. Given the number of lakes and rivers, General Otis conceived of the plan to convert captured steam launches to gunboats by adding armor and ord-

nance, including Gatling guns, three-inch Naval guns, and Hotchkiss guns. Feuer, *America at War*, 121.

5. Ibid., 125–26.

6. General Orders No. 19, Hdqrs. First Division, Eighth Army Corps, Manila, P. I., April 6, 1899, Annual Reports of the War Department for the Fiscal Year Ended June 30, 1899, Part 3, 32–33; Feuer, America at War, 126. The standard field ration consisted of bacon, hard bread, coffee, sugar, beans, and rice or hominy. If possible, potatoes, onions, and canned tomatoes were added. Risch, *Quartermaster Support*, 528; Scott, "Gunner in Luzon," Part 4, 217. According to Scott, fresh fruit was rare, butter and jam were "unknown," and "canned tomatoes were a much sought-after luxury." The latter were packed in heavy cans, yet a soldier would gladly carry one all day long "for the delight of drinking from it in the evening."

7. *New York Times*, April 17, 1899, p. 2.

8. Another form of native watercraft. A small, traditional wooden fishing vessel with outriggers.

9. During the operation, the members of the press volunteered the use of the steam launch *Oriente* to tow some cascos across Laguna de Bay, thus "rendering valuable assistance." H. W. Lawton to Adjutant General, Department of the Pacific and Eighth Army Corps, Report, April 10, 1899, *Annual Reports, 1899*, Part 3, Appendix 10, 43–44.

10. Robert Dexter Carter diary, Saturday, April 8, 1899, Robert Dexter Carter Papers.

11. Linn, *Philippine War*, 102; *New York Times*, April 10, 1899, p. 1.

12. William M. McCammon to Adjutant General, Report, April 20, 1899, *Annual Reports 1899*, Part 3, Appendix 34, p. 64.

13. Linn, *Philippine War*, 102; H. W. Lawton to Adjutant General Department of the Pacific, Report, August 1, 1899, *Annual Reports, 1899*, Part 3, 34–35; H. W. Lawton to Adjutant General, Department of the Pacific and Eighth Army Corps, Report, April 10, 1899, *Annual Reports 1899*, Part 3, Appendix 10, 46–47.

14. H. W. Lawton to Adjutant General Department of the Pacific, Report, August 1, 1899, *Annual Reports, 1899*, Part 3, 31–43.

15. *New York Times*, April 17, 1899, p. 2.

16. Durand, *The Boys*, 76–77.

17. Reference to the Santa Cruz Campaign just completed.

18. The precursor to the bicycle. Eric Jaffe, *The King's Best Highway: The Lost History of the Boston Post Road, the Route that Made America*, 176–78.

19. Lawton's headquarters was located in Paco, a suburb of Manila south of the Pasig River.

20. Telegram, Lawton to MacArthur, May 9, 1899, *Annual Reports, 1899*, Part 3, 190–91; Telegram, MacArthur to Lawton, May 9, 1899, *Annual Reports, 1899*, Part 3, 192.

21. Walcutt was relieved of his duties as acting commissary by Captain Samuel B. Bootes on May 8, 1899. Telegram, Brainard to Lawton, May 8, 1899, *Annual Reports, 1899*, Part 3, 187; Adjutant General, *Register of General Officers, 1899*, 7.

22. Telegram, Lawton to Adjutant General (Palace, Manila), April 24, 1899, *Annual Reports, 1899*, Part 3, 131; Telegram, Walcutt to Adjutant General (1st Division), April 24, 1899, *Annual Reports, 1899*, Part 3, 132; Report, C. G. Starr to Adjutant General (1st Division), May 12, 1899, *Annual Reports, 1899*, Part 3, 127; Scott, "Gunner in Luzon," Part 4, 214.

23. Durand, *The Boys*, 253.

24. Report, Maj. Gen. H. W. Lawton to Adjutant General, United States Army, September 26, 1899, *Annual Reports, 1899*, Part 3, 78.

25. Telegram, Lawton to Adjutant General, Department of the Pacific and Eighth Army Corps, April 30, 1899, *Annual Reports, 1899*, Part 3, 151.

26. Report, Maj. Gen. H. W. Lawton to Adjutant General, United States Army, September 26, 1899, *Annual Reports, 1899*, Part 3, 87; Risch, *Quartermaster Support*, 538. For his part, General Funston had high praise for the civilian employees of the Quartermaster Department who handled the pack mules. Funston, *Memories of Two Wars*, 370–71. Many in the Army supported the use of Chinese bearers and considered them to be "patient, tireless and brave." However, as the war progressed, many, like Brig. Gen. Theodore Schwan, disapproved, referring to them as "great looters." For that and other reasons, the Army discontinued the use of Coolies as bearers in 1900. Mary C. Gillett, *Army Medical Department, 1865-1917*, 208–9.

27. Scott, "Gunner in Luzon," Part 4, 214–15.

28. Edwards to Commanding Officer 22nd Infantry, April 30, 1899, *Annual Reports, 1899*, Part 3, 150; Telegram, Barry to Lawton, April 30, 1899, *Annual Reports, 1899*, Part 3, 151; Telegram, Edwards to Walcutt, April 30, 1899, *Annual Reports, 1899*, Part 3, 151. The Quartermaster Department was also called upon to bury the enemy dead using its wagons and coolie labor. Funston, *Memories of Two Wars*, 309.

29. Telegram, Lawton to Adjutant General Department of the Pacific, May 3, 1899, *Annual Reports, 1899*, Part 3, 163.

30. Telegram, Walcutt to Adjutant General, First Division, May 4, 1899, *Annual Reports, 1899*, Part 3, 169.

31. Telegram, Walcutt to Adjutant General, First Division, May 5, 1899, *Annual Reports, 1899*, Part 3, 172; Telegram, Case to Adjutant General, First Division, *Annual Reports, 1899*, Part 3, 173.

32. Report, Maj. Gen. H. W. Lawton to Adjutant General, United States Army, September 26, 1899, *Annual Reports, 1899*, Part 3, 104.

33. Telegram, Lawton to Adjutant General Department of the Pacific, May 14, 1899, *Annual Reports, 1899*, Part 3, 223; Telegram, Acting Assistant Adjutant General to Lawton, May 15, 1899, *Annual Reports, 1899*, Part 3, 228.

34. Brig. Gen. Harry Clay Egbert (1839–99) was mortally wounded leading his 22nd Infantry at Malinta, north of Manila, and died March 26, 1899. Available at http:/www.arlingtoncemetery.net; Funston, *Memories of Two Wars*, 241; Egbert held the rank of colonel (22nd Inf.) in the Regular Army and brigadier general in the U. S. Volunteers. William H. Powell, *List of Officers of the United States Army from 1779 to 1900*, 298.

35. 1st Lt. John C. Gregg (U.S.M.A. 1887), 4th Infantry Regiment, was killed in action in the Mariquina Valley on March 31, 1899. Heitman, *Historical Register, vol. 2*, 23.

36. Slang for the Chinese porters or litter bearers employed by the Quartermaster Department and used to carry baggage and supplies, as well as wounded, during an offensive operation, due in part to a shortage of carts and pack animals. Risch, *Quartermaster Support*, 537–39.

37. Reference to a popular poem by Ernest Lawrence Thayer, first published in the San Francisco Examiner on June 3, 1888, under the pen name "Phin." Available at http://www.baseball-almanac.com/poetry/po_case.shtml.

38. Carter's observations are clearly sarcastic. On January 23, 1899, Aguinaldo declared Malolos the capital of the Philippine Republic in a formal, public ceremony. Carter continues to dismiss the courage and fighting qualities of the Filipino soldiers. This haughty attitude would catch many by surprise, as the war gradually moved to a guerilla phase and the Filipino, armed only with a Mauser or a bolo, proved to be quite a fierce and adaptive adversary. Moreover, the Philippine Scouts and the Macabebe Scouts, led by American officers, were very capable and loyal allies.

39. Funston and his small band seized the Bag-Bag Bridge on April 27, 1899. Telegram, MacArthur to Lawton, April 28, 1899, *Annual Reports, 1899*, Part 3, 146.

40. Scouts recruited by the Army from among the Macabebes, who were hostile to the predominant Tagalogs. Very loyal and good fighters, although sometimes given to excesses. Linn, *Philippine War*, 127.

41. Rio Grande de Pampanga.

42. For a description of the difficulty of evacuating the sick and wounded and their interim care during the San Isidro Campaign see, Gillett, *Army Medical Department*, 208–10.

43. Prior to the advance, Maj. Gen. Lawton issued strict orders prohibiting, "any straggling, looting, pillaging, burning, or the commission of any

unlawful excesses." General Orders No. 20, Headquarters First Division, Eighth Army Corps, April 19, 1899, *Annual Reports, 1899*, Part 3, 76.

44. Although for much of its short course, the Pasig River had numerous sand bars in many places, near Manila, it was deep and had a strong current. See reference to drowning of Pvt. Adolph Koplen in March 1899. Durand, *The Boys*, 221.

45. Durand, *The Boys*, 10; Telfer, *Manila Envelopes*, 35–36; John Clifford Brown, *Gentleman Soldier: John Clifford Brown & the Philippine-American War,* edited by Joseph P. McCallus, 203.

46. Linn, *Philippine War*, 1899-1902, 103; H. W. Lawton to Adjutant General Department of the Pacific, Report, August 1, 1899, *Annual Reports, 1899*, Part 3, 32 and 39; Telegram, H. W. Lawton to Adjutant General Department of the Pacific, Report, April 11, 1899, *Annual Reports, 1899*, Part 3, Appendix 23, 52.

47. Telegram, Adjutant General, Department of the Pacific and Eighth Army Corps to H. W. Lawton, April 12, 1899, *Annual Reports, 1899*, Part 3, Appendix 24, 53.

48. Telegram, E. S. Otis to H. W. Lawton to Adjutant General, Department of the Pacific and Eighth Army Corps, April 15, 1899, *Annual Reports, 1899*, Part 3, Appendix 32, 58; Durand, *The Boys*, 246.

49. Telegram, H. W. Lawton to Adjutant General, Department of the Pacific and Eighth Army Corps, April 11, 1899, *Annual Reports, 1899*, Part 3, Appendix 23, 52.

50. Scott, "Gunner in Luzon," Part 4, 215.

51. Major Clarence Ransom Edwards (1859–1931) (U.S.M.A. 1883), assistant adjutant general, 1st Division. Edwards, a West Point graduate (Class of 1883), rose to the rank of major general and had many responsible assignments throughout his long career. He also had many influential friends, including President Taft. Edwards was known as a very able administrator who earned the respect and admiration of those he commanded. He formed and led the 26th ("Yankee") Division in World War I, only to be relieved of command by General Pershing just weeks before the end of the war. Michael E. Shay, *Revered Commander, Maligned General: The Life of Clarence Ransom Edwards, 1859-1931*, 169.

52. Linn, *Philippine War*, 132–36; Miller, *"Benevolent Assimilation"*, 83–87.

53. The Casa del Ayuntamiento was a public building, a former palace, in the old walled section of Manila. It was the town hall, but it was also used by the chief quartermaster as his headquarters. Telfer, *Manila Envelopes*, fig. 109.

54. The "pike position," that is, sitting on his hindquarters with his forelegs touching his hind legs.

55. More than likely a reference to a contemporary vaudeville act or cartoon characters.

56. The Dhobi (Dhobie) Itch (referred to simply as the "Itch.") is a particularly uncomfortable form of ringworm (tinea cruris) affecting the crotch, armpits, and feet. It can spread, and the scratching of the sores, especially in filthy conditions, can lead to more serious problems, which, no doubt, was the case with Carter.

57. It would appear that Carter may have had some small success in getting an article printed back home, thanks to his father's typing and editing.

58. Villain in *Oliver Twist* by Charles Dickens. A miserly Jewish thief and fence who operates a criminal gang of young London boys. An obvious anti-Semitic stereotype.

59. Reference to telegram sent to General Lawton with orders from General Otis to suspend operations due to Aguinaldo's request for a truce; in compliance, Lawton withdrew from San Rafael on April 27, 1899, but, after the truce fell apart, he had to retake the town on May 1, with more loss of life. Linn, *Philippine War*, 113.

60. Chromolithograph or colored print.

61. 2nd Lt. Frederick B. Kerr (U.S.M.A. 1895), 22nd Infantry Regiment. Adjutant General, *Official Army Register for 1901*, 212.

62. Major Leopold O. Parker, 22nd Infantry Regiment. *Official Army Register for 1899*, 175.

63. Frederick Dent Grant (1850–1912) (U.S.M.A 1871) was an Army officer and politician, and the son of the former president. He also attended West Point, graduating a year behind Carter's father.

64. Joseph Wheeler (1836–1906) (U.S.M.A. 1859), former Confederate cavalry officer and later Member of Congress from Alabama, called out of retirement to serve in Cuba and later in the Philippines. In fact, while in the Philippines, due to his age and concerns for his health, Otis and MacArthur purposely kept Wheeler on inspection duty, finally relenting to his pleas in November, when he took part in some limited action at the front near Tarlac shortly before returning to the U.S. in January. John P. Dyer, *From Shiloh to San Juan: The Life of "Fighting Joe" Wheeler*, 256–58.

65. Brig. Gen. Thomas M. Anderson brought the first contingent of troops to the Philippines in June 1898. 1st Division commander until relieved by Lawton.

66. More than likely, the house fronted the Pasig River in the vicinity of the San Miguel District. The launch referred to was the *Maria*. See Robert Dexter Carter diary, April 8, 1899, Robert Dexter Carter Papers.

67. *Judge* was an American weekly magazine founded in 1881 by a group of artists and writers who had left Puck and were in direct competition with it.

It ceased publication in 1947. Available at http://www.en.wikipedia.org/wiki/Judge_(magazine).

68. 1st Lt. William Brooke, Aide de Camp to General Lawton.

69. Scott, "Gunner in Luzon," Part 4, 215. Scott discusses the various articles of a soldier's uniform, particularly the durability of the khaki.

70. Reference to Lawton's relentless campaign to capture the Apache leader Geronimo in 1886. Louis Kraft, *Gatewood & Geronimo.*

71. Captain Benjamin P. Lamberton (1844–1912) was in command of Dewey's flagship Olympia.

72. Maj. John Wyler Summerhayes. He was Depot Quartermaster at New York, where, according to his obituary, during the Spanish-American War, following transfer from his command at David's Island (later Ft. Slocum), he "inspected and outfitted the ships that were purchased by the Government for transport, supply, and hospital ships." *New York Times*, March 9, 1911; *Official Army Register for 1899*, 14. His wife, Martha, wrote a popular memoir of life as an Army spouse entitled *Vanished Arizona: Recollections of the Army Life of a New England Woman* (Salem, Mass.: Salem Press, 1911). See also, http://www.arlingtoncemetery.net/jwsummerhayes.htm.

Chapter Five June–July 1899

1. H. W. Lawton, Report of an Expedition to the Province of Morong, October 8, 1899, *Annual Reports, 1899*, Part 3, 289–92.

2. H. W. Lawton, Report of an Expedition to the Province of Cavite, June 10 to 22, 1899, October 9, 1899, *Annual Reports, 1900*, Part 3, 274.

3. Telegram, Edwards to Walcutt, June 10, 1890, *Annual Reports, 1900*, Part 3, 294; Telegram, Walcutt to Edwards, June 11, 1899, *Annual Reports, 1900*, Part 3, 297.

4. H. W. Lawton, Report of an Expedition to the Province of Cavite, June 10 to 22, 1899, October 9, 1899, *Annual Reports, 1900*, Part 3, 279.

5. H. W. Lawton, Report of an Expedition to the Province of Cavite, June 10 to 22, 1899, October 9, 1899, *Annual Reports, 1900*, Part 3, 278; Lawton to Adjutant General, Department of the Pacific, June 12, 1899, *Annual Reports, 1900*, Part 3, 298.

6. Telegram, Lawton to Adjutant General, Department of the Pacific, June 13, 1899, *Annual Reports 1900*, Part 3, 303.

7. Linn, *Philippine War*, 120.

8. Clarence R. Edwards to Officer in Charge of Casco Rations, June 13, 1899, *Annual Reports 1900*, Part 3, 306. Lawton ordered that "1,000 complete rations" be turned over to "Padre Gabino Lizo, to be distributed to the poor na-

tives" of Las Piñas. Telegram, Lawton to Adjutant General Department of the Pacific, June 15, 1899, *Annual Reports 1900*, Part 3, 313.

9. Linn, *U. S. Army and Counterinsurgency*, 129.

10. Brands, *Reckless Decade*, 321.

11. Gillett, *Army Medical Department*, 213.

12. Durand, *The Boys*, 168.

13. Gillett, *Army Medical Department*, 214.

14. Ibid., 216.

15. Brands, *Reckless Decade*, 321; Gillett, *Army Medical Department*, 216–19.

16. Gillett, *Army Medical Department*, 175–78; Silbey, *War of Frontier and Empire*, 113.

17. Brian McAllister Linn, *Guardians of Empire: The U. S. Army and the Pacific, 1902–1940*, 16.

18. Gillett, *Army Medical Department*, 210–12.

19. Linn, *U. S. Army and Counterinsurgency*, 128–29; Feuer, *America at War*, 176.

20. Brown, *Gentleman Soldier*, 145.

21. Durand, *The Boys*, 155–56.

22. Another letter writer referred to venereal patients as the "Asiatic Squadron." Telfer, *Manila Envelopes*, 61 and 93–94.

23. Ronald Schaffer, *America in the Great War*, 99.

24. As a young lieutenant, Guy Howard served on his father's staff during the Nez Perce fighting, and he was present when Chief Joseph surrendered at the Bear Paw Battleground in Montana, on October 5, 1877. Alvin M. Josephy, Jr., *The Nez Perce Indians and the Opening of the Northwest*, 629.

25. 2nd Lt. Frank Halstead, 4th Infantry Regiment. Adjutant General, *Official Army Register for 1899*, 123.

26. Captain, later Colonel, William Edward Birkhimer (U.S.M.A 1870). A classmate of Carter's father and an officer Lawton's staff, he went on to command the 28th Volunteer Infantry Regiment. Awarded Medal of Honor for actions at San Miguel de Mayumo on May 13, 1899. Linn, *Philippine War*, 115.

27. Hardtack.

28. A recurrent form of malaria, occasionally accompanied by episodes of delirium. Available at http://www.museumstuff.com/learn/topics/Cuban_fever.

29. Major John B. Rodman (U.S.M.A. 1868). Cullum, *Biographical Register, vol. 4*, 153.

30. Capt. Leonard A. Lovering, 4th Infantry Regiment (U.S.M.A. 1876). He refers to Lovering as regimental commander, but this is more than likely an

error. As a Captain, he would have been a company commander, unless thrust into the role temporarily. It is also possible that he was referring to his permanent rank as a Regular, and that he also held the rank of Colonel in the Volunteers. Cullum, *Biographical Register, vol. 4*, 264.

31. In this assessment, Lawton would ultimately be vindicated. Brian McAllister Linn, *U. S. Army and Counterinsurgency*, 12–13; Miller, "*Benevolent Assimilation*," 78.

32. Maj. Gen. William Rufus Shafter, commander of the American army in Cuba.

33. Brig. Gen. Charles P. Eagan, Commissary General of Subsistence. Adjutant General, *Army Register for 1899*, 18.

34. Carter is referring to the beginning of hostilities with the Philippine Army on February 4, 1899, as well as to the uneasy peace between those forces during the period starting with the surrender of the Spanish garrison at Manila and ending on that date.

35. The fighting actually began when William Grayson of the 1st Nebraska Volunteers, while on guard duty, fired the first shot. Linn, *Philippine War*, 46; Durand. *The Boys*, 194–98.

36. The bolo is a long, single-edge knife used by native Filipinos.

37. Lt. Col. James W. Pope (U.S.M.A.1868), Chief Quartermaster, 8th Army Corps, with headquarters at the Casa del Ayuntamiento, referred to as the "Palace," or town hall in the old walled city of Manila. Cullum, *Biographical Register, vol. 4*, 184–85.

38. Novelist M.A. Bengough. Author of *In a Promised Land* (Harper's 1893) and *So Near Akin* (1891). *New York Times*, May 28, 1893.

39. There was a very vocal anti-imperialist feeling in the United States at this time including elements of the press. In response, Lawton is quoted as having said: "If I am shot the gun will be loaded by our friends in the States." Brown, *Gentleman Soldier*, 243. The remark was eerily prescient.

40. Capt. Abraham S. Bickham, Assistant Quartermaster. Adjutant General, *Register of General Officers*, 6.

41. Brig. Gen. Frederick Dent Grant (U.S.M.A. 1871), son of Ulysses S. Grant.

42. Carter is wrong, Lawton was held at San Rafael which he had already captured, withdrew, and had to retake the next day. Linn, *Philippine War*, 113.

43. Term first used during the Cuban insurgency against Spain prior to American involvement, when the Spanish under General Valeriano Weyler relocated thousands of the population into fixed locations, where many died of starvation and disease. Ostensibly, the purpose of American intervention in Cuba was to stop the Spanish atrocities. Ironically, the United States Army

would adopt a similar practice during the Philippine War. Linn, *U. S. Army and Counterinsurgency*, 26–27, 154–55, and 158–59.

44. Once again, Carter is mistaken. Lawton, on his own initiative, distributed 1,000 rations, and, in addition, requested permission to purchase and distribute rice to the natives. See Endnote 8.

45. Another racial stereotype.

46. Major Clarence Ransom Edwards.

47. Mount Pleasant section of NW Washington, D. C.

48. Camp Thomas was located on the grounds of the newly dedicated Chickamauga National Battlefield in northwest Georgia, where various Volunteer regiments encamped during the War with Spain. It was named for Union Major General George H. ("Pap") Thomas, known as the "Rock of Chickamauga" for his heroic, last-ditch stand during that battle. In addition to problems with the mail, unsanitary conditions at the camp led to disease, including typhoid fever, prompting many soldiers to demand to be sent home. Gillett, *Army Medical Department*, 175–78; Lewis L. Gould, *The Presidency of William McKinley*, 102 and 124–25.

49. Reference to Commanding General of the Army, Nelson A. Miles and his unfounded accusations of "embalmed beef."

50. The Second Reserve Hospital was established in Manila in September 1898, in a building that originally housed a girl's school. It had walled gardens, and boasted 8 porcelain bath tubs. At first it had 300 beds for convalescents transferred from the First Reserve Hospital, and later treated more severe cases. It was closed in July 1901. Carter may be mistaken in describing the hospital as having "three stories," as photographs show only two. His initial admission covered the period June 29 through July 7. Gillett, *Army Medical Department*, 204–6.

51. Given the increase in troops in the Philippines and their disbursal throughout the country, the Army came to rely upon contract surgeons to meet the need. Gillett, *Army Medical Department, 1865-1917*, 318–20.

52. Major Francis M. Schreiner, Quartermaster. Adjutant General, *Register of General Officers*, 6–7.

53. Mary C. Gillett, *The Army Medical Department, 1865-1917* (Washington, D.C.: Center of Military History, 1995), 216.

54. Carter was readmitted to the hospital on July 11 and released on July 26.

55. Reference to P. T. Barnum's extraordinarily large elephant.

56. Frank W. Carpenter began his career as an Acting Hospital Steward, and later he served as the civilian Chief Clerk for Lawton. Naturally, he would have known Carter, as they both worked at 1st Division headquarters in Manila. He would remain in the Philippines, where he would serve as Executive Secretary. In 1913, he became the first civilian governor of the Moro and Sulu

Department, succeeding Brig. Gen. John J. Pershing. In the latter appointment, Carpenter received a boost from Brig. Gen. Clarence Ransom Edwards, formerly Lawton's Assistant Adjutant General, in his capacity as Chief of the Bureau of Insular Affairs. Shay, *Revered Commander*, 230n46. See also, http://www.arlingtoncemetery.net/fcarpenter.htm.

57. This is likely a reference to his schoolmates from the Business High School in Washington, D.C., which offered a program in drill and military science. The students who participated were referred to as cadets. Fred Kerr went on to West Point.

58. Reference to Laguna de Bay and the Santa Cruz Expedition.

59. A growth or cyst on the skin.

60. Reference to the Governor of New York, Theodore Roosevelt.

61. Secretary of the Navy John Davis Long.

Chapter Six August 1899

1. Linn, *Philippine War*, 122.

2. Telfer, *Manila Envelopes*, 40.

3. Linn, *Philippine War*, 26.

4. Roaming dogs were a problem in Manila. Durand, *The Boys*, 242.

5. Telfer, *Manila Envelopes*, 43; Durand, *The Boys*, 318. The high cost of things affected the Quartermaster Department in Manila, which saw the price of a pony to pull supply carts skyrocket from $15-$20 to $100-$150 each. Risch, *Quartermaster Support*, 537–38.

6. Telfer, *Manila Envelopes*, 102, 122–23; Durand, *The Boys*, 152.

7. *New York Times*, April 12, 1912.

8. Linn, *Philippine War*, 158–59.

9. According to Brigadier General E. D. Scott, Lawton's staff were quick to read the signs and generally absented themselves until the flare-up passed, sometimes leaving an unsuspecting junior officer to absorb the blow. Scott, "Gunner in Luzon," Part 6, 389.

10. Durand, *The Boys*, 268–74; Cullum, *Biographical Register, vol. 4*, 196.

11. Linn, *U.S. Army and Counterinsurgency*, 122.

12. The fight at Zapote Bridge was more complicated than simply forcing a passage across the span. The Insurgents were well dug in, and while holding that position, at the same time pressed a flank attack toward Manila Bay which, but for a heroic stand and fire from the gunboats, could well have ended badly for Lawton's forces. Lawton had anticipated the flank attack, and enlisted the aid of the gunboats in advance. Throughout, Lawton or his staff maintained complete control and shifted troops when necessary to meet the

challenge. As to Wheaton's apparent slowness, this, more than likely, was a reference to the days leading up to the battle, when stifling heat and snipers caused Wheaton's and Ovenshine's columns to become strung out and separated. Wheaton was known to be aggressive, which he soon demonstrated near Bacoor and Imus in the days following the fight at Zapote Bridge. Carter's defense of Lawton, as well as the newspaper articles criticizing him, both failed to look at the battle as a whole.

13. Reference to the Carter family residence on 3218 16th Street in Washington, D.C., 1900 U. S. Census, Washington, D.C., Series T623, Roll 158, Page 275.

14. Under the policy of benevolent assimilation, it was anticipated that the control would be gradually turned over to the Filipinos themselves. The Second Philippine Commission under the chairmanship of William Howard Taft was instrumental in this process. In fact, Taft would repeatedly clash with the military governor, Maj. Gen. Arthur MacArthur. The latter would lose that battle.

15. Captain William Brooke, Aide-de-Camp to Gen. Lawton.

16. Natalie Powell Carter, Carter's youngest sister.

17. Mary Wright (Mrs. Charles), Helen's mother.

18. Bessie Richardson Carter, the oldest of the Carter siblings.

19. Well-known photography studio in Washington, D.C.

20. A variant of a simple late eighteenth- and early nineteenth-century diplomatic code using a key word and the substitution of numbers for letters of the alphabet utilized by John Adams.

21. Major Clarence R. Edwards

22. Harpswell Center, small town 30 miles northeast of Portland on coast.

23. Short for "Slumgullion," a rough stew made from whatever meat and vegetables were available.

24. In this Carter is mistaken, as McKinley was re-elected in November.

25. Minister and journalist from Boston. As noted in the "Introduction" for Karl Irving Faust's Campaigning in the Philippines (San Francisco: Hicks-Judd, 1899), he assisted in gathering facts and materials. MacQueen achieved some notoriety when he accompanied Theodore Roosevelt and the Rough Riders at Kettle Hill, Cuba, in 1898.

26. Great Diamond Island. A part of the City of Portland, Maine, situated in Casco Bay. Site of Fort McKinley. Due to his many Army connections, Robert G. Carter was likely offered the use of one of the many residences on the post.

27. Col. Crosby P. Miller (U.S.M.A.1867), chief quartermaster. Cullum, *Biographical Register, vol. 4*, 167–68.

28. Throughout July 1899, Lawton's forces engaged in a series of small, largely unsuccessful actions in the region of Laguna de Bay to stop the contraband trade by insurgents. The most significant action was Lawton's capture of Calamba on July 26. E. S. Otis, *Report of Major-General E. S. Otis, U. S. Volunteers, on Military Operations and Civil Affairs in the Philippine Islands, 1899*, 141–42.

29. Brig. Gen. Marshall I. Ludington (1839–1919), the twenty-first quartermaster general of the Army. He served from 1898–1903. Available at http://www.qmfound.com/BG_Marshall_Ludington.htm.

Chapter Seven September 1899

1. It is possible that Carter was called upon to make a short trip to Cavite Province during late July or early August when Lawton's division carried on a series of minor operations against the insurgent supply operations. Given the time it took for Mamie Lawton's letter to reach the United States and the return query to Carter would seem to support this. The young man left the hospital on July 26.

2. William E. Horton to Adjutant General, Department of Southern Luzon, June 20, 1900, *Annual Report of Major General Arthur MacArthur, U. S. Volunteers, Commanding, Division of the Philippines, Military Governor in the Philippine Islands, vol. 1* (Manila: N.p., 1900), 101–4.

3. *New York Times*, October 24, 1899, p. 7; Linn, *Philippine War*, 145; Summary of Principal Events Connected with Military Operations in the Philippine Islands, September 1, 1899, to August 31, 1900, *Annual Reports, 1900*, 10.

4. Major John Thornton Knight (U.S.M.A, 1879). John T. Knight to Assistant Adjutant General, 1st Division, 8th Army Corps, February 15, 1900, *Annual Report of Major General Arthur MacArthur, vol. 1*, 94.

5. Most likely a reference to the 1st North Dakota Volunteers. The unit was assigned to Lawton's 1st Division.

6. Homer Davenport (1867-1912), native Oregonian and political cartoonist for William Randolph Hearst's New York Evening Journal. His familiar depiction of "Uncle Sam" is iconic. See article by Walt Curtis on the website of the Oregon Cultural Heritage Commission, available at http://www.ochcom.org/davenport/.

7. Sarcastic reference to General Otis.

8. See letters dated May 28, 1899 and June 1, 1899.

9. No doubt a reference to an Army officer of their mutual acquaintance who liked to interfere with and micromanage his subordinates.

10. The *Morgan City* was a small steamer carrying troops and mail bound from San Francisco to Manila, which sank in the Inland Sea of Japan during

the early morning hours of August 10, 1899. All on board were rescued. The same could not be said for the mail. She may have been somewhat of a "hard luck" ship, as midway on an earlier trans-Pacific voyage, she had a fire in a coal bunker that the crew was unable to extinguish until after the ship landed in Manila. Durand, *The Boys*, 57.

11. Assistant Quartermaster, Captain Abraham S. Bickham.

12. Dengue fever is a tropical and subtropical disease caused by one of four mosquito-borne viruses, characterized by, among other things, rash, headache, fever, muscle and joint pain, and a lack of energy. Death can result in some cases.

13. Given the prevalence of disease in Manila, this must have been a welcome luxury, if not a necessity.

14. James Creelman (1859-1915), editor and well-known journalist and war correspondent. During his career, he worked at the *New York Evening Journal* among other newspapers. Accompanied Lawton's forces at El Caney in Cuba, where he captured the Spanish flag and was wounded in the process of waving it at the garrison. *New York Times*, February 13, 1915.

15. Classic mystery novel, *The Woman in White* by Wilkie Collins, published in 1860.

16. It is possible that Carter made a short trip to Cavite Province during July or August when Lawton's division was conducting minor actions there. See endnote 1.

17. The family dog.

18. The German word for dog.

19. Reference to President William F. McKinley and Senator Marcus A. Hanna.

20. Apparently he resold some photos to that magazine.

21. Captain Edward L. King, aide-de-camp to General Lawton.

22. Captain William Brooke, aide-de-camp to General Lawton.

23. Major Charles G. Starr, Inspector General, United States Volunteers, served on General Lawton's staff.

24. Captain Robert Sewell served on General Lawton's staff.

25. Curiously, Carter does not mention Clarence R. Edwards, Lawton's adjutant, who was promoted from major to lieutenant colonel in the Volunteers about this time. Edwards was very close to Lawton. Perhaps Carter did not want to take a swipe at him.

26. Most likely a reference to the Lawtons' vineyard in California. During his career, Lawton had acquired a twelve-acre homestead at Redlands, California, east of Los Angeles in San Bernadino County.

27. This is an obvious comparison of the upcoming offensive into Central Luzon with the one conducted earlier in the year.

28. One of Major Howard's clerks must have been a Canadian.
29. Gillett, *Army Medical Department*, 216.
30. See letter to his father dated June 26, 1899.
31. Reference to inventor Thomas Alva Edison. That is, a genius.

Epilogue

1. Linn, *Philippine War*, 160–61.
2. Heitman, *Historical Register, vol. 1*, 288.
3. *Army List and Directory* (Washington, D.C.: G.P.O., 1920), 36.
4. Available at http://www.arlingtoncemetery.net/rdcarter.htm.
5. *Sixty-seventh Annual Report of the Association of Graduates of the United States Military Academy at West Point, New York, June 11, 1936* (Newburgh, N.Y.: Moore Printing, 1936), 78–81.
6. Robert Goldthwaite Carter, *Four Brothers in Blue: A Story of the Great Civil War from Bull Run to Appomattox* (Norman: University of Oklahoma Press, 1999).
7. Carter, *On the Border with Mackenzie.*
8. *New York Times*, January 1, 1900 and January 31, 1900.
9. *New York Times*, February 7, 1900.
10. *New York Times*, February 10, 1900, p. 8.
11. *New York Times*, April 14, 1907, p. 1. Originally located on the southwest corner of the County Courthouse grounds, the statue was moved to its present location in Garfield Park in 1915. The sculptor, Andrew O'Connor (1874-1941), studied under Daniel Chester French. "Historical/Biographical Sketch re Theodore Roosevelt Photographs, 30 May 1907," available at http://www.indianahistory.org/library/manuscripts/collection_guides/P0118.html.
12. Ossad, "Henry Ware Lawton," 21.
13. H. W. Lawton, Report, September 26, 1899, *Annual Reports, 1899*, Part 3, 88.
14. Clarence R. Edwards to Officer in Charge of Casco Rations, June 13, 1899, *Annual Reports, 1899*, Part 3, 306.
15. Available at http://www.arlingtoncemetery.net/hwlawton.htm.
16. *New York Times*, December 30, 1914; *Forty-sixth Annual Reunion of the Association of Graduates of the United States Military Academy at West Point, New York, June 11, 1915*, 142–47.
17. *Forty-sixth Annual Reunion of the Association of Graduates of the United States Military Academy at West Point, New York, June 11, 1915*, 74–83.
18. Available at http://www.arlingtoncemetery.net/wbirkhim.htm.
19. Available at http://www.arlingtoncemetery.net/ccwalcuttjr.htm.
20. Linn, *Philippine War*, 320–21.

21. Funston, *Memories of Two Wars*, x.

22. *New York Times*, April 12, 1912.; *Forty-third Annual Reunion of the Graduates of the United States Military Academy at West Point, New York, June 11, 1912*, 149–52.

23. Brands, *Bound to Empire: The United States and the Philippines*, 227.

24. Emilio Aguinaldo y Famy (1869-1964). Available at http://www.loc.gov/rr/hispanic/1898/aguinaldo.html

Works Consulted

Primary Sources

Adjutant General. *Official Army Register for 1899*, Washington, D.C.: G.P.O., 1899.

———. *Official Army Register for 1901*, Washington, D.C.: G.P.O., 1900.

———. *Register of General Officers and Officers of the General Staff, U. S. Volunteers, 1899*. Washington, D.C.: G.P.O., 1899.

Annual Reports of the War Department for the Fiscal Year Ended June 30, 1899, Part 3. Washington, D.C.: G.P.O., 1899.

Cullum, George W. *Biographical Register of the Officers and Graduates of the U. S. Military Academy at West Point, New York Since Its Establishment in 1802*, vol. 4. Cambridge, Mass.: Riverside, 1901.

Forty-third Annual Reunion of the Association of Graduates of the United States Military Academy at West Point, New York, June 11, 1912. Saginaw, Mich.: Sherman & Peters, 1912.

Forty-sixth Annual Reunion of the Association of Graduates of the United States Military Academy at West Point, New York, June 11, 1915. Saginaw, Mich.: Sherman & Peters, 1915.

Heitman, Francis B. *Historical Register and Dictionary of the United States Army, From Its Organization, September 29, 1789, to March 2, 1903*, vols. 1 and 2, Washington, D.C.: G.P.O., 1903.

MacArthur, Arthur. *Annual Report of Major General Arthur MacArthur, U. S. Volunteers, Commanding, Division of the Philippines, Military Governor in the Philippine Islands*, vol. 1. Manila: N.p., 1900.

Otis, E. S. *Report of Major-General E. S. Otis, U. S. Volunteers, on Military Operations and Civil Affairs in the Philippine Islands, 1899*. Washington, D.C.: G.P.O., 1899.

Powell, William H. *List of Officers of the United States Army from 1779 to 1900* (New York: Hamersly, 1900.

Sixty-seventh Annual Report of the Association of Graduates of the United States Military Academy at West Point, New York, June 11, 1936. Newburgh, N.Y.: Moore Printing, 1936).

Manuscripts and Special Collections

Library of Congress, Washington, D.C.
  Prints and Photographs Collection
Military History Institute, Carlisle, Penn.
  W. C. Brown Collection
  W. W. Dinwiddie Collection
  Louis Dunston Collection
  Luther R. Hare Collection
West Point Albums Collection
National Library of Medicine, History of Medicine Division, Bethesda, Md.
  Prints and Photographs
Pack Memorial Public Library, Asheville, N.C.
  North Carolina Collection
Rutherford B. Hayes Presidential Center Library, Fremont, Ohio
  Robert Dexter Carter Papers

Books and Pamphlets

Brands, H. W. *Bound to Empire: The United States and the Philippines.* New York: Oxford University Press, 1992.

———. *The Reckless Decade: America in the 1890s.* Chicago: University of Chicago Press, 2002.

Brown, John Clifford. *Gentleman Soldier: John Clifford Brown & the Philippine-American War*, edited by Joseph P. McCallus. College Station: Texas A & M University Press, 2004.

Carter, Robert Goldthwaite. *Four Brothers in Blue: Sunshine and Shadows of the War of the Rebellion: A Story of the Great Civil War from Bull Run to Appomattox.* Norman: University of Oklahoma Press, 1999.

———. *On the Border with Mackenzie; or, Winning West Texas from the Comanches.* College Station: Texas A & M University Press, 2011.

Cashman, Sean Dennis. *America in the Age of Titans: The Progressive Era and World War I.* New York: New York University Press, 1988.

Coffman, Edward M. *The Regulars: The American Army, 1898–1941.* Cambridge, Mass.: Belknap, 2004.

Crichton, Judy. *America 1900: The Sweeping Story of a Pivotal Year in the Life of the Nation.* New York: Henry Holt, 2000.

Davis, Richard Harding. *Cuba in War Time.* Lincoln: University of Nebraska Press, 2000.

Durand, John. *The Boys: 1st North Dakota Volunteers in the Philippines.* Elkhorn, Wisc.: Puzzlebox Press, 2010.

Dyer, John P. *From Shiloh to San Juan: The Life of "Fighting Joe" Wheeler*. Baton Rouge: Louisiana State University Press, 1992.

Feuer, A. B. *America at War: The Philippines, 1898–1913*. Westport, Conn.: Praeger, 2002.

Freidel, Frank. *The Splendid Little War: The Dramatic Story of the Spanish-American War*. Short Hills, N.J.: Burford, 2002.

Funston, Frederick. *Memories of Two Wars: Cuban and Philippine Experiences*. Lincoln: University of Nebraska Press, 2009.

Gates, John M. *Schoolbooks and Krags: The United States Army in the Philippines, 1898–1902*. Westport, Conn.: Greenwood, 1973.

Gillett, Mary C. *The Army Medical Department, 1865-1917*. Washington, D.C.: Center of Military History, 1995.

Golway, Terry. *Washington's General: Nathanael Greene and the Triumph of the American Revolution*. New York: Henry Holt, 2005.

Gould, Louis L. *The Presidency of William McKinley*. Lawrence: University Press of Kansas, 1980.

Jaffe, Eric. *The King's Best Highway: The Lost History of the Boston Post Road, the Route that Made America*. New York: Scribner, 2010.

Jones, Gregg. *Honor in the Dust: Theodore Roosevelt, War in the Philippines, and the Rise and Fall of America's Imperial Dream*. New York: New American Library, 2012.

Josephy, Alvin M., Jr. *The Nez Perce Indians and the Opening of the Northwest*. Boston: Houghton, Mifflin, 1997.

Kraft, Louis. *Gatewood & Geronimo*. Albuquerque: University of New Mexico Press, 2000.

Linn, Brian McAllister. *The Philippine War, 1899–1902*. Lawrence: University Press of Kansas, 2000.

———. *The U.S. Army and Counterinsurgency in the Philippine War. 1899–1902*. Chapel Hill: University of North Carolina Press, 1989.

———. *Guardians of Empire: The U. S. Army and the Pacific, 1902–1940*. Chapel Hill: University of North Carolina Press, 1997.

Marshall, George C. *Memoirs of My Services in the World War, 1917–1918*. Boston: Houghton, Mifflin, 1976.

Meinig, D. W. *The Shaping of America: A Geographical Perspective on 500 Years of History, Vol. 3, Transcontinental America, 1850–1915*. New Haven: Yale University press, 1998.

Miller, Scott. *The President and the Assassin: McKinley, Terror, and Empire at the Dawn of the American Century*. New York: Random House, 2011.

Miller, Stuart Creighton. *"Benevolent Assimilation": The American Conquest of the Philippines, 1899–1903*. New Haven: Yale University Press, 1982.

Morgan, H. Wayne. *William McKinley and His America*. Kent, Ohio: Kent State University Press, 2003.

Morris, Edmund. *The Rise of Theodore Roosevelt*. New York: Modern Library, 2001.

Musicant, Ivan. *Empire by Default: The Spanish-American War and the Dawn of the American Century*. New York: Henry Holt, 1998.

Phillips, Kevin. *William McKinley*. New York: Henry Holt, 2003.

Risch, Erna. *Quartermaster Support of the Army: A History of the Corps, 1775–1939*. Washington, D.C.: Center of Military History, 1989.

Roosevelt, Theodore. *The Rough Riders*. New York: Modern, 1999.

Schaffer, Ronald. *America in the Great War: The Rise of the Welfare State*. New York: Oxford University Press, 1994.

Sferrazza, Carl Anthony. *Nellie Taft: The Unconventional First Lady of the Ragtime Era*. New York: William Morrow, 2005.

Shay, Michael E. *Revered Commander, Maligned General: The Life of Clarence Ransom Edwards, 1859–1931*. Columbia: University of Missouri Press, 2011.

Silbey, David J. *A War of Frontier and Empire: The Philippine-American War, 1899–1902*. New York: Hill and Wang, 2008.

Telfer, George F. *Manila Envelopes: Oregon Volunteer Lt. George F. Telfer's Spanish-American War Letters*, edited by Sara Bunnett. Portland: Oregon Historical Society Press, 1987.

Thomas, Evan. *The War Lovers: Roosevelt, Lodge, Hearst, and the Rush to Empire, 1898*. New York: Little, Brown, 2010.

Trask, David F. *The War with Spain in 1898*. Lincoln: University of Nebraska Press, 1996.

Traxel, David. *1898: The Tumultuous Year of Victory, Invention, Internal Strife, and Industrial Expansion that Saw the Birth of the American Century*. New York: Knopf, 1998.

———. *Crusader Nation: The United States in Peace and the Great War, 1898–1920*. New York: Knopf, 2006.

Utley, Robert M. *Frontier Regulars: The United States Army and the Indian, 1866–1891*. Lincoln: University of Nebraska Press, 1984.

Washington, George. *George Washington: Writings*, edited by John Rhodehamel. New York: Library of America, 1997.

Wimmel, Kenneth. *Theodore Roosevelt and the Great White Fleet: American Sea Power Comes of Age*. Washington, D.C.: Brassey's, 1998.

Wooster, Robert. *Nelson A. Miles and the Twilight of the Frontier Army*. Lincoln: University of Nebraska Press, 1996.

Zimmermann, Warren. *The First Great Triumph: How Five Americans Made Their Country a World Power*. New York: Farrar, Straus, 2002.

Articles

Eberle, Edward W. "The 'Oregon's' Great Voyage." *The Century* 58, no. 6 (October 1899): 912–24.

Linn, Brian McAllister. "The Philippines. Nation Building and Pacification." *Military Review* (March–April 2005): 46–54.

Ossad, Steven L. "Henry Ware Lawton: Flawed Giant and Hero of Four Wars." *Army History* 63 (Winter 2007): 4–25.

Scott, Ernest D. "Gunner in Luzon," Part 1, *The Field Artillery Journal* 29, no. 6 (November–December, 1939): 513–24.

———. "Gunner in Luzon," Part 4, *The Field Artillery Journal* 30, no. 3 (May–June, 1940): 209–21.

———. "Gunner in Luzon," Part 6, *The Field Artillery Journal* 30, no. 6 (September–October, 1940): 384–93.

Index